343.73052
D 489t

DETROIT PUBLIC LIBRARY

3 5674 05049487 2

The Tax Lady's Guide

BEATING
THE IRS

— AND —

Saving
Big Bucks
on Your
Taxes

HUBBARD BRANCH LIBRARY
12929 W. McNICHOLS
DETROIT, MI 48235
578-7585

OCT - - 2009

The Tax Lady's Guide to

BEATING THE IRS

— AND —

Saving Big Bucks on Your Taxes

Learn How you Can Pay Less Money to the IRS by Beating Them at Their Own Game

RONI LYNN DEUTCH

BENBELLA

BENBELLA BOOKS, INC.
Dallas, TX

Copyright © 2009 by Niko & Inu, LLC

All rights reserved. No part of this book may be used or reproduced in any manner whatsoever without written permission except in the case of brief quotations embodied in critical articles or reviews.

THE TAX LADY and RONI DEUTCH TAX CENTER are registered service marks of Roni Lynn Deutch and used with permission.

BENBELLA

BenBella Books, Inc.
6440 N. Central Expressway, Suite 503
Dallas, TX 75206
www.benbellabooks.com
Send feedback to feedback@benbellabooks.com

Printed in the United States of America
10 9 8 7 6 5 4 3 2 1

Library of Congress Cataloging-in-Publication Data is available for this title.
ISBN 978-1933771-77-9

Proofreading by Yara Abuata
Cover design by Laura Watkins
Text design and composition by PerfecType, Nashville, TN
Printed by Bang Printing

Distributed by Perseus Distribution
perseusdistribution.com

To place orders through Perseus Distribution:
Tel: 800-343-4499
Fax: 800-351-5073
E-mail: orderentry@perseusbooks.com

Significant discounts for bulk sales are available. Please contact Robyn White at robyn@benbellabooks.com or (214) 750-3600.

I dedicate this book to my Mom, Aunt Ider, and Dana.

Today is a good day!

PLEASE NOTE: THE INFORMATION IN THIS WORK IS PROVIDED FOR GENERAL INFORMATIONAL PURPOSES ONLY. IT IS NOT A SUBSTITUTE FOR, AND IS NOT INTENDED TO CONSTITUTE, TAX, FINANCIAL, LEGAL OR OTHER PROFESSIONAL ADVICE.

ALTHOUGH IT IS HOPED THAT THIS WORK WILL BE HELPFUL AS BACK-GROUND MATERIAL, IT IS NOT INTENDED TO CONSTITUTE A COMPLETE ANALYSIS OF ALL TAX CONSIDERATIONS AND IS NOT GUARANTEED TO BE ACCURATE, COMPLETE, OR UP-TO-DATE, PARTICULARLY AS LAWS AND CIRCUMSTANCES CHANGE AFTER PUBLICATION. THE INFORMATION IN THIS WORK OMITS MANY DETAILS AND SPECIAL RULES, AND MAY NOT APPLY TO THE FACTUAL, TAX, FINANCIAL, OR LEGAL CIRCUMSTANCES OF ANY PARTICULAR INDIVIDUAL.

THIS WORK IS NOT A SOLICITATION FOR THE FORMATION OF ANY FINANCIAL ADVISOR-CLIENT OR ATTORNEY-CLIENT RELATIONSHIP, AND NO SUCH RELATIONSHIP IS CREATED THROUGH THE USE OF THIS WORK OR ANY INFORMATION HEREIN. ANYONE USING INFORMATION IN THIS WORK SHOULD NOT ACT UPON SUCH INFORMATION WITHOUT FIRST SEEKING COMPETENT PROFESSIONAL ADVICE.

THE AUTHOR AND PUBLISHER AND THEIR ASSOCIATED ORGANIZATIONS MAKE NO REPRESENTATIONS OR WARRANTIES WHATSOEVER WITH RESPECT TO THE INFORMATION IN THIS WORK OR IN ANY PROMOTIONAL OR MARKETING MATERIALS RELATING TO THIS WORK, AND EXPRESSLY DISCLAIM ALL WARRANTIES, WHETHER EXPRESS, IMPLIED, STATUTORY OR OTHERWISE, INCLUDING, WITHOUT LIMITATION, WARRANTIES OF MERCHANTABILITY OR FITNESS FOR A PARTICULAR PURPOSE.

THE AUTHOR AND PUBLISHER AND THEIR ASSOCIATED ORGANIZATIONS EXPRESSLY DISCLAIM ANY AND ALL LIABILITY FOR DAMAGES ARISING DIRECTLY OR INDIRECTLY FROM THE USE OF ANY INFORMATION IN THIS WORK.

REFERENCES TO ORGANIZATIONS OR WEBSITES IN THIS WORK ARE NOT ENDORSEMENTS OR SPONSORSHIPS OF SUCH ORGANIZATIONS OR WEBSITES. FURTHER, READERS SHOULD BE AWARE THAT WEBSITES LISTED IN THIS WORK MAY HAVE CHANGED SINCE THIS WORK WAS WRITTEN.

Table of Contents

These "Rounds" are my way of helping you go head-to-head with the IRS. Think of the book as a boxing match. Each chapter is another round, at the end of which you'll still be standing, taller and stronger than before. And you'll save money on your taxes, too.

➤ INTRODUCTION

Let's Fight Back

Do you want to pay less money in taxes? Do you want to keep more of the money you work so hard to earn? Of course you do! With the economy in the tank and the stock market and prices—gas and food—as unstable as ever, everyone needs more money just to survive. Most people I know—and probably many people you know—are sick and tired of being taxed to death by the IRS. Well, let's face it—you and I have two things in common: (1) we are all going to die—hopefully at a ripe old age—and (2) we all have to pay taxes to the IRS.

Everyone wants to pay less money to the IRS, but most people just don't know how. That's where I come in. I am Roni Lynn Deutch—aka the Tax Lady. I have two decades of experience fighting the IRS, and I have saved thousands of people—just like you—millions and millions of dollars.

That's right, I'm a tax attorney. I know tax laws, and I know how to save you money.

Has anyone ever told you that he or she owes back taxes to the IRS? Have you ever heard anyone say that he or she has been audited? Come on! It would be like wearing a Red Sox jersey to a

Yankees game—it takes real guts to do it. Why are so many people afraid to talk about taxes, afraid of the big, bad wolf? Well, *I'm* not afraid. I'm not afraid to talk taxes, and you shouldn't be either. After all, you have tax rights, too! Rather than living in fear of the bogey-man, you need to wake up and learn how to take advantage of all the laws that are out there—laws that allow you to save money on your taxes.

Listen: Congress and the IRS *intentionally* make taxes complicated and confusing. That's their job. They *want* you to live in fear of them so you will gladly pay whatever amount of money they tell you to pay. Did you know the average person overpays the IRS by almost $2,000 per year? Overpaying the IRS stinks, especially when you have kids to feed, rent to pay, and electric bills that increase monthly. The IRS is in business to collect as much of your money as they possibly can. But guess what? It is time for you to do something about it.

Here's the good news: you *really can* save money on your taxes. Say it with me—"I *really can* pay less money to the IRS!" Wow, doesn't that sound good? Doesn't that *feel* good? Well, it does to me because I know it. I believe it. And I have faith that you will know it and believe it, too, as you begin to navigate your way through taxes with this book as your guide.

So, the choice is yours. You can do nothing and continue to pay the IRS way too much money. Or you can follow the advice in this book and keep more of your hard-earned money. So, what will it be?

➤ ROUND 1

Feeling In*tax*icated? Dude, You Are Paying *Way* Too Much in Taxes

The Congress shall have power to lay and collect taxes on incomes, from whatever source derived, without apportionment among the several States, and without regard to any census or enumeration.
—Sixteenth Amendment to the U.S. Constitution

Former U.S. Supreme Court Justice Oliver Wendell Holmes once said that taxes are the price we pay for a civilized society.

While there is no shortage of critics who say we have been civilized enough already, I think Holmes was on to something.

After all, could society function without taxes? I don't want to get all philosophical on you—especially on the first page of a book that teaches you how to beat the IRS, tax-wise—but it is a question my professors used to ask us at law school. As you may know, the Constitution is filled with passages emphasizing the need for establishing a more perfect union, securing a common defense, and promoting the general welfare. And it's hard to do those things without a few bucks in your pocket! So we the people gather together every mid-April in post offices, around kitchen tables, and at accountants' desks, from sea to shining sea, to pay for the services the U.S. needs to get by for another year.

⟩⟩⟩ FAST FACT

Types of Taxes

While there is no shortage of ways that the U.S. government can lay claim to your money, the bulk of tax revenues comes from a handful of taxable income categories. Let's have a look at them:

Income Taxes

Taxes on earned income (salaries, wages, tips, commissions) and unearned income (interest from savings accounts, dividends if you hold stocks). Both individuals and businesses are subject to income taxes.

Federal Estate Tax

Sometimes known as the "death tax," the estate tax in recent years has been a controversial topic in Washington D.C., with some in Congress lobbying for its permanent demise and others clamoring for its fixed place at the taxable income table. Simply stated, the estate tax is a federal tax levied on the transfer of property from a deceased person to his or her heirs, legatees, devisees—any individuals or organizations bequeathed a portion of the deceased's estate.

Federal Gift Tax

A tax on the transfer of property by one individual to another when the first individual receives nothing, or less than full value, in return. The tax applies to the gift-giver (i.e., "donor") and applies whether the donor intends the transfer to be a gift or not. The gift tax does not apply to gifts given to a spouse and only applies to gifts to others (e.g., children) when the value of the gift exceeds a certain threshold (i.e., $12,000 in 2008).

Social Security Tax

The federal government imposes two types of taxes on employment—Social Security tax and unemployment tax. The Federal Insurance Contribution Act (FICA) imposes a tax on both an employee and his/her employer if the employee is eligible for Social Security and Medicare health insurance benefits. Proceeds from the FICA tax are used by the federal government to finance its payment of Social Security benefits. The Federal Unemployment Tax Act (FUTA) imposes a tax only on the employer. The FUTA tax revenues are used by the federal government to fund unemployment benefits programs.

Excise Tax

Taxes imposed on the production, sale, or consumption of specific goods, services, or resource usage. Common examples include luxury passenger automobiles, heavy trucks and trailers, wagering, water transportation, removal of hard mineral resources from deep seabeds, etc. Some states also impose excise taxes on the purchase of tobacco or alcohol.

Capital Gains Tax

Federal and state taxes levied on the profit received from the sale of an asset (i.e., stocks, bonds, and mutual funds). Profit is defined as the difference in the value of the asset at the time of sale and at the time it was acquired. The rate of the tax may also be dependent upon how long the asset was held before it was sold.

Franchise Tax

A tax that a business pays for the the privilege of forming a business and/or conducting business in a state or local municipality (i.e., a county or city). The amount of tax can differ depending on the tax rules within each jurisdiction—some states calculate the amount owed based upon the value of assets while others use the number of shares issued. Some states have significant franchise taxes (i.e., Delaware) while others (i.e., Nevada) have none.

Sales Tax

A state- or local-level consumption tax on the retail sale of goods or services. This tax is a percentage—set by the taxing jurisdiction—of the cost of the goods or services being purchased. Generally the purchaser pays the tax and the seller collects it as an agent for the taxing jurisdiction. Various taxing jurisdictions allow exemptions for purchases of specified items (e.g., in California, groceries are exempt from sales tax but prepared foods are not).

Property Tax

Tax assessed on real estate. The tax is determined by several factors, including the use of the land (residential, commercial, or industrial), the assessed value of the property, and the tax rate. The tax is usually assessed by one or more of the following local governmental entities: county or municipality government, school district, and water/sewer district. Usually deductible on federal income tax returns, property taxes are used by these entities for schools or transportation expenses (i.e., snow removal, road repair, etc.).

Source: Internal Revenue Service ◄

Where does our hard-earned money go? Well, it funds a full menu of societal needs, including the military, police and fire departments, the environment, Social Security, court systems, health inspection, transportation, and libraries. Then there's foreign aid, welfare, and programs that help the disabled.

Those are just some of the patriotic reasons for paying taxes. Don't forget there are legal reasons, too. The Sixteenth Amendment to the U.S. Constitution gives Congress the power to collect taxes. Congress has delegated those tax-collecting duties to the IRS. If that's not reason enough to fork over your dough, hefty fines and possibly a date with one of our other tax-funded entities—the U.S. prison system—await those who opt not to pay their taxes.

>>> **FAST FACT**

Notable Individuals Who Opted Not to Pay Their Taxes— and the Price They Paid

Who	What They Did/ Failed to Do	Price They Paid
Helio Castroneves	Failed to report to the IRS about $5.5 million in income between 1999 and 2004	Plead not guilty to these charges in October 2008, and was ordered released on $10 million bail; faces a maximum thirty-five-year prison sentence
Wesley Snipes	Failed to file tax returns from 1999 to 2004; claimed he had no requirement to pay taxes	Convicted in 2008; sentenced to three years in prison
Richard Hatch	Failed to pay taxes on the $1 million grand prize from winning *Survivor*	Convicted in 2006; sentenced to more than four years in prison
Heidi Fleiss	Failed to pay taxes on "escort services" income	Convicted in 1997; sentenced to three years in prison
Leona Helmsley	Claimed $2.6 million in phony business expenses	Convicted in 1994; served four years in prison

Who	What They Did/ Failed to Do	Price They Paid
Willie Nelson	Owed $16.7 million in back taxes	In 1990, the IRS confiscated and auctioned off his assets; released a double album, *The IRS Tapes: Who'll Buy My Memories*, with all profits going to the IRS; debt paid in full by 1993
Al Capone	Failed to pay four years of taxes on income earned illegally	Convicted in 1931; sentenced to eleven years in prison and an $80,000 fine

Few Americans enjoy paying taxes, usually ranking the chore somewhere between getting a root canal sans Novocain and hosting a birthday party for fifteen nap-deprived kindergartners. And there is little doubt that some of our tax money is spent in a less-than-judicious manner. In fact, a decent case can be made that our elected politicians have a monopoly on hare-brained schemes and pet pork projects that have little to do with the general welfare of our country. Perhaps that's why former Canadian prime minister W. L. MacKenzie King's observation that "The politician's promises of yesterday are the taxes of today" hits so close to home.

Nevertheless, as anyone who has ever benefitted from federally sponsored programs knows—and that includes anyone who's ever been to public school, received mail, or gone to a national park—taxes are critical to the public morality of a democratic society. No taxes means no justice system to punish and incarcerate the bad guys, no educational system to teach our young and give them hope for the future, and no environmental system to shield us from dangerous chemicals in our air and poisons in our water.

Perhaps the strongest reason of all for paying taxes? By and large, you cannot live in the United States of America, the greatest country of them all, without paying them.

Okay, now that I have flexed my patriotic muscles, honed in on softball fields all across the PAC-10 and along surf pipelines from Bondi Beach to Waimea Bay, let's get something straight. Although taxes are a part of our national and cultural fabric, if you are paying too much in taxes, then Uncle Sam is playing you for a sucker. The IRS will make a big show of going after you and taking all they can get, but in reality, the government is more like the tired old man behind the curtain in *The Wizard of Oz*: all bluster and bombast, but no real bite—*if* you know how to handle him.

And that, dear readers, is where I come in.

>>> FAST FACT

According to the Tax Foundation, the average American:

- Will work more than 2.5 hours out of every eight-hour workday to pay taxes. That means, in 2008, the average American worked 113 days just to pay his or her taxes.
- Will work 14.4 years out of a typical forty-five-year career to pay taxes.
- Sees taxes consume about 30.8 percent of his or her gross income— more than most Americans spend on food, clothing, and housing *combined.* ◄

Remember—*I am the Tax Lady!* I have spent my entire adult life helping people stand up to the IRS.

It is not always easy. Most clients I work with do not have a good grasp of their own tax picture. They fear the awesome clout of the IRS. It's as if they never realized *they could fight back.*

The Tax Monopoly Game

The mission of the IRS is a simple one: to collect taxes and enforce tax laws enacted by Congress. One of the world's largest money machines, the IRS collected almost $2.7 trillion in revenues for the most recently completed tax year (2006), and processed 236 million tax returns while doing so. The agency also helped more than 100 million taxpayers that year who either called the IRS's toll-free hotline, visited the agency online, wrote a letter, or visited one of the IRS's four hundred field offices spread throughout the U.S.

The agency's origins date back to 1862, right smack in the middle of the Civil War. At that time, President Lincoln, with the blessing of Congress, created a position called the Commissioner of Internal Revenue. The move was a boon to the war effort, as the newly created tax office sent roughly four thousand tax collectors out to hill and dale and townhouse and flophouse, collecting $28.15 million in 1863 and a total of $300 million by the end of the war. From the start, the IRS was incredibly diligent about collecting taxes: according to agency records, in 1864, President Lincoln overpaid his own taxes by $1,250.

The agency grew in measured steps over the next hundred or so years, hindered by mounting accusations of bloatedness and strong-arm tactics. Reforms came and went until 1998, when mounting consumer complaints caused Congress to convene hearings where average Americans lined up to bash the agency. That led to some minor changes that are yet to have a true impact in re-shaping the methods or means of the IRS as the largest and most powerful collection agency on the continent.

The IRS is just one piece of the tax-collecting puzzle, albeit a critical one. Its creation is one of the cornerstones of the U.S. tax landscape in the twenty-first century.

>>> **FAST FACT**

U.S. Tax Payments, Most Recently Completed Tax Year (2006)

Total Taxes Paid:	$2.691 trillion
Individual Income Taxes:	$1.366 trillion (50.8%)
Social Insurance Taxes:	$850 billion (31.6%)
Corporate Income Taxes:	$395 billion (14.7%)
Other (Excise, Estate, and Others):	$80 billion (3.0%)

Source: Internal Revenue Service ◄

The Impact of Taxes on Americans

As French statesman Jean B. Colbert once said, "The art of taxation consists in so plucking the goose as to obtain the largest possible amount of feathers with the smallest possible amount of hissing."

So, how much hissing is the average goose . . . er, taxpayer doing these days? Not as much as you might think. Sure, the family barbecue isn't complete until Uncle Jarret moans about this year's tax bill. But overall, Americans pay their taxes every year without too much muss and fuss.

Perhaps that's because most Americans don't consider taxes to be *their* money. In fact, when the Congressional Institute commissioned the Charlton Research Company to conduct a telephone survey about taxes in 1996, one question asked was to list the items in their household budget. Only 22 percent of 800 survey respondents mentioned taxes as a personal budget item. When asked why taxes were omitted, the overwhelming response was that taxes were not considered an expenditure. Instead, because the money is simply taken directly out of their paycheck and never seen again, taxes are viewed by most individuals as inevitable—something they had absolutely no control over.

Main Budget Items	
Expense	**Percentage of Respondents**
Mortgage/Rent	55%
Food	54%
Utilities	40%
Automobile	24%
Taxes	**22%**
Other	12%
Clothing	12%
Children	10%
Entertainment	9%
Savings/Retirement/Investment	7%
Travel	6%
Charities	4%
Don't Know	2%

Source: Charlton Research Company

Call it dread, confusion, or indifference, but Americans' avoidance of tax planning is costing taxpayers plenty. By postponing or ignoring the impact taxes have on our lives, and by failing to put an aggressive tax-planning campaign in place that will minimize what Uncle Sam gets and maximize what we keep, taxpayers are painting themselves into a corner that can cost us tens of thousands of dollars, if not more, over the course of our lifetimes.

How are Americans shortchanging themselves? Usually by not claiming exemptions, deductions, and credits they are entitled to. They also shoot themselves in the foot with untimely investment withdrawals (e.g., from a 401[k], IRA, etc.). These decisions and miscalculations are the result of either not understanding or being

>>> **FAST FACT**

How Taxes Rate as a Popular Pastime

When dinner with your mother-in-law ranks higher than tackling your taxes, you know the relationship between the IRS and taxpayers is a dysfunctional one. Here's how taxes rank against other loathsome activities:

Rank	Least Favorite Activity	Percentage of Respondents
1	Trip to the Dentist	29%
2	**Doing Taxes**	**26%**
3	Public Speaking	24%
4	Cleaning the Bathroom	16%
5	Dinner with In-Laws	5%

Source: TurboTax, Quicken.com, April 2005 ◄

indifferent to their personal tax situations. Over the course of a lifetime, a missed deduction here or a lost receipt there—repeated on an annual basis—can really add up.

Consider another recent study on taxes, this one by the U.S. General Accounting Office (GAO) in 2002. It reports that as many as 2.2 million people overpay their taxes annually because they claim the standard deduction instead of itemizing. The average overpayment to the IRS was $438. That may or may not seem like much, but nevertheless, that's extra money that could be used for food, clothing, entertainment, or maybe even one extra tankfull of gasoline (ha, ha). If that's still not reason enough for you, then think about this: $438 dollars invested every year with a modest 10 percent return would yield $72,435 in thirty years! That's money you could use for an extended vacation, to put your children through college, or to live off of in early retirement. Alternatively, in my case, you could go surfing for a year!

And that's not all. The study's results indicate that the less income earned, the higher the chance of needlessly overpaying one's taxes.

Income Level	# of Taxpayers Who Overpaid Taxes
$25,000 – $50,000	853,000
$50,000 – $75,000	774,000
> $100,000	62,000

By reviewing the above chart, you can begin to see how the people who can least afford it are being most penalized by detrimental tax behaviors—or by just not having a basic understanding of taxes. As you can see, more than 1.6 million of the 2.2 million people who overpay their taxes (roughly 74 percent) are those making less than $75,000 per year.

These are the same working-class Americans that another study says are selling themselves short in other tax-related areas. According to Lincoln, Nebraska–based Avalon Marketing & Communications, people who donate clothing, books, furniture, sporting goods, and other household items to charities typically value these items at only 20 percent of their fair market value, or 80 percent less than the IRS allows. The study, conducted between October 28, 2000, and November 18, 2000, surveyed one hundred people who donated non-cash items to Nebraska charities, including the Salvation Army and Goodwill. Study supervisors inventoried the donated items, then compared the value donors put on the items with fair market values.

Item	Result
Number of People Who Undervalued	91
Average Amount Undervalued	$1,697.40
Maximum Amount Undervalued	$3,680.00

Properly valued, these donations would have resulted in an average annual tax savings of $526.19 (applying an average 31 percent combined federal and state tax rate). There goes early retirement!

Numbers like these can add up fast. If the results of the Avalon study are projected against all 20 million American taxpayers who itemize deductions and claim non-cash donations, more than $10.5 billion in additional tax savings could be realized each year.

So why do people fail to take full advantage of the IRS's fair market valuation allowance? Simple: most people don't have any idea how to determine fair market value. But they don't want to risk an audit by overvaluing their contributions either.

▶▶▶ FAST FACT

What can $10.5 billion buy?

- 3.76 billion Big Macs
- 483 million toasters
- 252 million tires
- 4.2 million flat-screen televisions
- 1.74 million pairs of diamond earrings ◀

Paper Chase

Maybe it is not Americans' indifference to or unawareness of how taxes affect their lives that has made tax planning such a low priority. Maybe it is not the wasteful government spending that leads to a "You can't fight City Hall"–type attitude.

Maybe, just maybe, it is the process of researching, record-keeping, preparing, and ultimately filing our tax returns that vexes Americans the most. An alien observer who just flew in from outer space might well wonder what Americans have done to deserve such punishment. According to the IRS, there are at least 480 different tax forms, each with many pages of instructions. Even the most basic form, the 1040EZ, has thirty-six pages of instructions, all in miniscule fine print that would give Superman and his x-ray eyes a migraine.

That is just for starters. The IRS also produces 8 billion pages of forms and instructions each year—about 300,000 trees' worth. Laid end to end, they would wrap around the earth twenty-eight times.

The tax code is so burdensome and so confusing that American taxpayers spend $200 billion and 5.4 billion hours working to comply with federal taxes each year, more than it takes to produce every car, truck, and van in the United States. In fact, we are so in*taxi*cated that we cannot complete our taxes on our own—60 percent of taxpayers hire a professional to get through their own return.

But just as a tiger cannot change its stripes, the tax code is not going to change that much, not as long as politicians in Washington are calling the shots and working under the premise that the American taxpayer can bail anyone out. As we all saw in the past year, politicians are quick to volunteer taxpayers to foot the bill—even a $760 billion bill—instead of trimming spending. And the IRS is not leaving the racket either. Granted, if you went to the IRS today, they would tell you that they are changing, that they are becoming more "user-friendly" and "customer-service oriented." Well, I've got news for you—they have been pitching that same song-and-dance routine to American taxpayers for the last twenty years. They have not changed *one iota*. Instead, they are what they will always be—the unprepared taxpayer's number one nightmare.

So, what can you do, short of having your wealth sucked out of you by the IRS?

Simple: arm yourself with knowledge. You need to learn as much about taxes as possible so you can use that knowledge to reduce your exposure to the long fangs of the IRS. This will reduce your tax liability, which in turn keeps more of your hard-earned money out of Uncle Sam's pocket—and puts more into yours.

Well then, you ask, how am I going to do all that?

My response is one question—are you ready to rumble? Because the Tax Lady **is**.

**Inside the Ropes:
Niko, the "Tax Protester"**

By all appearances, Niko is your average American. Thirty-five years old, Niko owns his own graphic design business, employing four other individuals. He is married to his high school sweetheart, Dana, and they have two lovely children. Niko owns his own home in his boyhood hometown, and plays softball for the local bar league with his former high school and college cohorts. Everything about Niko appears perfectly normal.

However, Niko has a secret. He is a tax protester.

"I don't believe the government has the right to tax my income," Niko said when I first met him. "First, the Sixteenth Amendment [which gives Congress the authority to set an income tax] was never properly ratified. Second, 'income' was never defined within the amendment anyway. So who knows what the writers were talking about when they wrote the damn thing. And don't even get me started about the Internal Revenue Swindle. They don't have authority to do anything."

Notwithstanding Niko's—and every other tax protester's—argument to the contrary, the Sixteenth Amendment *was* properly ratified, income *is* properly defined, and the IRS *does* have the authority to collect federal taxes. All these tax protester arguments have been thoroughly debunked at every level of federal court.

During my initial conversations with Niko, it was apparent he was in complete denial that he had a possibly colossal problem at his feet. Niko was still stuck in the mindset that he did not owe the IRS properly assessed taxes. In fact, Niko had failed to file a tax return since starting his business five years ago, and never made necessary payroll deposits on his employees' wages paid. This was a big problem, because Niko's business was actually quite successful. It earned more than $7 million from services and sales in its first five years of operation, most of which was reinvested into the company (i.e., marketing, technology).

But the IRS had not gotten their share over the course of those five years. And they had come to his doorstep, with their arm outstretched and palm facing upward.

"I need an attorney who can get the IRS out of my life for good," Niko told me during our initial consultation. "I am sick of them harassing me, my family, and my employees. I mean, they come to my workplace unannounced, and expect me to set aside time for them. I just can't have it anymore; I've got a business to run."

Luckily for Niko, he came to our office, where we provided him with the education he sorely needed. Once we were able to get him beyond the acceptance stage—realizing that he had a tax problem—Niko became an enthusiastic client. We were able to get his tax returns prepared and filed, and a manageable monthly payment plan set with the IRS for his back taxes, which amounted to a staggering $385,000 in business tax liabilities and $135,000 in personal taxes. We also learned, four years after resolving his case, that Niko had been able to pay his business and personal taxes in full.

≫ ROUND 2

First Steps: Mama, Don't Let Your Kids Grow Up to Be Sloppy Record Keepers

Before anything else, getting ready is the key to success.
—Henry Ford

Remember—and I tell my clients this all the time—tax planning is a year-round activity.

What do I mean by that? Well, think of Michael Phelps and swimming. As he says, "Swimming is more than a once-every-four-years sport." It requires a daily commitment to practice and repetition—not to mention consuming more than 12,000 calories per day! Every single stroke, kick, and breath is dissected and perfected because each means so much to the end result of the race.

Becoming the "Greatest Olympian of All Time" required a legendary focus and commitment to honing the craft. Phelps exemplified that through sixteen years of practice—not to mention two prior Olympics, one at the age of fifteen.

And what accounts for that level of commitment? Well, go to Phelps himself for the answer to that question. "I think that everything is possible as long as you put your mind to it and you put the work and time into it. I think your mind really controls everything."

Now, the commitment to tax planning is not nearly as . . . taxing as it is to be an Olympic athlete in any sport. However, it does take more than a lackadaisical approach—because if you slack off, you are easy pickings for the IRS. You can't expect to show up at the Olympics and take home eight gold medals. Similarly, you can't expect to wake up on April 14 or 15 and meet your tax deadline while saving big bucks in the process. It just will not happen. Chances are you will rush your taxes, miss a boatload of exemptions, deductions, and credits, and promise yourself you will do better next year as you sprint to the post office before the clock strikes midnight.

Why go through that kind of pain and anxiety? Instead, treat tax planning as a year-long marathon rather than a one-week sprint. By taking a "big picture" approach to tax strategizing, you will save money, and alleviate tax headaches in the process.

Let's develop a plan together so you can develop such a strategy. I have some great ideas for you—ideas that have already been tried and tested with clients of my own who wound up saving serious money on their taxes.

Keeping Good Records

When it comes to preparing our tax returns, many Americans don't mind waiting until the last minute.

According to the IRS, 20 million Americans wait until the final week before April 15—tax deadline day—to square their accounts with the IRS. What's more, almost a third of the returns claiming refunds are not mailed until after April 1, despite the fact that the money could have been earning interest weeks before. And with more than 70 percent of taxpayers entitled to a refund, procrastination amounts to a great big interest-free loan for Uncle Sam.

That is a surprisingly large number of procrastinators, especially in a nation where drive-through restaurant windows, wireless

Internet, and instant text messaging are staples of the "hurry-up" culture. Normally, we like to take care of business, and fast.

Not with our taxes, though. We will come up with any reason to put off preparing our taxes. There is that "You May Already Be a Millionaire" mailer to complete and put in the mail. Maybe you need to check on that bid you made on eBay for the world's largest ball of string. Moreover, you know you will have to set aside an afternoon for the time-honored tradition of watching paint dry.

You get the picture.

Perhaps it would be easier to get our collective acts together and file our taxes with plenty of time to spare—and plenty of well-earned deductions included—if we were better prepared for the process. In tax planning, as in life, preparation is key. As basketball great Larry Bird once said, "If you don't do your homework, you won't make your free throws." Even Magic Johnson would agree to that.

This is particularly true in tax planning, where things can get complicated in a hurry if you're not ready. Interest deductions, non-reimbursed business expenses, and charitable contributions all call for extensive records to support them on your tax return.

If you do not have all this available come tax time, you will likely be leaving some money on the table. Money that the government—not you—will put to good use.

Why Keep Records?

The good news is that you have the opportunity to organize your financial records in a clear, smart way, so you know what you are doing when you sit down to prepare your tax returns.

Why begin with something as seemingly humdrum and bland as bookkeeping? Because a solid record keeping system is the foundation for a solid tax plan.

For example, reducing your taxes will typically involve one of two things (both of which you will learn more about later in this book): reducing your Adjusted Gross Income or increasing your tax deductions, exemptions, and/or credits. In order to do either, you will need documentation to show that you made contributions to an

IRA or paid student loan interest (i.e., reduced your Adjusted Gross Income) and/or have dependents, paid mortgage interest, or are eligible for education credits (i.e., increased your deductions, exemptions, and/or credits). Thus, you need a system to maintain records associated with those actions or statuses.

But keeping good records is not just a tax-reducing luxury—it is also a necessity. The IRS has a sweet deal set up with the legal system: income tax regulations place the burden of proof on you, the taxpayer. So, can you see why you need to maintain accurate records in order to prepare your tax returns? These records should verify the income and expenses you report. Largely, these are the same documents—check stubs, old tax statements, receipts, and the like—that you use to monitor your business or track your personal finances.

With an organized record keeping system, you will have the information on hand to claim the right deductions on your return and keep a few extra bucks in your pocket.

Creating the Perfect System

Before getting into the specifics of the perfect organizational system, remember and follow this simple rule: **keep it simple**. I cannot stress this enough. Keeping your system simple ensures that it will be easy to remember from day to day, month to month, and year to year. In addition, when the parties involved in managing your system expand due to growth of your family or growth of your business, it ensures that the system can be easily taught and easily understood by these new managers.

The key to any simple organizational system is centralization. This can be achieved by storing your key physical documentation in a single filing cabinet, located near a computer that has all your electronic records stored in a single file. This file can be on the hard drive or on a web-based program. And remember to back up any electronic copies on a CD or portable hard drive (also called a flash drive). We are in the age of the computer virus, where rogue contaminants can infiltrate any personal computer and destroy its contents in seconds.

TAX TIPS

Why Good Record Keeping Is Good and Bad Record Keeping Is Bad

- **Good record keeping leads to more money in your pocket**
  Efficient tax records can mean big tax savings. For example, by keeping track of allowable deductions and tax credits—and using them—you are keeping more of your hard-earned money.

- **Bad record keeping leads to a pain in the . . . er, audit**
  Bad record keeping can not only lead to an audit, but can also end up costing you a lot of money in the end. The key in any audit is backing up your tax statements with documented evidence. Without that evidence, deductions can be disallowed, leading to a substantial tax bill.

- **Good record keeping kills unnecessary stress**
  Who needs the headache of not knowing where that essential mortgage loan document is or what you earned on capital gains this year? A thorough record keeping system not only organizes your financial life, it helps you sleep better at night, too.

Finally, invest in a safe deposit box for the financial documents you absolutely cannot afford to lose. This should include your birth certificate, the deed to your house, any stocks or bonds, and your will and other estate-planning documents. If it makes you feel better, go ahead and stick that Mickey Mantle baseball card from 1957 in there, too. As I said, whatever is important to you. A bonus: the safe deposit box may be tax deductible if it holds income-producing or investment-related items

Please note—there is no universally acknowledged "perfect" system for tax record keeping. Every individual and/or business is its own unique breed. What follows is a system that I recommend and have found successful both individually and professionally, but you will need to figure out what works for you. Just remember to keep your tax filing system organized enough that you can put your hands on a key document in thirty seconds or less, every time. In other words, *keep it simple and keep it consistent.*

▶▶▶ FAST FACT

The Must-Have Tax Record Keeping Checklist to Get You Started:

☑	Item
☐	Safe deposit box
☐	Desk (preferably with filing cabinet to hold records)
☐	Two to three dozen file folders
☐	Two to three dozen white business labels
☐	Ball-point pen/felt marker
☐	Computer
☐	Back-up electronic filing (i.e., CD, flash drive, etc.)

Getting Started

Take your pen and begin recording the tax document headings on your file folders. Here is a list of suggested headings:

- **Income**
  - ▶ Wages (W-2 forms)
  - ▶ Interest and Dividends (1099 forms)
  - ▶ Investment Account Statements

- ➤ Supporting Statements for Capital Gains and Losses
- ➤ Social Security Payments
- ➤ Retirement Plan Distributions
- ➤ Alimony Received
- ➤ Annual Business Profit and Loss Statement (if self-employed or a business owner)
- ➤ Miscellaneous (unemployment insurance payments, hobby or gambling income, etc.)

- **Expenses**
  - ➤ Medical
  - ➤ Taxes: Property, State Income Tax, and Foreign Income Tax
  - ➤ Interest: Home Mortgage, Business, and Investment
  - ➤ Charitable Contributions
  - ➤ Childcare Expenses
  - ➤ Education Expenses
  - ➤ Adoption Expenses
  - ➤ Alimony
  - ➤ Wages Paid to Household Employees
  - ➤ Miscellaneous (union dues, tax-preparation fees, etc.)

- **Special Items**
  - ➤ Closing Statements on Real Estate Transactions
  - ➤ Moving Expense Statements
  - ➤ Copy of Prior Year's Tax Return
  - ➤ Partnership K-1s
  - ➤ IRA Contributions
  - ➤ Rental Property Statements (from a property management company)
  - ➤ College Loan Statements

What Tax Records to Keep

If I had a dime for every time a client told us that he or she couldn't find this or that form, I could buy my own tropical island and go surfing for the rest of my life.

While you do not have to keep every financial document that crosses your path—the receipt for this morning's donut and coffee come to mind—there are some tax records that take precedence over others. Let us have a look at the ones you should hang on to:

- **Basic Financial Documents**
  Hang on to pay invoices/receipts, W-2 forms, records of tips received, receipts for big-ticket items like your home or car, records of investments and contributions to retirement accounts, bank and brokerage statements, and 1099 forms.

- **Receipts for Deductible Items**
  Many people I know pay for everything they buy with a debit or credit card, or electronic funds transfer or check. If that's you, then you will need to record all the pertinent information—such as a check number, dollar amount, payee's name, and date of the transaction. If you use cash, make sure you have a signed and dated receipt showing the amount and reason for the payment.

- **Insurance and Medical Records**
  Keep paperwork regarding insurance claims and medical expenses, along with dates and specifics as to what was paid for and when.

- **Theft or Loss Documentation**
  If you have been the victim of a crime, then listen up. Any theft loss should be documented, including the value of what you lost, the date the property was first noticed missing, and verification that it was owned by you. If possible—and where appropriate—attempt to obtain a copy of the police report and an insurance report with a record of all reimbursements.

- **Gambling Records**
  If you hang out in Las Vegas or Atlantic City, you should document everything. Just state the type of gambling activity, the

amount won or lost, the address or location of the establishment, names of others present with you, and the date. Keep all ATM receipts and ask for a receipt when cashing in your chips.

- **Records of Charitable Contributions**
  Charitable contributions of goods or services over $75 require a receipt. You can only deduct a cash donation of $250 or more if you have written confirmation. Be sure to log out-of-pocket expenses for charitable work, such as mileage, parking fees, tolls, cost and cleaning of uniforms, and bus or taxi fares. Record the name of the charity, the date of the expenses, and the amount.

- **Small Business or Self-Employment Records**
  If you work for yourself or use your home for business, make room for a special set of records, things like 401(k) forms and Health Savings Account forms. Obviously, any tax forms, too.

Please remember to separate your tax records into active and inactive files, and remember what goes into each category. Otherwise you're going to mix up your W-2 from working the back fryer at Burger King in high school with your W-2 from working in the Merger & Acquisitions Department of Burger King Corp. Your active file will include all the items mentioned above for the current tax year (so if you received a bonus check from your employer in January, record it in the "active" general finance file). Your inactive file should be further separated by inactive years, and then broken down like your active file.

For your inactive file, you will need to hang on to at least six years' worth of tax returns (more on that below) and relevant supporting documents, along with home improvement receipts, cancelled checks, and pay stubs for the previous tax year.

The same goes for your personal and business records. If you own a home-based or other small business, keep your personal records separate from your business records. You will have a much easier time figuring out which deductions and credits you are entitled to as a business owner if you are working off the correct tax records.

Above all, remember to file your tax records in order by date, broken down by category. Organizing your receipts, pay stubs, and various financial forms as the year goes along will make it easier to get the numbers you need when it is time to file your tax return.

There are several web-based and software programs on the market designed to help you maintain good tax records. Even if you grab one, you should still keep original receipts and tax forms. In fact, it's a good idea to use a folder, envelope, or binder to keep all your records for the tax year together, and then store these yearly files away in boxes or on shelves for later reference.

 TAX TIPS

Tax Records to Keep

The list of financial records to hang on to is a lengthy one, ranging from household budgeting sheets to the receipt and warranty for your new barbecue grill. For tax purposes, though, records can be limited to the following:

- **Income**
    - ➤ Records of employment earnings and tips received (W-2 forms)
    - ➤ Records of interest, dividends, and state income tax refunds (1099 forms)
    - ➤ Records of self-employment (1099 forms, invoices, and receipts)
    - ➤ Alimony receipts (divorce decree, your ex-spouse's Social Security number, and bank statement)
    - ➤ Capital gains and losses (brokerage confirmation slips, receipts showing date acquired, cost and gross selling price, and form 1099-B)

» Bank statements (for all open accounts and accounts closed that year)
» Real estate rental income (lease agreements, closing statements with the cost of property, contracts and cancelled checks reflecting improvements and repairs made, and information on depreciation from previous tax years)
» Distributions from IRAs and retirement plans (until all funds in the account are withdrawn)
» Distributions from other tax-deferred plans (cancelled checks, withholding statements, and employer-supplied documents)
» Partnerships, S corporations, estates and trusts (K-1 forms and all investment records), nontaxable income, and gifts (records of the donor's basis, fair market value at date received, and tax paid on the gift if applicable)
» Unemployment compensation
» Social Security benefits
» Miscellaneous income (jury duty fees, gambling winnings, prizes, and hobby income, etc.)

- **Expenses**
  » Retirement plan contributions (contribution statements, a copy of the plan, and a statement of actuarial assumptions)
  » Alimony payments (cancelled checks, divorce decree or agreement, and your ex-spouse's Social Security number)
  » Medical and dental expenses (cancelled checks, receipts, copies of bills, doctors' statements, prescriptions, insurance policies, records for amounts deducted by employers for medical insurance, and expenses for which you were reimbursed, like car expenses and gas mileage)
  » Taxes (W-2 forms for state income tax withheld, state tax return for additional tax paid, cancelled checks, copies of estimated state tax returns and tax documents supporting deductions for both real and personal property taxes)
  » Home mortgage and investment interest expenses (statements, notes, and cancelled checks that outline the terms of a loan)

➠ Charitable contributions (cancelled checks, appraisals, any re-ceipts recording the name of charity and amount and date of gift, and the value of any items received in return, out-of-pocket expenses, and mileage incurred while providing services to the charitable organization)

➠ Casualty/theft losses (police and insurance reports, receipts for items, and any documentation showing the fair market value when destroyed or stolen)

➠ Non-reimbursed business expenses (credit card slips, receipts, cancelled checks, and a detailed business ledger of expenses)

➤➤➤ FAST FACT

Lost & Found

Here are some quick tips to getting yourself back in shape records-wise for tax season:

- If you've lost your W-2, just contact your employer for another, or, if you are having your taxes done professionally, ask your tax preparer for help. If you cannot get one before you file, use the information from your last pay stub for the year and prepare Form 4852. Please note that the IRS does not accept this form until February 15 of the filing season.

- If you've lost receipts, reconstruct the amounts as best you can. If you obtain additional substantiation after you have filed, you can always file an amended return if the numbers you reported were not accurate.

- If you need to retrieve a new IRS tax form or research a publication, log on to www.irs.gov and select "Forms and Publications." You can also ask your tax preparer for assistance. I'm sure he or she would love to help. ◄

How Long Should I Keep Records?

Some clients I work with keep their tax records indefinitely. You have probably seen a few of them. They are the folks forever down at the office supply store buying more filing cabinets to hold more paperwork. Nice people—but you do not want to emulate their record keeping habits.

You might have heard the story about Hollywood studio chief Samuel Goldwyn. One day his secretary, while cleaning out the office file cabinets, asked Goldwyn if she could throw out files that were ten years old or older. "Sure," he said. "Just be sure to make copies."

In an odd way, Goldwyn had a point. You certainly don't want to throw away your financial records too soon. Then again, unless you favor wallpapering your home office with fifteen-year-old telephone bills and bank statements, you don't want to hang on to them forever.

The IRS requires taxpayers to keep their tax records around for three years from the date the return was filed. By law, the IRS has three years to ring you up and question a return. If they find discrepancies they can go back six years, and if they find outright fraud they can dig as far back as their hearts desire. So to be on the safe side, hang on to your tax records for six years, particularly key documents like your tax forms, pay stubs, and checking account statements.

There are certain forms, though, that you really should hang on to indefinitely. For example, the IRS recommends that you keep copies of your W-2 forms until you are eligible for retirement, in case there is a discrepancy with the Social Security Administration records. In the event you become ill or pass away, you may need to prove earnings for retirement income or insurance purposes. Your W-2 forms are the best proof of those earnings.

It's also a good idea to store copies of your Form 8606 along with your tax returns. This is the form used to track the basis in your individual retirement account (i.e., total, nondeductible contributions made to your IRA that will be recovered tax-free when distributions begin). It is filed annually with your tax return, showing the on-going basis amount with any nondeductible contributions for that year's tax return. Investment brokerages and banks do not keep this information, and neither does the IRS. Thus, taxpayers should keep the basis information for any year of nondeductible contribution, even if it's decades old. Hopefully you have been saving copies of these forms in your safe deposit box, right next to your complete set of Bee Gees eight-tracks.

INVESTMENT TIP:
Go to a Professional

Unless you are qualified or have experience with IRAs, make sure you see your IRA custodian to determine your required minimum distribution. The calculation is fairly complex, and banks typically do a good job with it.

Also, hang on to copies of records from any purchase of investment assets or properties until at least three years after the assets are sold. Ditto for your home and home improvements.

Keep Tax Returns for Six Years, Then Shred

After six years, it should be safe to throw your tax documents away. If you are the ceremonial type, burn them in the fireplace while sipping champagne. But get rid of them.

You can shred any financial document that is dated, including expired insurance policies, credit card bills more than a year old, and receipts for items with expired warranties. Go ahead and junk those documents that are also stored elsewhere, like medical records (your primary physician has them).

> >>> **FAST FACT**

What You Can Safely Throw Away:

✓	Throw Away at Will
✓	Tax documents > six years old
✓	Expired insurance policies
✓	Non-tax-related checks (birthday money, consumer goods rebates, etc.)
✓	Records for things you no longer own
✓	Paycheck stubs > one year old
✓	Old wills and estate documents (keeping old wills and estate documents is a huge no-no for both tax and non-tax reasons)
✓	Quarterly mutual fund statements—just keep the year-end ones
✓	Cancelled checks > three years old
✓	Household bills > one year old

Pay Attention, Small Business Owners

Entrepreneurs are the kind of people who identify problems, solutions, and how much they're going to cost—but not always in that order. You want food on the road—invent fast food. You create a wallet-sized instrument for carrying an infinite collection of music—market the hell out of it and sell individual songs to fill it. You get the picture.

Unfortunately, innovation and record keeping are not typically bosom buddies. In fact, they are more like polar opposites, with the innovator being all about what is cutting-edge and the record keeper being all about what is tried-and-true. Thus, as an innovative business owner, calling the tax record keeping responsibilities tedious is like calling the Grand Canyon a cute little hole in the ground.

Still, to be a successful, innovative business owner, it is a responsibility that must be met. Good record keeping could be the difference between recording your annual balance sheets in red ink or black. In fact, the University of Maine Cooperative Extension claims you can save $100 per hour solely by keeping good records. How, you ask? Well, imagine you have a $20 business expense that you failed to record or maintain a receipt. This failure raises your business's net income by $20. Overstating your net income by $20 causes your Social Security tax to go up $3.06 (i.e., $20 times 15.3 percent for a self-employed person), your federal income tax to go up $4 (i.e., $20 times 20 percent—assuming you are in the 20 percent tax bracket), and your State Income tax to go up $1 (i.e., $20 times 5 percent—assuming you are in the 5 percent tax bracket for your state).

As you can see, this $20 oversight has now cost you $8.06 more in taxes (i.e., Social Security, federal, and state). Now, how much time do you think it would have taken you to record this expense or maintain this receipt? Five minutes, tops, right? So, had you spent this five minutes recording this expense or saving the receipt, you would have saved $8.06 in taxes in 1/12 of an hour of work. Or, put another way, a savings of $96.72 per hour. And that kind of savings can mean a *lot* to any struggling company. In addition to cost savings, maintaining good records provides (1) an accurate reflection of financial performance, (2) ability to monitor business performance in specific areas, (3) complete and accurate income and expense data, and (4) the basis for future planning of your business's growth.

Just because you are a business does not mean you have to have a record keeping system that rivals Google. Just use the same tools you would for personal records. That means some kind of filing system, online or offline, where your records can be kept in a safe, dry place.

As a business owner, you will also be keeping many of the same documents you would as an individual taxpayer, but you will be adding to that list. For instance, receipts, cancelled checks, and credit card bills are invaluable items to a small business owner. They all provide evidence of business-related expenses, which will come in handy when you are looking for tax deductions and credits.

You do not have to keep every scrap of paper—the IRS does not require receipts, for example, for less than $250 in value. When you do save a receipt, make sure to jot on the receipt or in your business expense ledger the amount, date, time, place, description, and business purpose. Make sure you label all your bank deposit slips. They provide a good record of sources of income and backup sales records.

If you use your car for business purposes, you will need a separate automobile expense ledger to record dates, mileage, tolls, parking fees, and general upkeep costs. Do not be reluctant to record too much information—better to have too much data than too little at tax time.

If your business has other employees on the payroll, you will also have to keep track of your payroll tax deposits for the quarterly payroll tax return.

Also, *keep your record keeping system updated*. Do not wait until the end of the year to collect your receipts and other records. Conduct a monthly review to make sure you have everything in order. Keep your records in one place, using envelopes to store receipts by month. Make sure receipts are labeled, dated, and can be read. If you forget a receipt or can't get one, make one of your own to remind you of the expense.

Use the Calendar to Your Advantage

Break the year down into seasons, just like Mother Nature does.

From January through March, set up your tax strategy for the coming year. In April, complete your taxes and check off the list you made for what to do by April 15. That includes things like deductions taken, forms filled out, checks sent out on time if you owe money to Uncle Sam, payments for retirement accounts if you're self-employed—all those "to do" items you have accumulated throughout

TAX TIPS

Essential Records That Small Business Owners Should Keep on File:

☑	ITEM
☐	**Checkbook:** it is advisable—scratch that, *mandatory*—to keep a separate bank account for your business
☐	**Income Receipt Records:** tabulated daily, weekly, or monthly
☐	**Expenses:** keep monthly summary listings of expenses
☐	**Asset Purchase Records:** i.e., computer equipment, automobiles, real estate leased or purchased, etc.
☐	**Employee Compensation (Payroll) Records:** if you have employees

the past twelve months in anticipation of having a clean, financially beneficial tax experience come tax day.

After the tax deadline, kick back. Fire up them grills, turn up the music, and take a breather. Use the summer months to reorganize your records and get ready for the busy season. Beginning in mid-autumn, begin to tally up your earnings for the year, including salary, interest, dividends, investment profits, self-employment, rental income, and any other income sources.

In early November, before filling your face with turkey, Grandma Nuny's stuffing, and pumpkin pie, take a piece of paper or a computer spreadsheet and a good calculator, and figure out your estimated income for the remaining two months of the year (based on your calculations from the first ten months). Once you have that final figure of taxable income for the year in place, begin chopping away at your taxable income before Uncle Sam gets his grabby paws on your money. With a fix on your taxable income, check the tax rates that apply. That tells you exactly how well you will be paid for maneuvers that reduce taxable income.

By December, you will not only be checking off gifts bought for loved ones, you will also be checking off your year-end planning lists. For example, begin planning for year-end tax deadlines, determining how much money you are going to sock away in your 401(k), whether you make a contribution to an IRA, or whether you should sell stocks or mutual funds to gain capital losses for the year (there is much more on taxes and investing in Round 7). On or before December 31, you will have completed your year-end financial paperwork so it is reflected on the current year's tax bill. January 1 starts the ball rolling all over again for the new tax year.

I will say this again and again: staying on top of your tax situation is not difficult if you have good records, a good tax-planning system in place, and a healthy appetite for keeping more of your money away from Uncle Sam.

Also, remember why you are expending all this energy to tackle your tax situation. Buried within thousands of pages of tax laws is a cornucopia of tax-saving opportunities. Whether it is moving income from one year to the next, selling a stock or two that lost money to balance out gains from your portfolio winners, or plowing a grand or two into your child's college account, the savings you realize on a year-to-year basis could reach thousands, if not tens of thousands, of dollars, depending on your income level. So reviewing your tax situation on a regular basis throughout the year may be the smartest financial decision you will ever make.

Know Your Tax Dates

One last item before your new tax record keeping system is complete: keep a copy of the IRS's annual tax calendar on hand so you know the key dates during the tax year. Pin it on your bulletin board, tape it to your refrigerator, or keep a copy on your computer's calendar function.

It would be a pity to organize all those receipts, invoices, and auto mileage records only to miss a key IRS filing date. Here is a copy to get you started. (Please note that these dates are always subject to change due to weekends and holidays. Typically, if the date below falls on a weekend or holiday, use the first business day thereafter.)

Key IRS Dates

☀ January ☀	
DATE	**EVENT(S)**
1	Start of Tax Season—Oh yeah, Happy New Year!
15	• Individuals/corporations make the **fourth estimated tax payment for the preceding year** if not paying—*or not paying enough*—income taxes through withholding; individuals use IRS Form 1040-ES • *(Employers)* **File Form 941** for fourth quarter for preceding year • *(Employers)* Deposit fourth quarter federal unemployment taxes (if more than $500) for preceding year
31	• *(Employers)* **W-2s are due/Forms 1099 are due**; send them out to your employees and contractors • *(Employers)* **File Form 941** for fourth quarter for preceding year • *(Employers)* Deposit fourth quarter federal unemployment taxes (if more than $500) for preceding year • *(Employers)* **File Form 940, 940EZ** for federal unemployment taxes

☁ February ☁	
DATE	**EVENT(S)**
14	• Happy Valentine's Day! My favorite!
28	• *(Employers)* **File Form 1096** accompanied by copies of Form 1099 • **File reconciliation on Form W-3** accompanied by 'A' copies of Form W-2 • *(Employers—Restaurant)* **File Form 8027**, Employer's Annual Tip Income Return • *(Employers—Mortgage Lender)* **File Form 1098**, Mortgage Interest Received Exceeding $600 • *(Employers—Casino)* **File Form W-2G**, Gambling Winnings

☂ March ☂	
DATE	**EVENT(S)**
15	• **Corporate Tax Day!** Corporation returns and taxes are due for corporations using the calendar year • Due date for postmarked automatic six-month extension for corporate returns (new deadline is September 15 for same calendar year); use Form 7004 for a six-month extension and pay tax due (if not paying, still disclose the amount due)
17	• Happy St. Patrick's Day!

April	
DATE	**EVENT(S)**
15	• **Tax Day!** Individual and partnership returns and individual taxes due • Due date for postmarked automatic six-month extension for individual returns (new deadline is October 15 for same calendar year); use IRS Form 4868 • Due date for gift tax returns and payment of gift taxes • Due date for IRA contributions • Individuals/corporations make the **first estimated tax payment for current year** if not paying—*or not paying enough*—income taxes through withholding; individuals use IRS Form 1040-ES
30	• *(Employers)* **File Form 941** for first quarter • *(Employers)* Deposit first quarter federal unemployment taxes (if more than $500)

May	
DATE	**EVENT(S)**
2nd Sunday	• Happy Mother's Day!
15	• Due date for information return for tax exempt organizations

⌖ June ⌖

DATE	EVENT(S)
2nd Sunday	• Happy Father's Day!
15	• Due date for individuals living abroad (and/or in the military) to file returns and pay taxes • Individuals make the **second estimated tax payment for the current year** if not paying—*or not paying enough*—income taxes through withholding; use IRS Form 1040-ES

○ July ○

DATE	EVENT(S)
31	• *(Employers)* **File Form 941** for second quarter • *(Employers)* Deposit second quarter federal unemployment taxes (if more than $500) • *(Employers)* **File Forms 5500, 5500-EZ**, Employee Benefit Plans

○ August ○

Nothing going on tax-wise, so here is your chance to head out for an end-of-summer vacation.

⌖ September ⌖

DATE	EVENT(S)
15	• If your corporation filed for an extension, due date to file corporate return and pay any and all tax, interest, and penalties due • Individuals/corporations make the **third estimated tax payment for the current year** if not paying—*or not paying enough*—income taxes through withholding; individuals use IRS Form 1040-ES

DATE	☁ October ☁ EVENT(S)
1	• Deadline for establishing SIMPLE IRA for this calendar year
15	• If you filed for an extension, due date to file return and pay any and all tax, interest, and penalties due
31	• *(Employers)* **File Form 941** for third quarter • *(Employers)* Deposit third quarter federal unemployment taxes (if more than $500) • *(Employers)* Deadline to give employees notice of employer match for a SIMPLE plan • Boo! Happy Halloween!

☁ November ☁

Not much going on tax-wise, so relax and watch the Giants
crush the Yankees in the World Series.

DATE	☃ December ☃ EVENT(S)
Throughout Month	• Happy Holidays!
31	• Deadline for establishing many self-employed retirement plans for this calendar year

Inside the Ropes: How Hannah Got Her Organizational Groove Back

Hannah is a highly trained marketing executive working for a Fortune 500 company. At work, she is a notorious neat freak. Her co-workers joke that the sheen from Hannah's freshly polished desk could act as a tracking point for the U.S. Space Shuttle. Hannah's mandate was that she would never go home for the evening until her desk was clean.

However, this past tax season, Hannah had some difficulty. Due to a variety of professional and personal changes—she was both promoted and transferred to a subsidiary of her business and, as a result, had to relocate—Hannah's famed tidiness failed to carry over to her home.

While Hannah continued to use a centralized location for her documents, she failed to maintain internal organization of those receipts and statements. Specifically, paycheck stubs, investment statements, and work-related expense receipts were all being stored in the same folder in her filing cabinet. She also failed to even file the documents as they arrived, and instead stored them as a large stack of documents in the "to do" pile.

By the time April 15 came around, Hannah had a lot of difficulty preparing her returns. In fact, Hannah was sure she could have claimed additional deductions, but could not find the appropriate records. As a result, she ended up having to pay the IRS instead of qualifying for a deduction. On April 16, Hannah was on a mission to ensure that this did not happen again.

"I read an article in the newspaper about reducing paper clutter and decided to apply it to my financial records," said Hannah. "So I went out and purchased two fireproof file cabinets, one for current stuff and another for information I would need over the long haul. I also bought a home safe for my vital records, just like the article said."

Using the article's advice as a blueprint, Hannah created a vastly improved record keeping system where everything was tabulated and filed individually for easy access. "I built an active file for things like recent bank and brokerage statements, insurance policies—anything I thought I'd need to pay my taxes next year. Then I created an inactive file where I put my last three tax returns and all the supporting documents for those returns. I put my birth certificate, passport, and some heirlooms from my grandmother in the safe."

Hannah also complemented her system by storing electronic copies of documents she received from her bank and investment firms on her personal computer in a similar file structure. She backed that system up through use of a USB flash drive.

Now Hannah has a financial record keeping system that is simple and consistent. "I know where things are and I know how long I should keep them. Next year, preparing my tax returns will be a snap. And Uncle Sam will be the one writing me a check."

➤ ROUND 3

Armed & Dangerous: The More You Know, the Less You Pay

The hardest thing to understand in the world is the income tax.
—Albert Einstein

Look at who said the above—Albert freaking Einstein. This from the man who had an IQ higher than our cholesterol counts!

Nevertheless, if you organize your records and bone up on the bedrock foundations of the IRS tax code—things like taxable and nontaxable income, filing status, and personal exemptions and withholdings—you are going to be way ahead of the game.

Why? Because having a basic knowledge of the tax code enables you to create a tax-planning strategy that takes full advantage of opportunities, loopholes, and options allowed within the tax code.

And that's where the real money can be found. After all, there's no getting around it—the key to fighting back against the IRS is to arm yourself.

No, not with brass knuckles or a bullwhip like the one Indiana Jones uses. If you're going to go twelve rounds with Uncle Sam, you need to arm yourself with *knowledge*. In tax planning, like most other walks of life, knowledge is power.

That is part of my "fighter" mentality for tax planning. You cannot and will not take advantage of your opponent—the IRS—and identify the thousands of tax breaks available to you in the tax code without first understanding how taxes work. That is the basis of this Round—training you to become familiar with taxes and taxable income so you can put that knowledge to good use. Then, when I tackle deductions, credits, and other tax breaks later in this book, you will know how to capitalize on them so they will help you change your financial life.

What Is Taxable Income?

By definition, taxable income is the amount of income subject to income taxes each year, usually calculated by subtracting the appropriate deductions (IRA contributions, alimony payments, non-reimbursed business expenses, some capital losses, etc.) from your total income. In more user-friendly terms, it is the money you earn throughout the year. Good examples of taxable income include salaries, wages, tips, commissions, interest and dividends, rental payments—even gambling and lottery winnings.

In IRS land, there are two types of income, **earned** and **unearned**. What's the difference?

- **Earned Income**
  Money you receive in exchange for goods or services. Typically this is compensation for work, including salary, wages, tips, commissions, and bonuses. But it also includes income you get from things like unemployment benefits and sick pay. Fringe benefits your employer provides are considered earned income, too. So if you enjoy a company car, a country club membership, or box seats at the World Series, Uncle Sam wants a piece of the action.

>>> **FAST FACT**

It's on You, Babe

Make no mistake about it, the government counts on you—and your income. In fact, the majority of the federal government's revenue is derived from income taxes. According to the IRS, personal income taxes generate roughly three times as much revenue as corporate income taxes.

Source: Internal Revenue Service ◄

- **Unearned Income**
  Money you receive that is not in exchange for goods or services. Typically this is the income generated by your financial investments or from selling your house or car. Even that $2,000 you won in Las Vegas is considered unearned income and is taxable as a result. So, too, are alimony payments received, rental income, and royalties earned from business ventures. Example: if this book you are holding in your hands sells well—and I sure hope it does!—it will likely earn royalties, which means I'll get a bill from the IRS for the taxes on those royalties.

Taken together, the sum of your earned and unearned income is your **gross income**.

Income Uncle Sam Considers Taxable

☑	**TAXABLE INCOME**
☑	**Wages/salaries**
☑	**Bonuses/tips/stipends**
☑	**Vacation/sick pay** (including third-party sick pay)
☑	**Employer supplemental unemployment benefits**
☑	**Employee contributions to** tax-deferred **retirement plans and** tax-deferred **annuity plans** (i.e., 401[k], 403[b], 457[b], etc.)
☑	**Employee contributions to costs of fringe benefits**
☑	**Employer-provided educational assistance**
☑	**Employer-paid premiums for group term life insurance** over $50,000
☑	**Contributions made by/on behalf of employees to cafeteria plans** (i.e., Section 125, etc.)
☑	**Contributions made on behalf of employees to** tax-deferred **annuity plans**
☑	**Net rental income**
☑	**Net farm income**
☑	**Net business income** (i.e., sole proprietorships, partnerships, corporations, hybrid business entities [LLCs, LLPs, etc.])
☑	**Trust/estate income**
☑	**Ordinary gains**
☑	**Income from wage continuation plans** (i.e., retirement incentive plans, severance pay, short-term disability, etc.)
☑	**Stock options** when exercised
☑	**Compensation paid in goods, services, property usage**
☑	**Prizes and gifts,** when connected with employment

☑	**TAXABLE INCOME**
☑	**Jury duty income**
☑	**Gambling/lottery winnings**
☑	**Strike pay**
☑	**Profit sharing**
☑	**Uniform, automobile, and travel allowances**
☑	**Reimbursements in excess of deductible expenses**
☑	**Social Security payments** (under some circumstances)
☑	**Pensions/retirement plans**
☑	**And more** (director fees, punitive damages, federal code section 89, union steward fees, etc.)

 T A X   T I P S

Punitive vs. Compensatory Damages

Hey, what can I say—the IRS likes to collect money. So when it comes to judgments, the IRS wants a piece of the pie.

The typical distinction is between compensatory damages—which cover the cost of physical injuries or loss—and punitive damages. This includes:

- **Interest earned on damages**—taxable as interest income
- **Punitive damages (i.e., punish the other party)**—taxable as other income
- **Emotional distress or mental anguish**—taxable as to the amount that exceeds medical costs, as other income
- **Physical injuries**—taxable as to the amount that exceeds medical costs, as other income
- **Injury to reputation**—taxable as other income
- **Loss-of-use/Loss-in-value of property**—taxable as to the amount that exceeds the basis in the property, as a capital gain

Income Uncle Sam Considers Nontaxable

☒	**Nontaxable Income**
☒	**Life insurance proceeds**
☒	**IRA rollovers**
☒	**Child support payments**
☒	**Inheritances**
☒	**Gifts**
☒	**Workers compensation**
☒	**Disability payments,** when you paid the premiums on the policy
☒	**Damages for personal physical injuries**
☒	**Health and accident benefits**
☒	**Federal income tax refund**
☒	**Scholarships and fellowships** for a degree candidate
☒	**Foreign earned income,** up to $85,700 in the most recently completed tax year
☒	**Foster care payments**
☒	**Social Security payments,** under certain conditions
☒	**Gain on sale of personal residence,** up to $250,000 in certain circumstances
☒	**Qualified Roth IRA distributions**
☒	**Department of Veteran's Affairs benefits or disability**
☒	**Welfare benefits**

TAX TIPS

On Tips

Making a few extra bucks these days bartending or driving a cab? Good for you. Just remember that Uncle Sam considers any tips you earn on the job taxable income, so they must be reported to the IRS.

If you do not log all the tips you make—an onerous process, to be sure, but a beneficial one—the IRS offers you help on tips and taxes with IRS Publication 1244: Employee's Daily Record of Tips and Report of Tips to Employer.

If you earn more than $20 a month in tips, the tips are subject to Social Security and Medicare taxes. Yuck!

Who Has to File a Tax Return?

All it takes to become a taxpayer is an income and a pulse—and the latter is not even needed to pay the estate tax. Old Benjamin Franklin was right on the ball when he said that "The only certainties in life are death and taxes."

There are, of course, exceptions—just not many. If you live in your parents' basement, you probably do not qualify to pay taxes. Lucky you—maybe.

But in general, if you earn an income, you have to pay taxes. The IRS bases the amount you must pay on three criteria:

Criteria for Determining Filing Requirement	
1	Filing Status
2	Age
3	Income

The good news is that you only need to file one federal income tax return each year, regardless of how many jobs you had, how many W-2 forms you received, or how many states you lived in during that year.

What complicates things is the *rate* of tax. Here are the current (2008) tax brackets for a single, unmarried person:

Rate	Bottom Income	Top Income
10%	$0	$8,025
15%	$8,026	$32,550
25%	$32,551	$78,850
28%	$78,851	$164,550
33%	$164,551	$357,700
35%	$357,701	+

Source: Internal Revenue Service

The above chart takes an overly simplistic view of the rates, though. If you take into account the standard deduction (worth $5,450) and one personal exemption (worth $3,500)—both of which we will address later—it clarifies the tax brackets quite a bit and introduces an additional bracket: the 0 percent tax rate bracket (again, this is for a single, unmarried person with no dependents):

Rate	Bottom Income	Top Income
0%	$0	$8,950
10%	$8,951	$16,975
15%	$16,976	$41,500
25%	$41,501	$87,800
28%	$87,801	$173,500
33%	$173,501	$366,650
35%	$366,651	+

Source: Internal Revenue Service

These are always subject to change, year by year, election by election. In 2001, President Bush and a Republican Congress pushed through a tax cut that called for a gradual reduction of tax rates. So the top rate, which was 39.6 percent in the Clinton era, fell all the way down to 35 percent in 2008. However, the tax cut had a sunset date of January 1, 2011, which will result in the top rate returning to 39.6 percent at that time. That is, unless Congress extends that tax cut into the future or makes it permanent.

>>> **FAST FACT**

Top Tax Brackets Over the Years

Year	Income (Single)	Income (Married— Joint)	Income (Married— Separate)	Rate
2000	$288,350 +	$288,350 +	$144,175 +	39.6%
2001	$297,350 +	$297,350 +	$148,675 +	39.1%
2002	$307,050 +	$307,050 +	$153,525 +	38.6%
2003	$311,950 +	$311,950 +	$155,975 +	35.0%
2004	$319,100 +	$319,100 +	$159,550 +	35.0%
2005	$326,450 +	$326,450 +	$163,225 +	35.0%
2006	$336,550 +	$336,550 +	$168,275 +	35.0%
2007	$349,700 +	$349,700 +	$174,850 +	35.0%
2008	$357,700 +	$357,700 +	$178,850 +	35.0%

Source: Internal Revenue Service

Dude, What's My Filing Status?

A tax filing status is like a nose or an opinion—every taxpayer has one. It's critical that you know what yours is, because that can mean the difference between paying a lot or a little in taxes. Since each status is treated differently by the IRS, you could cheat yourself out of thousands of dollars by selecting the wrong tax filing status.

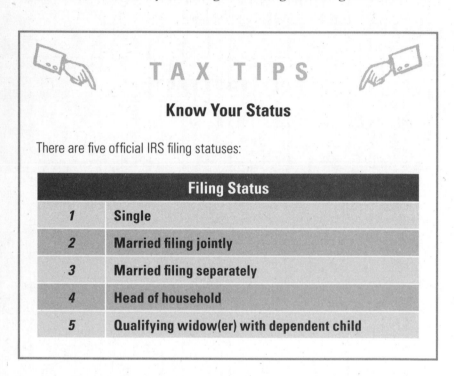

TAX TIPS

Know Your Status

There are five official IRS filing statuses:

Filing Status	
1	Single
2	Married filing jointly
3	Married filing separately
4	Head of household
5	Qualifying widow(er) with dependent child

Let's take a closer look at each category:

- **Single**

    This means you are unmarried, divorced, or legally separated, either according to your state law or under a separate maintenance decree.

    Your friend Shawn, the day-trading, nightspot-hopping playboy working the bookstore clerk for some digits right now is one of more than 60 million American taxpayers who files single.

- **Married Filing Jointly**

  This means that you were married by the last day of the tax year (December 31) and have elected to prepare your returns jointly.

  Jay and Judy, your classmates who fell in love at school, got married shortly thereafter, and have both been working comparable-paying jobs as they built their lives together, would be a perfect representation of the more than 105 million American taxpayers who are married filing jointly.

 TAX TIPS

Screw a New Year's Day Wedding—Elope Already!

To file jointly, you don't have to be married for all 365 days of the year. Rather, your marital status on the last day of the year determines your status for the entire year. So if your wedding was Dec. 29, you can file a joint return for that tax year—even though you'll only have been married for forty-eight hours of it.

- **Married Filing Separately**

  This means you and your spouse are married by the last day of the tax year and elect to file separate tax returns.

  Married couples often elect to file separately when it cuts their tax bill. However, you will only know whether it cuts your tax bill if you figure your taxes both separately and jointly, then assess which method saves you the most money. Married couples also may elect to file separately if one of the two spouses brought an IRS tax debt into the marriage or engages in risky tax-filing tactics—unsurprisingly, these attributes typically go hand in hand!

  Your coworkers, Farrell and Tracy, who met and married later in their lives, may elect to file separately, as they have decided to keep their assets and income separate. As such, they would be among the more than 2 million American taxpayers electing this filing status.

- **Head of Household**

  Individuals may use this status if (1) they are unmarried and (2) they have provided more than half the cost of keeping up a home for themselves and a qualifying relative. Tax rates for head of household filers are more favorable than for those in the single or married-filing-separately categories. In some cases, married people who have not lived with their spouses at any time for the last six months of the year may qualify for this status. Head of household is also the most complicated filing status. You should carefully examine the qualifications to make sure you are eligible.

  Your cousin Sue Ann would be a candidate for head of household, as she is a Superwoman—an unmarried working mother of two. As such, she joins the more than 20 million American heads of households, who not only put food on the table for their families, but also cook it, wash the dishes, walk the dog, and tuck their children in for good measure.

- **Qualifying Widow(er) with Dependent Child**

  When a spouse dies, a taxpayer may still file a joint return for that tax year. After that, a widow or widower who supports a child and does not remarry will probably want to use the qualifying widow(er) status, which is allowed for the two years following the death of a spouse and applies the same rate as that afforded married joint filers. This is generally more beneficial than the head of household rates. More than 75,000 American taxpayers use this status every year.

Tax Brackets—Where Do You Fit In?

Tax brackets have changed dramatically in the last hundred years, but their formula has not. Based on the premise that not every dollar

TAX TIPS

Considered Unmarried

To qualify for head of household status, you must be unmarried or considered unmarried on the last day of the year. You are considered unmarried on the last day of the tax year if you meet all the following criteria:

- You file a separate return.
- You paid more than half the cost of keeping up your home for the tax year.
- Your spouse did not live in your home during the last six months of the tax year (your spouse is considered to live in your home even if he or she is temporarily absent due to special circumstances).
- Your home was the main home of your child, stepchild, or foster child for more than half the year.
- You are able to claim an exemption for your child.

Please note: there is an exception to that final requirement. You may still be considered unmarried for head of household purposes if the only reason you cannot claim an exemption for your child is because the child's other parent qualifies for the exemption instead of you under the special rules for children of divorced or separated parents.

of your income is taxed at the same rate, tax brackets mean that portions of your income fall into different brackets, which are assigned tax rates that increase on a graduated scale. Generally speaking, the first dollar you make will be taxed at a lower rate than the last dollar you make.

It is also worth noting that your taxable income is not the amount your boss said you would be making when she hired you, but the amount of income left over after you have subtracted the tax breaks to which you are entitled.

Income ranges that define tax brackets are adjusted for inflation, change yearly, and differ depending on your filing status. And tax rates can change as well, as we have seen with the Bush administration from 2001 to 2008.

Here is an example of how income is taxed:

> Let's say Shawn is filing his 2008 tax return. He did not marry by the end of 2008, but he did score the bookstore clerk's digits and has started a relationship. Shockingly, his budding relationship cut into his time day-trading, as well as his nightclub hopping. But although he saved a bundle in fewer gin martinis throughout the rest of 2008, he lost more through a weak stock market and not putting in enough hours at the office. So Shawn only earned $160,000 in salary in 2008. In accordance with the income ranges defining federal tax brackets for single filers that year (based on 2008 figures), here is how Shawn's income is taxed:

From	To	Rate
$0	$8,025	10%
$8,026	$32,550	15%
$32,551	$78,850	25%
$78,851	$160,000	28%

Source: Internal Revenue Service

> This means that the first $8,025 of Shawn's income is taxed at 10 percent; dollars $8,026 through $32,550 are taxed at 15 percent; dollars $32,551 through $78,850 are taxed at 25 percent; and dollars $78,851 through $160,000 are taxed at 28 percent.

Marginal Tax Rate

Just as you should know your Social Security number, your blood type, and, in my case, the San Francisco Giants' schedule—especially when the Dodgers come to town—you should memorize your **marginal tax rate**. That is the rate that applies at the margin, to your top dollar of income earned. Under the IRS's graduated income tax system, as income rises, your tax goes up, and the percentage of that income claimed by the government also increases.

It's actually a pretty simple concept to understand. When people ask you what your tax bracket is, they are really asking for your marginal tax rate, or the percent at which the highest portion of your income is taxed. In the example above, Shawn's marginal tax rate is 28 percent—dollars $78,851 to $160,000 were taxed at this rate. The current marginal tax rates for all income levels are listed earlier in this Round, but for the sake of maintaining your momentum, I have reproduced them below:

Rate	Bottom Income	Top Income
10%	$0	$8,025
15%	$8,026	$32,550
25%	$32,551	$78,850
28%	$78,851	$164,550
33%	$164,551	$357,700
35%	$357,701	+

Source: Internal Revenue Service

Now, a much more interesting and, unfortunately, difficult concept to understand is your **effective rate**. This is the overall percentage of your taxable income that was actually paid in income taxes. And that rate may be lower than your marginal tax rate.

A savvy tax planner is also aware of his or her **combined tax rate**. That is the sum of your federal tax bracket and your state tax bracket. (If your top federal rate is 30 percent and your top state tax rate is 6 percent, your combined bracket is 36 percent.)

>>>> **FAST FACT**

The Official Tax Rates (2008 Figures)

Below are charts for all the filing statuses (note that married filing jointly, and qualifying widow[er] use the same rates). First, find the appropriate chart given your filing status. Second, find where your income falls. Third, multiply your income by the rate for your income range. Finally, the fourth column of each chart represents the tax already calculated from income that was taxed at the lower rates. Add that to what you just calculated to find out how much you would owe in taxes—if there were no exemptions, deductions, or credits.

Filing Single			
RATE	**APPLIES FROM**	**APPLIES TO**	**PLUS**
10%	$0	$8,025	$0
15%	$8,026	$32,550	$802.50
25%	$32,551	$78,850	$4,481.25
28%	$78,851	$164,550	$16,056.25
33%	$164,551	$357,700	$40,052.25
35%	$357,701	+	$103,791.75

Married Filing Jointly and Qualifying Widow(er)			
RATE	**APPLIES FROM**	**APPLIES TO**	**PLUS**
10%	$0	$16,050	$0
15%	$16,051	$65,100	$1,605
25%	$65,101	$131,450	$8,962

Married Filing Jointly and Qualifying Widow(er)			
28%	$131,451	$200,300	$25,550
33%	$200,301	$357,700	$44,828
35%	$357,701	+	$96,770

Married Filing Separate			
RATE	APPLIES FROM	APPLIES TO	PLUS
10%	$0	$8,025	$0
15%	$8,026	$32,550	$802.50
25%	$32,551	$65,725	$4,481.25
28%	$65,726	$100,150	$12,775
33%	$100,151	$178,850	$22,414
35%	$178,851	+	$48,385

Head of Household			
RATE	APPLIES FROM	APPLIES TO	PLUS
10%	$0	$11,450	$0
15%	$11,451	$43,650	$1,145
25%	$43,651	$112,650	$5,975
28%	$112,651	$182,400	$23,225
33%	$182,401	$357,700	$42,755
35%	$357,701	+	$100,604

Source: Internal Revenue Service

More on Tax Brackets

By design, tax brackets are fluid and ever-changing. The IRS adjusts them each year because the dollars you earn decline in purchasing power due to inflation. For example, if the inflation rate in 2007 is 3 percent, the top of each bracket will rise by 3 percent, meaning more dollars will be taxed at lower rates.

In IRS vernacular, these are the "official rates" because, as noted below, there is more here than meets the eye. In the table for head of household, you will see that taxable income between $43,651 and $112,650 falls in the 25 percent bracket. Does that mean if you make $100,000 that 25 percent of it—$25,000—goes to Uncle Sam? Well, no.

First of all, only the dollars earned from $43,651 to $100,000 will be taxed at 25 percent. The first $43,650 will be taxed at the preceding lower rates. When added up, the amount of tax on those dollars is $5,975 (see the fourth column on previous page).

Secondly, part of your earnings is not taxed at all. For instance, if Evelyn claims exemptions for herself and her two children on her 2008 return, that knocks $10,500 off of her taxable income because exemptions are worth $3,500 each in 2008. Her deductions will reduce her taxable income by at least $7,850 more.

So, Evelyn's hypothetical $100,000 earnings have now been pared down to $81,650 of taxable income.

Withholding and Estimated Taxes

April 15 is tax day, right? Well, yes and no.

Yes, your tax return is due on that date every year (though sometimes it falls on a Sunday and you get an extra day to file). But no, it is not the only date that taxes are collected.

Taxes are actually due as income is earned, and employers have become the country's primary tax collectors by withholding taxes from our paychecks. Most of the money paid in individual income taxes each year is withheld from employees' paychecks. The government also expects its share of income not covered by withholding—including income from self-employment, investments, and alimony—in installments throughout the year. Social Security taxes as well as income taxes are due on a pay-as-you-go basis.

As part of your year-end planning, compare your tax payments so far with what you expect to owe. If your payments will be at least as much as the tax you owed for the previous year, or at least 90 percent of what you will owe this year, you are probably safe from penalty. If you are going to fall short, however, some year-end maneuvering can save you money.

Are You Overpaying Uncle Sam?

I expect you would rather arm-wrestle a gorilla than overpay the government. Hey, I feel the same way, although from my experience, dealing with the IRS is actually a lot like arm-wrestling a gorilla.

Yet despite all the worrying and grousing we all do about high taxes, and all the planning and conniving we do to minimize what we owe Uncle Sam, the millions of tax-refund checks the treasury mails out each spring are proof positive that employees have too much withheld from their payroll checks.

But you can keep your withholding down to the legal minimum. After all, the point is for you to get the use and enjoyment of more of your money when you earn it, rather than making an unintentional—albeit generous—interest-free loan to the government.

How much are Americans overpaying the IRS? In one recent sample year, the government churned out almost 118 million tax-refund checks. The total amount returned to appreciative taxpayers was more than $292 billion. The average check was almost $2,500.

On the flip side, a growing number of taxpayers are tripped up each year by having too little withheld or failing to pay enough estimated tax, leading to a higher tax bill come April 15. This is a particular problem for two-earner married couples.

So why adjust your withholdings? Well, if you are single and earn $20,000 a year, one additional exemption allowance slices the amount the government takes from your paycheck by about $30 a month. That adds up to $360 a year. Add five additional withholding allowances, and you can stash an extra $1,500 in your pocket every year.

TAX TIPS

"The Double Whammy"—Another Reason to Reduce Withholdings

When you over-withhold your income to pay for taxes, you are, in effect, giving the federal government an interest-free loan. The federal government accumulates billions if not trillions of dollars this way, and by making a simple, low-risk investment, can take the overwithholdings of all American taxpayers and make billions more.

Why should you adjust your withholdings? I think the better question is why not! Lord knows you have your own bills to worry about. And your debts are probably not interest-free. So when you overwithhold, you are not only losing an opportunity to make extra money—by investing that additional cash yourself—but you are also actually losing money. If that's not a double whammy, I don't know what is!

Now, be mindful that this is a tricky business. There is a science to withholdings. You will need to complete the Form W-4 worksheet in order to ensure you withhold the correct amount, so as not to cause a large tax bill come April 15. Thus, this might be something best reserved for your tax professional (I'll cover that in Round 11).

However, just because you've decreased your withholdings, that doesn't mean you've cut the tax you will pay the IRS in April. You are just putting more cash in your wallet now, instead of getting it later in the form of a fat refund.

So the goal here is to balance your withholding and estimated payments so you pay Uncle Sam just enough cash every year to avoid getting whomped with a penalty. In doing so, you are taking control of your money—you earn the interest accrued on your income, not Uncle Sam.

Generally, it's a good idea for anyone who received more than a $500 refund or owed more than 10 percent of his or her overall tax bill to adjust his or her withholding. To change your withholding, ask your employer to change your IRS Form W-4. That is the form on file with your company that determines the amount of tax withheld from your paychecks.

Most folks fill out their W-4 on their first day on the job and then never give it another thought. Big mistake! Like many tax documents, W-4s can be changed at any time and as often as you like.

TAX TIPS

Inter-Office Bureaucracy

Do not let your Human Resource Department get in the way of changing your withholding! IRS Publication 15 provides specific instructions on how employers are supposed to handle requests for W-4 changes. It states:

> Encourage your employees to file an updated Form W-4 for the current year, especially if they owed taxes or received a large refund when filing their last tax return. Advise your employees to use the Withholding Calculator on the IRS website at www.irs.gov/individuals for help in determining how many withholding allowances to claim on their Form W-4.

Aside from the above, your Human Resource Department should leave you alone when it comes to taxes.

Did you have a new baby? Change your W-4 to reflect that extra mouth to feed so you will have less taken out of your paycheck. Did you buy a new house? Those mortgage payments change your tax status, too. Tough year on Wall Street? Those investment portfolio losses impact your withholdings. Remember, the more allowances you claim, the less is withheld.

Even if you are reading these words in late summer or in the fall, you can still get in on the good stuff. Remember, withholdings from your paycheck are considered to be made evenly throughout the year. That means overwithholding in November and December can make up for earlier underpayments. If you have a job, arrange with your employer to withhold extra amounts from the final paychecks of the year. In addition, remember in January to have your withholding readjusted downward.

 Inside the Ropes: Josh Tracks Down His Paycheck Deductions

Who is FICA and why are they taking money out of Josh's paycheck?

My nephew Josh is a student at Sacramento State, studying to be a classical pianist. He makes a few extra bucks bussing tables at the local Pluto's restaurant.

"I didn't really have time for a job in high school, and in the summer I did a few unpaid internships," he explains. "So the bussing job was really my first chance to get a paycheck. But when I ripped open the envelope containing my first check, I noticed that some of my money went to something called 'FICA.'"

Josh brought up his confusion with me when he came over for a family reunion. I have to admit, I kind of laughed about it.

"Yeah, Aunt Roni sat me down and gave me a mini-tax lecture," says Josh. "She explained to me that FICA was just another way of saying 'Social Security,' and that the money taken out was money I'd get back when I retire someday."

Josh learned that under the Federal Insurance Contributions Act (FICA), 12.4 percent of his earned income up to $97,500 (for 2007; $102,000 in 2008) must be paid into Social Security, and an additional 2.9 percent must be paid into Medicare. "Roni told me that since I was considered a wage or salaried employee, I'd only pay half the FICA bill [6.2 percent for Social Security + 1.45 percent for Medicare], and that my employer must contribute the other half."

I also had an additional nugget of information for Josh—part-time students who are employed by colleges and universities that they attend are not subjected to FICA. So long as the student works less than forty hours per week, is not considered full-time, is taking the equivalent of a full-time course load, and falls into some additional specific safe harbor provisions, the IRS provides that collegiate employers need not pay or withhold FICA tax.

At first, Josh shrugged off the deduction fairly quickly. However, when I last spoke with his father, I found out Josh has been putting out feelers for a job as a busboy with the university's dining hall.

1040 Treasure Map or 1040 Survival Guide? You Decide

Tax avoidance is legal tax planning. Tax evasion is fraud.

—Anonymous

Have you seen the two *National Treasure* movies? I did. I loved how the Nicholas Cage character followed the clues laid out for his team and beat the bad guys to the hidden treasure. To me, an IRS Form 1040 is full of hidden treasure, if you know where to look.

The 1040 is the basis for squaring our annual accounts with Uncle Sam. Like our Constitution, it helps establish and preserve our identities as Americans. Young and old, rich and not so rich, we are all asked to contribute something to the common good, and the 1040 is the document we use to do that. In the tax world, Form 1040 is the one document that trumps all others, striking fear and confusion into the hearts of many taxpayers but offering abundant money-saving opportunities to the tax savvy.

The 1040 dates back to 1914, when the Bureau of Internal Revenue hired Nina Wilcox Putnam—of the Putnam publishing family—to create the 1,040th form to be published by the IRS. Ms. Putnam, co-screenwriter of the 1924 stage drama *Dracula* and storywriter for the 1932 film *The Mummy* with Boris Karloff, delivered a complete four-page form, with instructions, and the 1040 form was born.

Imagine the 1040 having its roots in the horror genre! To be honest, it doesn't surprise me a bit.

>>> **FAST FACT**

On the Clock

According to the Internal Revenue Service, the average taxpayer takes 11.6 hours to complete a 1040 form. ◄

Whether you hire a professional or prepare your return on your own, you need to know the 1040 inside and out.

Why? Because the 1040 giveth and the 1040 taketh away. It rewards certain tax behaviors while mitigating others. Consequently, knowing where to find the gold mines—and the land mines—can go a long way toward saving you big bucks off your tax bill. All you have to do is figure out where to look.

To help you along the way, we devised Round 4 as a walk through the 1040 tax form. We are going to define each item that appears on the form, and hopefully provide a helpful tip or two along the way. By taking you through the document point by point and line by line, you will gain a greater understanding of how to use the form to your advantage when preparing your tax return.

Before you start, it is a good idea to have the actual 1040 form on hand as we walk through it. If you can't dig one out of your old records (which means your organizational skills may be lacking—go back to Round 2), you can download a PDF at www.irs.gov, keyword "1040".

A Short Word on Short Forms

Unless you are a non-resident alien required to file the 1040-NR, you will file your return on one of three versions of the IRS Form 1040:

- IRS Form 1040EZ
- IRS Form 1040A
- IRS Form 1040

The 1040 is the default form. Thus, to be eligible for the 1040A or 1040EZ, special requirements must be met. Below, please find a chart explaining the eligibility for each of these "short form" versions of the 1040.

IRS Form 1040EZ	
#	YOU MUST MEET ALL REQUIREMENTS:
1	Filing status is single or married filing jointly
2	Do not claim any dependents
3	All income comes from the following five sources: • wages/salaries/tips • taxable scholarships/grants • unemployment compensation • Alaska permanent fund dividends • interest income
4	Do not claim any adjustments to income
5	Taxable income < $100,000
6	Taxable interest income < $1,500
7	Only tax credit claimed is the Earned Income Credit
8	No household employment taxes on wages
9	Not a debtor in a Chapter 11 bankruptcy case
10	Do not owe alternative minimum tax

Source: Internal Revenue Service

For more information, please see instructions to IRS Form 1040EZ (www.irs.gov, keyword "1040EZ").

IRS Form 1040A	
#	**YOU MUST MEET ALL REQUIREMENTS:**
1	**All income comes from the following eight sources:** • wages/salaries/tips • interest/ordinary dividends • capital gain distributions • taxable scholarships/grants • pensions/annuities/IRAs • unemployment compensation • taxable Social Security/railroad benefits • Alaska permanent fund dividends
2	**All income adjustments come from the following four sources:** • educator expenses • IRA deduction • student loan interest deduction • tuition/fees deduction
3	**Must claim standard deduction**
4	**Taxable income is < $100,000**
5	**All tax credits come from the following seven sources:** • child tax credit • additional child tax credit • education credits • Earned Income Tax Credit • credit for child and dependent care expenses • credit for the elderly or disabled • retirement savings contribution credit
6	**Did not have an alternative minimum tax adjustment on stock acquired through an incentive-based stock option**

Source: Internal Revenue Service

For more information, please see instructions to Form 1040A (www.irs.gov, keyword "1040A").

Here is a suggestion: for purposes of learning about the tax law and how to use it to your advantage, forget the short forms. Sure, they have fewer lines than the full 1040, but that also means they contain fewer opportunities to save money.

>>> **FAST FACT**

When to Use It

To determine when the IRS Form 1040 must be used—instead of Form 1040A or 1040EZ—please see the below chart:

	If Any of the Below Apply, You Must Use the 1040
✓	**Received any of the following four types of income:** • income from self-employment (i.e., farm, business, etc.) • tips not reported to employer • income received from partnership/S corporation/trust • dividends on insurance premiums
✓	**Received or paid interest on securities transferred between interest payment dates**
✓	**Claiming a tax credit for any of the following three types of income:** • foreign earned income as U.S. citizen or resident alien • Puerto Rican income (if bona fide Puerto Rican resident) • American Samoan income (if bona fide American Samoa resident)
✓	**Had an alternative minimum tax adjustment on stock acquired through an incentive-based stock option**
✓	**Have a financial account (i.e., bank account, securities account, etc.) in a foreign country**

If Any of the Below Apply, You Must Use the 1040	
✓	Received a distribution from a foreign trust
✓	Owe excise tax on insider stock compensation from an expatriated corporation (very rare)
✓	Reporting an original issue discount in an account more or less than the amount shown on IRS Form 1099-OID
✓	Owe household employment tax
✓	Eligible for health coverage tax credit
✓	Claiming adoption credit
✓	Received employer-provided adoption benefits
✓	Employer did not withhold Social Security and Medicare taxes
✓	Received a qualified health savings account funding distribution from your IRA (very rare)
✓	Debtor in a bankruptcy case filed after October 16, 2005—as part of the Bankruptcy Abuse Prevention and Consumer Protection Act of 2005, this requirement was added for all bankruptcies filed after this date

Source: Internal Revenue Service

Form 1040—A Primer

I have long held that the best approach to tax planning is "inch by inch." That *really* applies to your 1040 tax form. Each section—in some cases each *line*—of the 1040 gives you an opportunity to put more of your hard-earned money back into your pocket.

So let's take a look, line by line.

- **Header**

  Name and address and Social Security number. If you are filing for yourself at home, you can just use a label. Always make sure to check the label for accuracy.

- **Filing Status** *(lines 1–5)*

  We went over each status in detail in Round 3, but here are a few additional tips.

  First, if you are single or separated and have been living apart from your spouse for the last six months of the tax year, you may qualify as a head of household. Head of household filing status requires that you provide a home for someone in addition to yourself—usually a child, parent, or other family member. This filing status puts more of your income in lower tax brackets than if you file using the single filing status, saving you money. Moreover, you get a bigger standard deduction: as of 2008, head of household receives $8,000 versus the $5,450 a single filer receives.

  Head of household is the most beneficial check-off in this area, but it's also the most abused. Because of the multitude of benefits and credits available to heads of household, the IRS takes its definition and eligibility very seriously. So be careful.

  In addition, it is generally better, if you're married, to file jointly as opposed to separately. Quite a few tax breaks are disallowed for married taxpayers filing separately.

  However, there are specific situations when filing separately will actually save you and your spouse tax dollars. So it's always in your best interest to prepare your return—or have your tax professional prepare your return—both ways, and then determine which method will result in the smallest tax bill.

  But in reality, your primary consideration for choosing whether to file jointly or separately might be who you're married to. If your spouse has a history of past-due filings or

TAX TIPS

Gone, Baby, Gone

When considering whether to file separately or jointly, remember that the following tax exemptions, deductions, and credits are only available for married people filing jointly (*note*—most are available for single, qualifying widow[er], and head of household as well):

Tax Breaks for Joint Filers
♥ Child and dependent care tax credit
♥ Adoption expense credit
♥ Hope and Lifetime Learning Education credits
♥ Credit for the elderly or the disabled
♥ Qualified education loan interest deduction
♥ Deduction for contributions to your IRA
♥ Excluding adoption assistance payments from an employer or any interest income from series EE savings bonds that you used for higher education expenses
♥ Tax-free Social Security benefits—If one half of Social Security plus all other income is under $32K, then the benefits are tax-free

Source: Internal Revenue Service

payments to the IRS, has a tendency to overstate expenses or understate income, or has been suspiciously eyeing Rio de Janeiro flights and purchasing Portuguese dictionaries and Rosetta Stone tapes, then it might be in your interest to file

TAX TIPS

Whoop, There It Is!

Married individuals can actualize tax savings by filing separately when one spouse makes considerably more than the other, and the spouse making less has a lot of the following:

- Medical expenses
- Casualty losses
- Miscellaneous deductible expenses

Medical expenses, for example, are deductible only to the extent that they exceed 7.5 percent of your Adjusted Gross Income (AGI), and only the portion of casualty losses that exceeds 10 percent of AGI is deductible. Miscellaneous itemized deductions, which include a variety of deductions such as investment expenses (other than investment interest), non-reimbursed employee expenses, and tax return preparation costs, are deductible only to the extent their combined total exceeds 2 percent of AGI (often referred to as a "2 percent floor").

However, please note that the sizes of most of these deductions taper off when income levels are met or exceeded. These income levels are much lower for married couples filing separately than those filing jointly.

Source: Internal Revenue Service

separately. This is because inherent in the joint filing status is that you are both agreeing to become *joint and severally liable* for the return and the claims therein. This means that the "offendee" (i.e., the complainant, plaintiff, or, in this case, the IRS) can seek all the damages (collect all the overdue taxes) from either of those who committed the offense. Thus, if your spouse is the designated tax-handler in your marriage, and he or she files a joint return with excessive deductions or under-claims your income, when he or she runs off to South America, you could be stuck with a hefty bill, a painful audit, or even a criminal investigation by the IRS.

TAX TIPS

Don't Fret, Just Regret

The IRS does provide relief to those individuals who fall victim to unscrupulous people who file fraudulent joint tax returns without the spouse's intentional participation. It is called Innocent Spouse. See Round 10 or IRS Publication 971 for more information.

If your spouse had a tax debt prior to the marriage, and your joint tax return refund was used to pay down a portion of that tax debt, you also need not worry. You can apply for Injured Spouse Relief, where the IRS will refund your portion of refund, as the tax debt was incurred before the marriage, so you are not obligated to pay it. Again, see Round 10 or IRS Publication 971 for more information.

My final tips deal with the death of your spouse. If you are facing this devastating event, first, let me say that I am very sorry for your loss and I send you warm thoughts and hope, wherever you are in your grieving process. Unfortunately, the IRS will not be sending any condolences. Thus, while you deal with all the emotional, social, and familial changes that will now take place, it is important that you not allow your tax obligations get lost in the shuffle. Otherwise, you may miss some tax savings and could actually cause some additional complications along the way.

If your spouse died during the current tax year, you can still file jointly. This will let you take advantage of the lowest tax rates. If your spouse died before the current year, you no longer can file a joint return. However, if you have a dependent child, you may file as a qualifying widow(er), which also allows you to use joint-return rates.

When a member of your family dies, it is important for the administrator of the estate—or anyone in the family—to file a final return for the deceased in the year of death. Even if the income level of the departed does not require a return, the

---

▶▶▶ FAST FACT

Community Property Alert!

Forty-one of the fifty states use a concept called *common law property* when classifying property within a marriage. In these states, each spouse treats his or her income (i.e., property) as his or her own. For example, assume you have a married couple, Miles and Alexis. Miles's wages are considered his own taxable income. Alexis's teaching pension is considered her own taxable income. Thus, for purposes of filing separate income tax returns, each spouse looks to his or her own income and relevant deductions when preparing the return.

The other nine states (Arizona, California, Idaho, Louisiana, Nevada, New Mexico, Texas, Washington, and Wisconsin) use a concept called *community property* when classifying property within a marriage. In these states, only income earned prior to the marriage is considered separate property owned solely by one spouse. Income earned during the marriage is treated as community property, owned 50 percent by each spouse. Thus, for example, assume another married couple, Chris and Madison, who are married prior to 2008. Chris earns $50,000 in wages in 2008, and Madison doesn't work, so she earns no money in 2008. Yet, according to community property law, Chris owns $25,000 of the income earned by the marriage and Madison owns the other $25,000.

Where am I going with this? Well, community property complicates the preparation of "married filing separately." Instead of each spouse entering the income they separately earned, each must enter half the income he or she earned and half the income his or her spouse earned throughout the year.

Please keep this in mind when determining which filing status will save you the most in taxes. ◀

IRS may have withheld income tax, so you may want to file to get a refund.

If there is a surviving spouse, he or she can file a joint return as a surviving spouse for the year of death, writing DECEASED across the top of the return. The surviving spouse should sign the return and file it, which will signal to the IRS that the refund should be issued in his or her name alone.

If there is no surviving spouse and a refund is due, IRS Form 1310 must be filed with the return to prevent the refund from being issued in the name of the deceased. This form can designate the administrator of the estate as the refund recipient.

• Exemptions *(line 6)*

Exemptions are worth their weight in gold. You will learn more about these in Round 5, but it is important that you know that each one you claim knocks $3,500 off your taxable income.

There are two kinds of exemptions: personal—for you and your spouse (if you have one and are filing jointly)—and dependent. Dependent exemptions are typically family members. However, a person need not be related to you to be your dependent. You may be able to claim someone who lives with you if you provide more than half of his or her support. There are actually up to eight tests that need to be met to claim a dependent on your return (see Round 5). The IRS instructions for line 6c also describe each test in detail.

To short-circuit attempts to claim pets or non-existent people as dependents, the law now demands that you provide the Social Security number for any dependent you claim. Exemptions, in the eyes of the IRS, are a zero-sum game. If you can be claimed as a dependent on someone else's return—such as your parents'—you cannot claim a personal exemption.

In addition, for the record, I believe that dogs should be exempt—they bring lots of people joy and happiness. So, why not exemptions, too? But the IRS hasn't indicated that they agree.

Form 1040—Income

In this section of the form, you are claiming all your income (and your spouse's, if filing jointly) that you received for the year. Most of the information you provide will come directly from forms that are provided to you by your employer, investment firms, banks, governments, benefit administrators, and other third parties who are under a reporting requirement with the IRS.

- **Wages, Salaries, Tips, Etc.** *(line 7)*
  For the majority of individuals, this comes right off the W-2 that you receive from your employer(s) around January 15–31. However, it could also include income from the following sources:

  - Money earned as household employee, where the employer did not issue a W-2 (if you did not earn above $1,500 per year, your employer is not required to report it)
  - Unreported tips received
  - Scholarship and fellowship grants not reported on a W-2 and not used for qualified education expenses
  - Unused dependent care benefits over $5,000
  - Employer-provided adoption benefits
  - Disability pensions (if the taxpayer has not reached the plan's retirement age)
  - Corrective distributions from a retirement plan

- **Taxable Interest** *(line 8a)*
  This includes all taxable interest from banks, savings and loan associations, credit unions, savings, bonds, etc. You must attach a Schedule B if the total amount exceeds $1,500.

- **Tax-Exempt Interest** *(line 8b)*
  These are amounts earned from interest-bearing investment devices like municipal bonds. This income is not taxed, but must be reported.

INVESTMENT TIP:
It's in Your Interest

If you report substantial taxable interest income here, it may be a sign that you should consider tax-free bonds or mutual funds. A 5 percent tax-free yield is worth almost as much as a 7 or 8 percent taxable return if you are in a higher tax bracket. Additional benefit—this does not count any possible state tax savings.

- **Ordinary Dividends** *(line 9a)*
  Dividends are distributions of money, stock, or other property a corporation pays you because you own stock in that corporation. You may also receive dividends through a partnership, estate, trust, sub–chapter S corporation, or an association taxed as a corporation. Ordinary dividends are paid out of the earnings and profits of the corporation. Again, you must attach a Schedule B if the total amount exceeds $1,500.

- **Qualified Dividends** *(line 9b)*
  To be a qualified dividend, the investor "must have held the stock for more than sixty days during the 121-day period that begins sixty days before the ex-dividend date." The tax rate on

⟩⟩⟩ FAST FACT

Non-Dividend Distributions

Different from an ordinary dividend, non-dividend distributions are typically a return of capital—a return of all or some of your investment through shares of stock in a company. The value of the return of capital reduces your cost basis in your original stock or investment. It is not considered a taxable event until the entire cost basis is recovered. ◄

qualified dividends is 5 or 15 percent, depending upon the individual's marginal tax rate. If the individual has a marginal tax rate of 25 percent or higher, then the qualified dividend tax rate is 15 percent. If the individual's income tax rate is less than 25 percent, then qualified dividends are taxed at the 5 percent rate. As you can see, qualified dividend status is very lucrative, as it saves taxpayers quite a bit, regardless of their marginal tax rate, when compared to ordinary dividends. Typically, the corporation will report the portion of ordinary dividends that are qualified in a properly filed Form 1099-DIV.

- **Taxable Refunds, Credits, or Offsets of State and Local Income Taxes** *(line 10)*
  These are returns of income taxes withheld or collected by state or local taxing authorities. Although you may receive an IRS Form 1099-G for these refunds, think twice before you report a state tax refund as taxable income. Yes, your state sends both you and the IRS a notice of how much you got back in taxes each year. However, refunds are tax-free for most taxpayers for the year of the refund. That includes you if you did not itemize deductions on your federal tax return. Even if you did itemize, part of the state refund may not be taxable.

- **Alimony Received** *(line 11)*
  These are payments received from your spouse or former spouse required under a divorce decree or separation instrument. This does not include voluntary payments made.
  Not all payments under a divorce decree or separation instrument are considered alimony. Alimony does not include:

  » Child support
  » Non-cash property settlements
  » Payments to keep up property

- ➤ Use of property (personal or real)
- ➤ Receipt of own community property

TAX TIPS

Prioritizing Payments

If the divorce decree or separation instrument provides for both child support and alimony payments, and the payee fails to completely pay what is due, then what is paid is first considered child support.

- **Business Income or Loss *(line 12)***

  In this line item, you report your income—or loss—from your business. To calculate this, complete a Schedule C, where you report your business income and expenses. Business income and expenses are examined in greater detail later in the book.

- **Capital Gains or Loss *(line 13)***

  The big issue for this line item is whether you are required to attach a Schedule D to account for your capital gains and losses throughout the year. You do not have to file a Schedule D if both of the following apply to you:

  - ➤ The only amounts to report are from IRS Form 1099-DIV, box 2a—total capital gain distributions (e.g., mutual fund distributions, etc.)
  - ➤ There are no amounts to report from box 2b (unrecaptured section 1250 gain), box 2c (section 1202 gain), or box 2d (collectibles gain)

TAX TIPS

Wherever They Can Get It

In a tough economy, bartering becomes a bigger piece of the action. As you can guess, people do not always have the money to go to the dentist—but maybe they can trade plumbing work, for example. In addition, the Internet has provided a medium for new growth in the bartering exchange industry.

But it is important to note that income from bartering is taxable. The fair market value of goods and services received must be included in the income of both parties in the year in which the bartered income (i.e., goods and/or services) was received.

The Schedule D is notoriously complex, and avoiding it will save you a headache and a half. But don't fret if you have to complete one—the result is a lower tax. See, you win both ways!

- **Other Gains or Losses** *(line 14)*
  Use this line item to report the sale or exchange of specified miscellaneous items, such as property used in your trade or business, depreciable/amortizable property, or mineral deposits (i.e., oil, gas, geothermal, etc.), among others.

TAX TIPS

Losers Are Winners, Too!

By law, you can deduct up to $3,000 in net capital losses per year.

- **IRA Distributions** *(lines 15a and 15b)*

  These are amounts of money distributed or withdrawn from your Individual Retirement Account (IRA). This includes traditional, Roth, simplified employee pension (SEP), and savings incentive match plan for employees (SIMPLE) IRAs.

  Distributions from traditional IRAs are usually taxable. There are specific rules concerning distributions from the other types of IRAs. For simplicity's sake, always enter all your IRA distributions in line 15b—leaving 15a blank—unless any of the following apply to you:

  - ➤ You rolled over part or all the distribution from (a) one IRA to another IRA of the same type or (b) SEP IRA or SIMPLE IRA to a traditional IRA
  - ➤ You received a distribution from any IRA—except a Roth IRA—and made nondeductible contributions to any traditional or SEP IRAs
  - ➤ You received a distribution from a Roth IRA
  - ➤ You converted all or part of a traditional, SEP, or SIMPLE IRA to a Roth IRA
  - ➤ You had contributions made this year or last year returned to you
  - ➤ You had excess contributions made in prior years returned to you this year
  - ➤ You re-characterized all or part of a contribution to a Roth IRA as a traditional IRA contribution (don't try this at home, kids; see your investment bank before re-characterization)
  - ➤ All the distribution is a qualified charitable contribution
  - ➤ All the distribution is a qualified health savings account funding distribution

- **Pensions and Annuities** *(lines 16a and 16b)*

  This includes all pension and annuity payments received during the current tax year, including distributions from 401(k) and 403(b) plans.

  You should include all your payments received on line 16b if they are considered "fully taxable." This means that:

➤ You did not contribute to the cost of your pension or annuity

➤ The amount of after-tax contributions was repaid to you prior to the current tax year

---

 TAX TIPS

Honoring the Blue Line

Eligible retired public safety officers (law enforcement officers, firefighters, chaplains, members of a rescue squad or ambulance crew) can exclude from income any and all distributions made from eligible retirement plans that are used to pay the premiums for insurance (i.e., accident, health, long-term care). This includes premiums for the taxpayer, spouse, or dependents.

- **Rental Real Estate, Royalties, Partnerships, S Corporations, Trusts, etc.** *(line 17)*
  Use Schedule E to calculate your income—or loss—from rental real estate, royalties, partnerships, S corporations, and trusts. Total up each separate section and enter the net total income—or loss—from these activities for the taxable year.

- **Farm Income or Loss** *(line 18)*
  Use Schedule F to report your income and expenses from farming. Calculate your net income—or loss—and report it here.

- **Unemployment Compensation** *(line 19)*
  Report distributions you received from your state unemployment income fund here. It also includes railroad unemployment compensation benefits, and disability benefits paid as a substitute for unemployment compensation, but not workers

TAX TIPS

An Army of Taxmen

Remember—there are taxing authorities other than Uncle Sam, Congress, and the IRS. So, remember that your farming activity may subject you to additional taxes on a local or state level. These other governments may also have licensing requirements that, while not a tax, are still just as annoying.

compensation. Unemployment compensation is reported to you on a Form 1099-G.

- **Social Security Benefits** *(lines 20a and 20b)*
  "Just in case" has to be the mindset of the IRS when it comes to taxing Social Security benefits. They do so "just in case" the recipient has other sources of income that exceed certain thresholds. This spawned a complicated calculation, which is not always in the taxpayer's favor. Especially when you consider that before 1984, all benefits were tax-free. Now, depending on your income, either 100 percent of your benefits are tax-free, up to 50 percent of the benefits can be taxed, or up to 85 percent of the benefits can be taxed.

  If your Adjusted Gross Income plus one-half of your benefits is less than $25,000 on a single return or $32,000 on a joint return, all your benefits are safe. But if your Adjusted Gross Income plus one-half of your benefits is more than $34,000 on a single or $44,000 on a joint return, up to 85 percent of the benefits are taxable. When income falls between those amounts, no more than half of your benefits can be taxed.

- **Other Income** *(line 21)*

Do not be intimidated by the all-encompassing sound of "other income." Although the IRS might like a shot at every dollar that passes through your hands, there are limits.

In the below charts, please find what is included, and what is not:

Other Taxable Income	
$	Distributions from Coverdell education savings accounts, qualified tuition programs, and health savings accounts not used for qualified expenses
$	Prizes and awards
$	Gambling/lottery winnings
$	Jury duty pay
$	Alaska Permanent Fund dividend
$	Income from activities not engaged in for profit (hobby income)
$	Cancelled debt

Nontaxable Income	
☒	Child support received
☒	Life insurance benefits received due to death of insured
☒	Gifts
☒	Inheritances

Gifts and inheritances are not taxable for the recipient, however, the payee may have to pay a tax if the amount exceeds certain thresholds.

>>> **FAST FACT**

"Miscellaneous"

Receiving a 1099-MISC may mean you have been paid for work you did as a self-employed individual. This income is reported on Box 7—Non-Employee Compensation. You must report that income on Schedule C and claim any expenses associated with making that money. If you believe you received the income as an employee, there are procedures for having the IRS determine your status (employee vs. self-employed), and you should contact a tax professional for assistance. If the income is for any other kind of compensation, such as a settlement, report it on line 21 as "other income." ◄

- **Total Income** *(line 22)*

  Here, add the amounts listed in items 7 through 21 to calculate your Total Income.

Form 1040—Adjusted Gross Income

The next section of the IRS Form 1040 calculates Adjusted Gross Income (AGI). AGI (aka *net income*) is your total income minus specified deductions. The IRS uses AGI for a multitude of calculations, including limits on certain deductions and credits. It is one of—if not *the*—most important figures on the tax return.

The deductions used to calculate AGI are called "above the line" deductions because they are taken while computing a taxpayer's AGI. In using this common distinction, always remember that the calculated AGI is "the line." Itemized deductions or your standard deduction are "below the line." Generally, "below the line" deductions are not favored because typically the size of the deduction is dependent upon a fixed percentage of the AGI. For instance, only business expenses over 2 percent of AGI and medical expenses over 7.5 percent of AGI were eligible for deduction in 2008.

>>> **FAST FACT**

Do Not Mix Up the Deductions

As mentioned above, AGI is calculated by subtracting gross income from specific deductions. However, these deductions are not all the available deductions. Most notably excluded is the itemized or standard deduction. They are not used to calculate AGI. ◄

>>> **FAST FACT**

AGI Over the Years

Here is a chart showing the average tax return's AGI from year to year (for individuals, not adjusted for inflation):

Year	AGI
1996	$37,689
1997	$40,579
1998	$43,407
1999	$46,079
2000	$49,202
2001	$47,373
2002	$46,385
2003	$47,952
2004	$51,342
2005	$55,238
2006	$58,028

Source: Internal Revenue Service ◄

Now let's explore some of the bigger above the line deductions that make up this section of the Form 1040:

- **Educator Expenses** *(line 23)*

    If you are an eligible educator (i.e., K–12 teacher, counselor, principal, or school aide who worked at least nine hundred hours during the school year) and you spend some of your own money to purchase "qualified education materials" for your classroom, you can deduct up to $250 of your out-of-pocket expenses. This means that if you are a first-grade teacher and buy crayons for your class, the crayons are deductible—yippee! If both you and your spouse are eligible educators, you can claim up to $500—a maximum of $250 apiece.

    Make a note, though: This deduction is not permanent. It has to be renewed each year.

≫≫≫ FAST FACT

Qualified Education Expenses

Expenses that qualify include books, supplies, equipment, software, services, etc. They have to be ordinary (common and accepted in the educational field) and necessary (helpful and appropriate for the profession of an educator).

Qualified education expenses do not include:

- Expenses for home-schooling
- Non-athletic supplies for courses in health or physical education ◄

- **Certain Business Expenses** *(line 24)*

    The following types of taxpayers receive special treatment of certain business expenses listed in IRS Form 2106:

    - Members of National Guard and National Guard Reserve who traveled more than 100 miles to perform duties

➤ Qualified performing artists

➤ Fee-basis state or local government officials

➤ Disabled employees with impairment-related work expenses

- **Health/Medical Savings Account Deduction** *(line 25)*
  A Health Savings Account (HSA) or Medical Savings Account (MSA) are tax-advantaged plans for the self-employed and employees of small firms. They combine a high-deductible health insurance policy with a savings account similar to an IRA. Money contributed to an MSA is deductible and withdrawals are tax-free when used to pay medical bills.

- **Moving Expenses** *(line 26)*
  You could get a big break here if you moved to take a new job. To earn the deduction, the move must be in connection with taking a job at a new location, and the new job has to be at least fifty miles farther from your old home than your old job was. So, if your current job is eight miles from your home, your new job will need to be fifty-eight miles from that home to qualify for this deduction—even if you move right next door to your new job.

  Making this write-off available to those who use the standard deduction is especially important to new graduates who move to take their first jobs.

➤➤➤ FAST FACT

What If You Had No Prior Job?

If you had no former workplace before moving, the new workplace must be at least fifty miles from your old home. ◄

- **Self-Employment Tax** *(line 27)*
  To ease the pain of the self-employment tax, the self-employed get to deduct half of what they pay in self-employment tax on line 58, Form 1040. This tax—the equivalent of the Social Security and Medicare taxes paid by employees and employers—is 15.3 percent of 92.35 percent of the first $102,000 of 2008 self-employment income and 2.9 percent of income over $102,000. The 2.9 percent represents the Medicare taxes that do not have an income cap like Social Security taxes.

- **Self-Employed SEP and SIMPLE Plans** *(line 28)*
  Here is another chance for a last-minute tax break. If you had self-employment income during the tax year, you can shelter part of it inside a Keogh plan, a Simplified Employee Pension (SEP), or a SIMPLE plan. Contributions to any of these accounts—up to $6,000 of self-employment income into a SIMPLE plan, up to $25,500 into a SEP, and up to $30,000 into a Keogh—can be made as late as the April 15 filing deadline and still earn a write-off from the previous tax year. (In addition to the dollar cap, contributions to Keogh and SEP plans are based on a percentage of your self-employment income.) Although Keogh and SIMPLE plans have to be opened during the tax year (by December 31) to qualify for a deduction, you can open a SEP right up to April 15 of the following year and still get credit for the previous tax year. You can open these plans at banks, brokerage firms, and mutual fund companies.

- **Self-Employed Health Insurance Deduction** *(line 29)*
  The self-employed are allowed to deduct 100 percent of what they pay for medical insurance. You may be able to deduct the amount you paid for health insurance for yourself, your spouse, and your dependents if any of the following applies.

  ➤ You were self-employed and had a net profit for the year
  ➤ You used one of the optional methods to figure your net earnings from self-employment on Schedule SE

>>> **FAST FACT**

Not So Fast ...

You cannot deduct any insurance costs for any months you were eligible to participate in a group health insurance plan through your or your spouse's employer. So if you paid for twelve months of private health insurance coverage for yourself and your family, but you became eligible to participate in your spouse's group health insurance in December, then you can deduct only eleven months' worth of insurance premiums.

Source: Internal Revenue Service ◄

> » You received wages in 2008 from an S corporation in which you were a more than 2 percent shareholder

- **Penalty on Early Withdrawal of Savings** *(line 30)*
  Yes, if you accrued a penalty due to an early withdrawal from a Certificate of Deposit or any other time-sensitive savings account, you can claim the penalty as a deduction here. You should receive a Form 1099-INT or 1099-OID, which will instruct you on the penalty.

- **Alimony Paid** *(lines 31a and 31b)*
  Alimony payments you make under a divorce or separation instrument are deductible if all the following requirements are met:

  - » You and your spouse or former spouse do not file a joint return with each other
  - » You pay in cash (including checks or money orders)
  - » The divorce or separation instrument does not say that the payment is not alimony
  - » If legally separated under a decree of divorce or separate maintenance, you and your former spouse are not members of the same household when you make the payment

➤ You have no liability to make any payment (in cash or property) after the death of your spouse or former spouse

➤ Your payment is not treated as child support

You need to include the Social Security number of the person
to whom you are making the payments on line 31b.

➤➤➤ FAST FACT

What About Child Support?

Child support is never deductible. If your divorce decree or other written
instrument or agreement calls for alimony and child support, and you pay
less than the total required, the payments apply first to child support. Any
remaining amount is considered alimony. You will only receive a deduction
on that remaining amount. Ouch! ◄

- **IRA Contribution Deduction** *(line 32)*
  Contributions to a traditional IRA might be deductible or
  nondeductible, depending on your age, AGI, and whether you
  are covered by a retirement plan through your employer. For
  phase-out limits and other restrictions on the deductible portion of your IRA contributions, see IRS Publication 590, Individual Retirement Arrangements.

  If you do qualify to deduct contributions, deposits you
  make right up to April 15 can be deducted on your previous
  year's return.

  If you do not qualify to deduct contributions, choose a
  Roth IRA over a traditional IRA. A Roth IRA is easier to manage and still retains the other advantages of a traditional IRA.
  Also, if you later convert your traditional IRA to a Roth IRA,
  all the converted non-basis amounts in the traditional IRA are
  exposed to taxation. Yikes!

>>> **FAST FACT**

Hey Grandma Dottie, Think About IRA Withdrawals, Too!

You must start taking the minimum required distribution from your traditional IRA by April 1 of the year after the year in which you turn 70½. While you are trying to figure out when that will be, let me tell you why: If you don't, you may have to pay a 50 percent tax on the amount that should have been distributed. ◄

- **Student Loan Interest Deduction** *(line 33)*
  You can deduct up to $2,500 of interest on student loans here, even if you do not itemize deductions. The deduction is for interest on almost any loans (not just federal student loans) taken to pay qualified higher education expenses (including room and board) for yourself, your spouse, or your dependent who is at least a half-time student. However, you cannot deduct interest on loans from relatives or from company retirement plans.

 TAX TIPS

Phase-Out Frustrations

In my experience, student loan interest is one of the most disallowed deductions due to high AGI. For the most recent tax year, the deduction begins to phase out at $55,000 for single (as well as head of household and qualifying widow[er]) and $110,000 for married filing jointly. The deduction is completely phased out at an AGI of $70,000 for singles (as well as head of household and qualifying widow[er]) and $140,000 for married filing jointly.

- **Tuition and Fees Deduction** *(line 34)*

  You may be able to claim a deduction here for tuition and fees paid for yourself, spouse, or dependents. Whether or not you qualify depends upon a variety of factors, including your filing status, the expense type, and your income level. Also, you cannot claim both the deduction and closely associated tax credits (i.e., Hope and Lifetime Learning Credits). To claim, you need to complete an IRS Form 8917.

- **Domestic Production Activities Deduction** *(line 35)*

  Complete IRS Form 8903 to determine whether or not you can claim a deduction of up to 6 percent (in 2008) of income from the following activities:

  - Construction of real property in the United States
  - Engineering or architectural services performed for the above
  - Lease, rental, license, sale, exchange, or other distribution of certain types of property (e.g., software, sound recordings, film, etc.)
  - Lease, rental, license, sale, exchange, or other distribution of certain types of resources (e.g., electricity, natural gas, water, etc.)

- **Add Lines 23 through 31a and 32 through 35** *(line 36)*

  Here, total up all your "above the line" deductions—i.e., all adjustments to your total income.

- **Adjusted Gross Income** *(line 37)*

  Here, you will calculate your Adjusted Gross Income by reducing your Total Income (i.e., line 22) by the total of your adjustments or "above the line" deductions (i.e., line 36).

Form 1040—Tax and Credits

After determining your AGI, we then move on to your "below the line" deductions. For your "below the line" deductions, the most

TAX TIPS

Write-In Candidates

If you have any additional adjustments to income that qualify as "above the line" deductions, you can write them in. For example, you may be able to claim a deduction for Jury Pay, if you gave the pay to your employer because your employer paid your salary while you served on the jury. In such a situation, list "Jury Pay" in the space provided (i.e., dotted line leading up to the line 36 blank) and the amount. Make sure to include this amount in your calculation for line 36.

▶▶▶ FAST FACT

Feeling the Standard Deduction Blues?

Do not feel cheated if you claim the standard deduction. After all, it saves you the hassle of itemizing your deductions and completing an additional schedule (Schedule A). And besides saving you time, the standard deduction saves you money. The reason to use it is when your itemized deductions for the year are less than the standard deduction for your filing status.

In other words, the standard deduction gives you credit for more than you actually spent on deductible expenses. About two-thirds of all returns filed claim the standard deduction.

However, owning a home will be what finally moves you beyond the standard deduction. It is at that point that your itemized deductions will finally exceed the standard deduction amount. ◄

---

notable is either the standard deduction or your total itemized deductions, either of which is claimed on line 40.

We will be exploring the deductions on Schedule A, Itemized Deductions in great detail in the next Round. So, hold your horses!

- **Amount from Line 37 (Adjusted Gross Income)** *(line 38)*

  This is used for easy reference to your AGI on the second page of the Form 1040. Merely carry the number forward from line 37 to here so that you can conduct calculations more easily later down the form.

- **Check Boxes** *(lines 39a, 39b, and 39c)*

  Line item 39a contains a couple of check boxes that are used to determine whether or not you or your spouse qualify for a higher standard deduction. The two determining factors are: (1) whether you or your spouse are 65 years or older by the end of the tax year and (2) whether you or your spouse are blind. If both you and your spouse are 65 years or older and blind, you qualify for a standard deduction of $14,900 if you file married filing jointly.

  Alternatively, line item 39b contains a check box to determine whether you qualify for a standard deduction at all. If your filing status is (1) married filing separately and your spouse itemizes his or her deductions on his or her return or (2) a dual-status alien, you do not qualify for the standard deduction, and instead, are required to check the box and itemize your deductions.

  Finally, line item 39c is to be checked if you will be claiming real estate taxes paid and/or disaster loss in addition to the standard deduction. This is a recent change to the Form 1040, just passed into law in 2008.

- **Itemized or Standard Deduction** *(line 40)*

  Here is where you enter your claimed deductions. If you itemize your deductions, you will complete a Schedule A. If you claim the standard deduction and no boxes are checked in line items 39a, 39b, or 39c, then you will claim the following amount on this line item, dependent on your filing status (as of 2008):

Filing Status	Amount of Standard Deduction
Single	$5,450
Married Filing Separately	$5,450
Head of Household	$8,000
Married Filing Jointly	$10,900
Qualifying Widow(er)	$10,900

Source: Internal Revenue Service

After deducing your deductions, move on to calculating your preliminary tax due. This is done by subtracting your "below the line" deductions and exemptions from your AGI to calculate your taxable income. Then, using your taxable income, your preliminary tax due is calculated. This may or may not include the Alternative Minimum Tax and other taxes from special forms.

- **Subtract line 40 from 38 *(line 41)***
  Here, you subtract your deductions (either itemized or standard) from your AGI and enter the remaining amount.

- **Exemptions *(line 42)***
  This line item is a little unclear, but it is where you claim your exemptions for yourself and your dependents. Take the number listed on line item 6d and multiply it by $3,500 (as of 2008). However, this amount can be reduced depending upon the size of your AGI and filing status:

Filing Status	Phase-Out AGI Amount for Exemptions
Married Filing Separately	$119,975
Single	$159,950
Head of Household	$199,950
Married Filing Jointly	$239,950
Qualifying Widow(er)	$239,950

Source: Internal Revenue Service

Also, in 2008 and 2009, the Midwestern Disaster Tax Relief Act of 2008 provides an additional personal exemption for those who house a "midwestern displaced individual." In order to qualifiy, the individual(s) had to have been displaced from their home and stayed in your home for free for at least sixty consecutive days in the tax year for which you are claiming the deduction.

- **Taxable Income** *(line 43)*
  Here, you subtract your exemptions (line 42) from the amount calculated for line 41 (i.e., AGI less your "below the line" deductions).

- **Tax Due** *(line 44)*
  You can calculate this two ways: (1) using the Tax Table if your taxable income < $100,000 and (2) using the Tax Computation Worksheet if your taxable income > $100,000. Both the table and worksheet are found within the Instructions to the IRS Form 1040, Individual Income Tax Return.

  However, whatever is calculated using the table or worksheet is only your preliminary tax due because (1) you have yet to apply any tax credits to reduce your tax due and (2) you have not yet added additional taxes due. So we still have some work ahead of us.

Note that there are also some additional boxes here. Those are used to signify that special types of taxes (i.e. lump sum distributions, Health Savings Accounts) are due and that the IRS forms associated with those taxes are attached.

- **Alternative Minimum Tax** *(line 45)*

The Alternative Minimum Tax (AMT) sets a minimum tax rate of either 26 or 28 percent on the amount of the taxpayer's alternative minimum taxable income, as adjusted. This monstrosity disallows many deductions and exemptions allowable in computing tax liability.

Affected taxpayers are those who have what are known as "tax preference items." These include some long-term capital gains, accelerated depreciation, certain medical expenses, percentage depletion, certain tax-exempt income, personal and dependent exemptions, and the standard deduction. The AMT is a monstrosity because it is not indexed to inflation and recent tax cuts. As a result, in recent years an increasing number of upper-middle-income taxpayers have been finding themselves subject to this tax. Yuck!

To determine whether you are required to file IRS Form 6251, use the AMT Assistant worksheet found on www.irs.gov.

- **Add Lines 44 and 45** *(line 46)*

Use this line item to add the Alternative Minimum Tax to the Preliminary Tax Due calculated.

Next, we are on to tax credits. We will explore tax credits in greater depth in the next chapter, but remember, credits are your friend. They are a dollar for dollar reduction in your tax due.

- **Foreign Tax Credit** *(line 47)*

No, you do not have to move to a foreign country to qualify for the foreign tax credit. You may qualify, for example, if you own shares in a mutual fund that invests in foreign securities. If your 1099-DIV from the fund shows that foreign taxes were paid on your behalf, for example, you can treat that amount as an itemized deduction or claim this credit. We will explore this in a little more detail in the next Round.

- **Child and Dependent Care Credit** *(line 48)*
  If you pay for childcare assistance for your children, including daycare, you may be able to claim a tax credit on your annual return. To qualify for this credit, you (and your spouse, if you are married) must work at least part-time, unless you are a full-time student or are disabled. Your children must be under the age of thirteen, or physically or mentally disabled.

- **Elderly or Disabled Credit** *(line 49)*
  This credit is based upon the taxpayer (and/or spouse, if filing jointly). You qualify if, by the end of the tax year, the taxpayer(s) were either (a) sixty-five years old or older, or (b) retired on permanent and total disability and yet had taxable disability income. You cannot claim this credit as an individual if your AGI exceeded $17,500, or, as married filing jointly, if the AGI exceeded $20,000 and only one of the two spouses were otherwise eligible, or if the AGI exceeded $25,000 and both spouses were otherwise eligible.

- **Education Credits** *(line 50)*
  The Hope credit and the Lifetime Learning credit can mitigate the pain of paying for college by helping you reduce your tax bill. The Hope credit is worth up to $1,800 for each qualifying student in the first two years of college or vocational school. The Lifetime Learning credit is worth up to $2,000 a year for expenses for students beyond sophomore year, including the cost of classes parents take. Although you cannot claim both credits for the same student, you can claim a Hope credit for each qualifying student and a Lifetime Learning credit for

qualifying expenses for a different student. We will review these credits in more detail in Round 7.

- **Retirement Savings Credit** *(line 51)*
  Also known as the saver's credit, this credit is designed to encourage retirement savings by lower- and middle-income individuals and families. Consequently, its availability is tied to AGI levels (less than $26,500 for individuals, $39,750 for head of household, or $53,000 for married filing jointly).

  Although it is restrictive about who is eligible, it is flexible as to the type of savings plan funded. Traditional and Roth IRAs, 401(k), 403(b), 501(c)(18)(D), governmental 457, SEP, SIMPLE plan, and federal Thrift Savings plan contributions all qualify for this deduction.

- **Child Tax Credit** *(line 52)*
  The IRS allows a $1,000 credit for each dependent child under seventeen. Like so many tax breaks, this one disappears as income rises above certain limits. The phase-out begins when the AGI passes $110,000 on a joint return or $75,000 on a single or head of household return.

- **Miscellaneous Credits** *(line 53)*
  This line item captures credits for the following items:

  - Mortgage Interest Credit—*complete IRS Form 8396*
  - Adoption Credit—*complete IRS Form 8839*
  - Residential Energy Credit—*complete IRS Form 5695*

  The last one actually consists of two credits—non-business energy property credit and residential energy-efficient property credit. The non-business energy property credit is for improvements to your main home made in the current tax year that meet certain energy-efficiency requirements. The residential energy-efficient property credit is for paying for any of the following:

  - Solar electric property improvements

TAX TIPS

Kids & Social Security

If you just had a baby—congratulations! Now, while loading up on diapers, do not forget to get your child a Social Security number before you file your tax return. The IRS will not allow you to claim a dependency exemption, the Earned Income Tax Credit, or head of household filing status without a valid Social Security number for your child.

Hospitals routinely give the application to the mother right after the child's birth. The Social Security number is then issued to the mother by mail soon after. However, if you used the application to light your celebratory cigars—*not advised*—applications are available on the web at SSA.gov, keyword "application".

> Solar water heating property improvements
> Fuel cell property improvements

All improvements, for either credit, must have been made to your main home, and that home must be located within the United States.

- **Other Credits** *(line 54)*
This line item captures credits for the following items:

> General Business Credit—*complete IRS Form 3800*
> Prior Year Alternative Minimum Tax—*complete IRS Form 8801 and enter amount calculated from its line 28*

It also has a space (see 55c) for you to fill in additional credits not listed on the Form 1040. There is a very long list of eligible credits, the most common being the following:

> Alternative Motor Vehicle Credit—*complete IRS Form 8911*
> Alcohol Used as a Fuel Credit—*complete IRS Form 6478*
> Qualified Electric Vehicle Credit—*complete IRS Form 8834*

- **Total Tax Credits** *(line 55)*
  Add the amounts claimed in line items 47 through 55. These are your total tax credits.

- **Preliminary Tax Due After Credits** *(line 56)*
  Then, subtract your total tax credits (line 56) from line 46. This is your preliminary tax due after the AMT is added and tax credits are removed. If this amount is less than zero, you will enter "0" here.

Form 1040—Other Taxes

The next section adds additional taxes to preliminary taxes due. These taxes come from a variety of sources. Below, we examine the major participants:

- **Self-Employment Tax** *(line 57)*
  The self-employment tax is no picnic, financially. The 15.3 percent rate to pay for Social Security and Medicare applies to the first $102,000 of self-employment income. From that point on, only the 2.9 percent Medicare part of the tax applies. If you have income from a job from which Social Security taxes are withheld, that income counts toward the $102,000 limit. Thus, if you have $60,000 in salary from an employer in addition to $70,000 in income from self-employment, the full self-employment tax would apply only to the first $42,000 of your self-employment income.

  Remember: half of what you pay in self-employment tax is deductible on line 27.

- **Unreported Social Security and Medicare Tax** *(line 58)*
  The Social Security and Medicare tax from two types of unreported income are entered here: unreported tips and wages from an employer who failed to withhold. You will use Form 4137 and 8919, respectively, to calculate the tax due.

- **Additional Tax on Retirement Plans** *(line 59)*
  This is the IRS's way of penalizing taxpayers who break the retirement plan rules. However, don't jump to the conclusion that you are guilty of an early withdrawal. For example, it's okay to take money from a company retirement plan as early as the year you reach age fifty-five, if you get the money after you leave the job. And you can get company plan or traditional IRA money at any time, without penalty, if the payout is part of a string of annual payments based on your life expectancy. The penalty is also waived if you use IRA money to pay medical bills that exceed 7.5 percent of your AGI, or to buy medical insurance during a period of extended unemployment.

⟫⟫⟫ FAST FACT

Early Returns on Early Withdrawals

"Early" IRA withdrawals are also now penalty-free if the money is used to pay college expenses for yourself, your spouse, or your child or grandchild, and up to $10,000 can be withdrawn penalty-free to buy a first home for yourself, your children or grandchildren, or even your parents. ◄

- **Additional Taxes** *(lines 60a and 60b)*
  This consists of two additional taxes:

  ➤ Advanced Earned Income Tax Credit payments:

  These are payments of the Earned Income Tax Credit earned prior to filing your income tax return, received through your paycheck. You can ask your employer for an advance on your anticipated Earned Income Tax Credit. The total of your advance is shown on your W-2 wage statement in box 9. If there are any amounts, you must report them on Form 1040 using line 60a.

➤ Household Employment Tax:

Here is where various payroll or employment taxes assessed on wages paid to household employees are recorded, including FICA (Social Security, Medicare), FUTA, SUI (SUTA), SDI (State Disability Insurance), and others.

➤➤➤ FAST FACT

Employing the Young

Amounts paid to employees under the age of eighteen who are also students do not count toward determining whether a household employment tax is necessary. ◄

- **Total Tax** *(line 61)*
  Here, add up all the other taxes entered in this section plus the preliminary tax due after credits (i.e., line item 57). This is your total tax.

Form 1040—Payments

This section records the tax payments you made throughout the year. These payments determine whether you have a refund coming or will have some taxes you still need to pay when you file your return.
  Here is a breakdown of some of the major types of payments:

- **Income Tax Withheld** *(line 62)*
  This information comes right from your Forms W-2 and 1099.

- **Prior Year Refund/Estimated Tax Payment** *(line 63)*
  This is a reminder from Uncle Sam on refunds. It means that if, rather than claiming a refund due on your last year's tax return, you had the IRS apply the amount to your current tax bill. Remember to take credit for that payment.

Also, remember to include any and all estimated tax payments that you made throughout the current tax year. It's a little tricky, almost as if the IRS doesn't mind if you forget. Hmm.

- **Earned Income Tax Credit** *(lines 64a and 64b)*
  The Earned Income Tax Credit (EITC) is for lower- and middle-income individuals and married couples who work. The eligibility for the credit is tied to AGI, filing status, and number of children.

  For example, in 2008, a single individual may be able to claim the EITC if his or her AGI is less than $38,646 (two children), $33,995 (one child), or $12,880 (no children). Alternatively, a married couple filing jointly may be able to claim the EITC if their AGI is less than $41,646 (two children), $36,995 (one child), or $15,880 (no children).

  This is only the tip of the iceberg for the EITC. We will explore it in greater detail in the next Round.

- **Excess Social Security Tax Payments** *(line 65)*
  So, say you're a moonlighter, and you worked more than one job last year. Alternatively, maybe you changed employers during the year. In either case, ask yourself this question: did your combined pay exceed $102,000? If you answered yes, too much Social Security tax may have been withheld from your paychecks. Line 67 is the place to go to get a tax credit. How much? The difference between what you paid in Social Security taxes (6.2 percent of your wages) and $6,375, the maximum amount anyone is supposed to pay in Social Security taxes.

- **Additional Child Tax Credit** *(line 66)*
  Additional child tax credit arises when there is no preliminary tax to reduce when applying the tax credit (see line 57). This permits you to claim the credit solely to increase the size of your refund. You need to complete IRS Form 8812 to see if you do in fact qualify for this additional credit, and to determine its size.

TAX TIPS

Drowning in Forms

Sometimes it seems like D-Day was planned with less paperwork than your income tax returns. And when it comes time to send in your return, you might leave out a form that Uncle Sam really wants. If you forget to mail a required form with your tax return, simply wait until the IRS contacts you with instructions, and send it in at that time.

- **Amount Paid with Request to File Extension** *(line 67)*
  If you filed a request for an extension—IRS Form 4868—and paid any amount with the filing of that form, enter the amount paid here.

- **Payments from Miscellaneous IRS Forms** *(line 68)*
  If you made payments on your taxes using one of these IRS forms, check the appropriate box and enter the amount paid here:

  » IRS Form 2439—reports undistributed long-term capital gains to shareholders of regulated investment companies or real estate investment trusts
  » IRS Form 4136—reports federal taxes paid on gasoline and other fuels when the fuel was used for allowable nontaxable purposes
  » IRS Form 8801—reports a credit for those individuals who paid penalties and interest on an Alternative Minimum Tax liability due to the exercise of stock options from tech companies that later became worthless; it is line 30 of the form
  » IRS Form 8885—reports a tax credit for certain displaced workers who paid for continued health insurance after being laid off

- **First-Time Homebuyer Credit** *(line 69)*

  This is a new tax credit, included in the Housing and Economic Recovery Act of 2008. It applies to home purchases between April 8, 2008, and July 1, 2009, in the United States, and reduces the tax bill—or increases the refund—dollar for dollar. For newly constructed homes, the purchase date is considered the date on which you first inhabited the home.

  The credit phases out for higher income families and individuals. For couples filing as married, filing jointly, the phase-out begins for those with a modified AGI of $150,000 and is completely phased out for those with a modified AGI of $175,000. For all other taxpayers (i.e., those filing single, head of household, married filing separately, or qualifying widow[er]), the phase-out begins at $75,000 and is completely phased out at $95,000.

  However, unlike other tax credits, this one needs to be repaid. That's right, Congress wants their money back, eventually. They do this through assessing an additional tax on taxpayers for the next fifteen years after the credit is claimed. Thus, for example, if an eligible taxpayer claims the full credit on his or her 2008 return (i.e., $7,500 or 10 percent of the purchase price—whatever is less), he or she will have to repay 1/15 of that amount every year thereafter in additional taxes (i.e., $500 per year) until the credit is paid back in full.

  To claim the credit, eligible taxpayers must complete an IRS Form 5405.

- **Recovery Rebate Credit** *(line 70)*

  As part of the Economic Stimulus of 2008, this line item was inserted to ensure that more individuals qualified for the benefits. It allows individuals who meet the requirements (i.e., have a valid Social Security number, total earned income of at least $3,000, and net income tax liability—regular tax plus AMT, less any nonrefundable credits—that is greater than zero) to claim a credit of up to $600–$1,200 if filing married filing jointly.

The size of the credit was dependent upon AGI requirements (i.e., phase-out begins at $75,000 for single, $150,000
for married filing jointly), the size of the tax liability (i.e., size
of credit could not exceed net income tax liability), and most
important, whether or not the individual received the Economic Stimulus payment in 2008. If he or she did, then he or
she was not eligible to also receive the credit.

If the credit they could have claimed exceeded the amount
of the stimulus payment received, then they can claim the difference as a credit. If the reverse was true and the payment
exceeded the credit they are now eligible for, taxpayers do not
have to refund the difference.

- **Total Payments** *(line 71)*

   Here, add up all the payments already made (i.e., lines 64
   through 71) to calculate your total payments.

Form 1040—Refund, Amount You Owe

This section can either be good or bad. Why? Well, many people
think refunds are a good thing, and only think that owing the IRS
additional money and having to enclose a check with the return
is bad. However, both owing and being owed are bad. In fact, the
refund is actually proof of Uncle Sam's deviousness. It is basically
the government saying "Whoops! I guess we took too much from
you. . . . Well, here is what we owe you, but we'll just keep the interest we earned on it."

The amount you owe is just ugly because it can result in interest
and penalties if you do not pay the balance due immediately. And
even if you pay it immediately, you may be subject to an estimated
tax payment penalty.

As we have done with the previous sections, let's now review the
essential line items of these two final sections:

- **Amount Overpaid** *(line 72)*

   If line 72 exceeds line 63, it means that you overpaid your
   taxes and are due a refund. While this is better than the

opposite, it is not entirely good. Rather, it means that you were coughing up money to the IRS throughout the year that could have been put to work for you. So, if the amount overpaid is large, now would be the time to make adjustments to what you are withholding or paying to the IRS throughout the year.

- **Direct Deposit of Refund** *(lines 73a, 73b, 73c, and 73d)*
  I do not want to wait for a refund. You do not want to wait for a refund. *Nobody* wants to wait for a refund in this age of instant gratification. We all feel entitled to get things as soon as they become available. Money is no different.

  So, if you have a refund coming, tell the IRS to put your money right into your checking or savings account. This can save you time and hassle. You should get your money at least a few days sooner than if you had to wait for a check. There is also no chance that an electronic deposit can be lost in the mail or stolen on the way to the bank. It is also the patriotic thing to do—direct deposit saves the IRS, and therefore all of us taxpayers, money. It is much cheaper to zap a refund to a bank account than to print and mail a check. One downside: you have to check with your bank or wait for a statement to know when your money has arrived.

- **Applied to Next Year's Estimated Tax** *(line 74)*
  You could always take your refund and get a jump-start on paying your taxes for the next year. This can be useful to those who are self-employed or are expecting a lot of taxes because of an increase in income or change in filing status in the present year. Also, you do not have to apply the full amount, but any portion that you elect.

- **Amount You Owe** *(line 75)*
  D'oh! If there is monetary value listed here, then it is proof positive that you need to make adjustments.

TAX TIPS

Charge It

Typically, it is not a good idea to use plastic when you can cut a check. However, if owing money at tax time leaves you in a pinch, it is good to know that you can use a credit card if you need to. Also, you may be able to build rewards points this way, which you can use on flights or other items. For more information on IRS payment methods, including credit cards, see Round 9.

- **Underpayment Penalty** *(line 76)*

  If you owe $1,000 or more—beyond what you paid through withholding and estimated tax payments—and the amount due is more than 10 percent of your tax bill for the year, look out. The IRS will also assess you a penalty for failing to pay enough during the previous tax year. Jerks!

 ## Inside the Ropes: Tackling the 1040

Jamie had never done her own taxes before. The thirty-three-year-old psychologist had always relied on her husband to do them. Now divorced, she is tackling them on her own for the very first time.

"I read some books, visited some tax websites," she explains. "But when I sat down to study my 1040, I realized that I needed to use some extra tax forms to get every deduction owed to me."

A visit to a local tax-preparation office confirmed that. There, Jamie learned the importance of Form 1040's Schedule A, the form for itemized deductions. "It wasn't that difficult once a professional tax preparer explained it to me," she adds. "I could itemize all my charitable contributions, medical expenses, investment interest, and mortgage interest all on one form."

Emboldened by the experience of saving money on deductions, she asked for help from her tax professional on Schedule D for all her mutual fund deductions. "I had some capital gains issues and I wasn't sure if was going to have to pay taxes or not."

Another e-mail from her tax specialist revealed that Jamie had some capital gains to contend with after redeeming some mutual fund shares for a profit the previous year. "I never would have known it otherwise," says Jamie. "If I hadn't done my homework and gotten some good tax advice, who knows where I would have been?"

➤ ROUND 5

Addition by Subtraction:
The Sweet Science of Tax Deductions,
Exemptions, and Credits

Money will not buy happiness, but it will pay the salaries of a large research staff to study the problem.

—Bill Vaughn

If there is one thing that I have learned in the tax game, it is that there is the haphazard taxpayer and then there is the scientific taxpayer.

The haphazard taxpayer always prepares his tax return—like his life—without a complete plan in place. He comes up with a lot of numbers, scenarios, and what-ifs that do not make sense, and he gives himself a headache in the process because there just is not enough time.

Let me give you a "for instance":

Justin is an up-and-coming, hotshot corporate attorney. Negotiating contracts left and right, Justin gets himself a big raise and a fancy corner office to boot. He is a mover and a shaker with that income, and he dabbles in the fine art of Internet stock and bond trading in between conference calls.

Justin is also having the time of his life. He loves the big city he lives in—and the women who inhabit it. He wants to stay near the scene, so he rents a big studio apartment in a trendy part of town.

Things could not be sweeter—until tax time. Turns out all that income has led to a very large tax liability. In addition, the Internet stock trading had tax consequences to boot. As Justin scrambles to offset some of his taxes with deductions, he learns that he missed out on large deductions by (1) not purchasing a parcel of property instead of renting, and (2) not setting up an office in said home. Also, by never settling down, he missed out on not only the advantages of a joint tax return, but also—more important to Justin—the large exemptions and possible credits that would have been available to him had he raised a family.

Needless to say, April was not Justin's favorite month. You try cutting a $47,000 check to Uncle Sam with a smile on your face!

Justin found out the hard way why it is cool to be a scientific taxpayer and to learn the "sweet science" of uncovering tax deductions, exemptions, and credits. To avoid Justin's fate, you need to learn a very simple lesson—that every dollar you save in taxes is a dollar you get to keep in your wallet. Working from that premise and motivation, you can set out to create a tax plan that takes advantage of as many deductions, exemptions, and credits as possible.

After all, why would you want to give almost 40 cents of every dollar you earn to the government when, oftentimes, you don't have to?

Understanding the IRS's standard deductions, how and when to itemize deductions, and claiming essential exemptions and tax credits is the way to establish your tax-planning strategy. That is why you want to understand deductions, exemptions, and credits, so you will never again wonder if you've missed something you could have taken.

Let's start by getting some definitions out of the way.

- **Deduction**
  A reduction in taxable income due to a type of expense incurred by a taxpayer. Deductions are subtracted from gross income, so tax deductions lower the overall taxable income and the amount of tax paid. However, the amount of savings from a particular deduction is dependent upon the tax rate.

- **Exemptions**
  A reduction in taxable income due to a status or circumstance of the taxpayer (or, sometimes, the status or circumstance of the taxpayer's property). Exemptions, like deductions, are subtracted from gross income. Consequently, tax exemptions similarly lower the overall taxable income and the amount of tax paid. As with deductions, the amount of savings from a particular exemption is dependent upon the tax rate.

- **Credit**
  A dollar for dollar reduction in the required tax payment. Deductions and exemptions only reduce the amount of your income that is taxable, whereas tax credits reduce the actual amount of tax owed. They are not dependent upon the tax rate.

Basically, deductions, exemptions, and credits are the different ways to reduce what goes into Uncle Sam's back pocket.

Deducing Deductions

Before we delve into the world of deductions, let's focus on the good news. As mentioned above, the larger your tax deduction, the lower your taxable income.

Let that roll off the tongue one more time. The larger the deduction, the lower your taxable income.

Okay, we have the motive. Now we need a game plan.

It starts with the star of Round 4—the IRS 1040 Tax Form. When you file a federal income tax return, you either take a standard deduction or itemize your deductions. By IRS statutes, you can take the larger of the two.

The standard deduction is dynamic, growing each year to account for constant rises in inflation. In fact, thanks to higher standard deductions, fewer taxpayers than in the past get any benefit from itemizing. (The standard deductions are even higher for taxpayers age sixty-five and older, and those who are legally blind.) Thus, itemizing pays off only if your qualifying expenses total more than the standard deduction for your filing status.

But if you have enough expenses—and most taxpayers probably do—then it is smart to do something about defraying their cost.

What You Can Deduct

While the IRS encourages you to take deductions, and even goes out of its way to show you where they are, it is ultimately your responsibility to claim them on your tax returns.

No worries. With a little digging and some research, you will leave no deduction unturned.

For starters, check out the following list of common deductions:

- **Alimony Payments & Income**
  The IRS is a huge factor in deciding which spouse in a divorce gets what—and which one does not. Big surprise, right? Largely, money paid out as alimony by an ex-spouse is viewed as deductible by Uncle Sam. That is not the case with child support, where the IRS will not allow a deduction.

Other marital money issues abound. If you receive stocks, real estate, or other investable assets after a divorce, the IRS considers it static. That is, any gain or loss from the investment while you were married is passed along to the receiving ex-spouse. That goes the same for tax liability from the investment. One caveat: you must own the asset long-term to qualify for the deduction.

 T A X   T I P S

On-the-Job Deductions

Any money used to help you retain or improve your skills in your current job or career is usually deductible.

- **Charitable Contributions**
  I encourage all readers to get involved with a charity of their choice. It doesn't matter which, just pick one (or many!) that supports a cause you agree with. Contributing what you can to charity enables you to do good. For example, I donate to my favorite charity, The Hannah Rose Foundation, which educates parents and other caregivers about the dangers of Shaken Baby Syndrome. (To learn more information about this foundation, please visit www.dontshakeyourbaby.com; my beautiful sixteen-month-old niece, Hannah, was shaken and died. In fact, a portion of the proceeds of this book you hold in your hand will go straight to this foundation.)

  While your motives for donations may be tied to someone or something you love, there is a financial and tax benefit as well. In addition, like most other financial and tax moves, timing is everything. For example, if you are thinking of making a substantial gift to your church, doing so before the end of the year locks in the deduction for the current year. If you normally give $100 a month to your church, making the January contribution by December 31 boosts your write-off by that amount. If you make a pledge to make future contributions, however, you do not get the deduction until you actually make the gifts.

 # TAX TIPS

Check Out These Other Charitable Deductions:

- There is a special advantage to giving away appreciated property—such as stock—rather than cash. You can earn a write-off for the current value of the stock rather than what you originally paid for it, and you avoid having to pay tax on the profit that built up while you owned it. That is, if you made a profit.
- If you routinely go through your closet for used clothing to give away, find time for a year-end sweep. Making the donation by New Year's Eve earns you a deduction for the current year.

• Medical Expenses

Ouch, those aching knees! You can alleviate some of the pain by deducting your doctor bills. Remember this when you go about it: since medical bills are deductible only if they total more than 7.5 percent of your Adjusted Gross Income, timing your payments may be the only way to garner a tax benefit from these costs. By the end of the year, you will know where you stand with your total adjustable gross income. But you may want to resist squaring any medical tabs until next year, when the tax benefits could be even more advantageous. However, if you know your medical bills will exceed 7.5 percent of your Adjusted Gross Income, then put your entire medical bill onto a low-interest credit card by the end of the year instead of making payments. This will ensure that you receive as large as a deduction as possible.

- **Miscellaneous Expenses**

Similar to a health care bill, a deduction in the miscellaneous expenses category kicks in only after you exceed a benchmark established by the IRS; here, it is 2 percent of your Adjusted Gross Income. The list of qualifying expenses is long, but you get no tax savings unless you pass the 2 percent test. As you creep close to year-end, see how close you are to the benchmark. Not going to make it? Then delay paying qualifying expenses, like association and professional fees and the cost of subscriptions to tax or investment publications. If it is likely your expenses will pass 2 percent of your AGI, speed up such spending to exploit the tax subsidy.

 TAX TIPS

Giving It Away Can Pay

If you believe that charity begins with family and friends (hey, that's how my business got started!), you can give away as much as $12,000 a year to any number of people without triggering the federal gift tax (as of 2008). In other words—tax-free. And the limit doubles to $24,000 if your spouse joins you in doling out the cash. Just be careful—you do not get a tax deduction for these gifts unless the recipient of your largesse is a qualified charitable organization.

While actually not a deduction in a technical sense, assets given away during your life—and any future appreciation—will not be in your estate to be taxed after you shuffle off your mortal coil (you know—die). Income generated by the gift is taxed to the gift recipient, not to you. (If you give assets to your own children, however, the income from those assets can be taxed in your tax bracket until the children reach age eighteen.)

- **State and Local Taxes**
  Imagine getting a deduction on the state taxes you pay. Here is how it works: if you make estimated income-tax payments, sliding the fourth-quarter installment into the mail by December 31 earns you the deduction for the current year—even if a portion of that check to the IRS is returned to you via a state tax refund a few months into the new year. Note that your state tax payment has to be a reasonable estimate—in the eyes of the IRS—of your formal state tax bill. In other words, you cannot pump up your fourth-quarter payment so you can claim the write-off on your federal return.

 TAX TIPS

Keeping Tabs

Try to keep track of your itemized deductions each year even if you are in the habit of taking the standard deduction. I know it's a pain, but I see too many people who do not bother with itemized deductions and end up paying more tax than they owe.

Often-Overlooked Tax Deductions

As I have been saying, there are plenty of deductions that taxpayers miss—repeatedly. Here is a list of the most commonly overlooked tax deductions. I want to make sure that, for you at least, they are not overlooked anymore.

- **Vehicle Personal Property Tax**
  So you get a tax levy each year from your state or local government for owning a car or other vehicle? The good news is that you may be able to deduct it from your tax bill. And that's not all. You also earn the tax deduction if you lease a car and

your finance company sticks you with the tax bill. The rule is that you can deduct the tax if it depends on the value of your vehicle. Some states, like California, include a breakdown of how the tax is calculated on your bill from the Department of Motor Vehicles. However, if you are fuzzy about how the tax was calculated, check with a good tax specialist.

- **Valuation of Donated Goods**
  Many people underestimate the thrift-store value of household goods they donate to charity. But your donated goods do have value. And it is important to calculate the value of the goods donated properly in order to maximize your deductions—and not to run afoul of the IRS.

  To determine the proper value of goods, first you must determine each item's fair market value. The fair market value is the price the good is worth on the date on which it was donated. The fair market value for household goods is usually much lower on the date it is donated than on the date it was originally purchased. IRS Publication 561—Determining the Valuation of Donated Property—is a good source of information on how to properly value different forms of donated property.

- **Job-Hunting Expenses**
  Whether you're working like an eager beaver or in between jobs, it pays to save your receipts for job-hunting expenses

---

>>> **FAST FACT**

The Volunteer State

Be a volunteer. It pays tax-wise, as well as soothes your conscience. Any cash you dish out for gas and oil (or the applicable mileage allowance), plus parking and tolls, or bus and taxi fares, to obtain medical care or perform volunteer work for a charity are all tax deductible. ◄

because they are deductible as a miscellaneous itemized expense if you used them to find a new job for yourself in a similar line of work. For example, cell-phone bills, printing your cover letter, or your transportation tab to and from job interviews may all be deductible.

- **Real Estate Taxes**

  Yes, the real estate market has been tough recently. All the more reason to note that real estate taxes are deductible. In addition, don't forget taxes you paid indirectly, such as through a mortgage escrow account. If you bought a house, check your settlement statement for any taxes for which you reimbursed the seller at the closing. Those are deductible, too.

- **Cost of Tax Preparation**

  Believe me—we see this one all the time—clients forget that they can deduct tax-preparation costs. Tax tools, tax books, tax classes, tax software, or even tax-preparation services rendered by yours truly, are all deductible as a miscellaneous itemized deduction. Just make sure to claim your tax service deduction on the return for the year in which you paid the bills for those services.

- **Reinvested Dividends**

  Brokerage houses and mutual fund firms manage your accounts, so they automatically reinvest dividends in additional share purchases. If you sell a stock or shares of a fund, your basis—the number you subtract from the sales price to figure your gain or loss—should cover these reinvested dividends. And remember, it is your responsibility to monitor the tax impact of the reinvested dividends. Best bet: ask your investment firm to handle it for you.

- **Credit for Excess Social Security Tax**

  Many people work for more than one employer during the year. If that's you, read up on the credit for excess Social

Security tax. Here's the deal: any company you work for will withhold Social Security tax as if they were your sole employer. Once your wages reach the Social Security limit—$102,000 in 2008—any Social Security tax withheld after that is treated as a credit against the regular tax you owe for the entire tax year. And if your regular tax owed is $0, the credit is refundable.

⟫⟫⟫ FAST FACT

My Kingdom for a Deduction!

Certain taxpayers must itemize, even if their deductions are less than the standard deduction. You must itemize your deductions if:

- Your filing status is married filing separately, and your spouse itemizes
- You are a U.S. citizen who can exclude income from U.S. possessions
- You are a nonresident or dual-status alien
- You file a short-period return because of a change in your accounting period

Source: Internal Revenue Service; Quicken.com ◄

- **Home Improvements**

  If you have a disabled and medically impaired friend or family member, or suffer from impairment yourself, my heart goes out to you. But tax-wise, at least, you may benefit from a deduction in the tax code that enables you to build special equipment or otherwise improve your home to accommodate your situation—even if the improvement increases the home's value. In such a situation, the amount of the cost that exceeds the increase in value is deductible.

- **Student Loans**

  Curse those monthly bills from the bank for your college loan!
  But take some relief from the fact that you can deduct interest on student loans regardless of the age of the loan. The law
  used to state that you could deduct interest on student loans
  only during the first sixty months of required interest repayments. However, starting in 2002, student-loan holders were
  allowed to deduct interest on loans that were more than five
  years old. That is a big benefit for students with large loans
  that will take many years to repay. Note that deductions
  are allowable based on your income—if you make less than
  $55,000, you get the full deduction. Anything higher is only
  partially deductible, based on your filing status.

>>> FAST FACT

Rolling Convoy

Are you on the road a lot for your job? The IRS says that qualified work-
related transportation expenses are deductible. If you keep mileage records,
you can usually claim a mileage allowance plus parking and tolls. ◀

- **Self-Employed Individuals**

  So you run your own home or small business? Great—besides
  being your own boss, you qualify for the self-employment
  health insurance deduction. That enables you to deduct part
  of your health insurance premiums even if you don't itemize.

Examining Exemptions

Exemptions are actually a pretty simple concept to understand.
They're just like deductions, except that they're not based upon an
event—notwithstanding marriage or childbirth. No, instead they are
dependent upon an individual household member's status in relation to the taxpayer of the household.

TAX TIPS

Deduct Your Home Office

If you turn a portion of your home into an office, you may qualify for the home office deduction.

The IRS can be a stickler about this one. But even so, it's well worth looking into. The deal is this: Uncle Sam insists that your home office area must be used regularly and exclusively for your business needs. In other words, you can't plop a computer down in a spare bedroom, send out invoices for your eBay sales, and claim the room as a home office. The business portion of your home must be either your principal place of business or where you meet or deal with patients, clients, or customers in the normal course of your business. The good news is that a separate office in the garage can qualify for a home office deduction.

That means the taxpayer has to be worthy—in the IRS's eyes—of an exemption of tax. Exemptions are quite large—when compared to deductions—in that you can exempt $3,500 of income from taxation for each exemption you claim. Thus, if you were entitled to two exemptions for 2008, you would deduct $7,000 ($3,500 × 2).

You can usually claim exemptions for yourself, your spouse, and each person you can claim as a dependent. Thus, there are in fact two types of exemptions—personal exemptions and exemptions for dependents. While they're worth the same amount, there are different rules governing the taxpayer's eligibility to claim each.

- **Personal Exemptions**

  You are generally allowed one exemption for yourself and, if you are married, one exemption for your spouse. These are called personal exemptions.

  You can take one exemption for yourself unless you can be claimed as a dependent by another taxpayer. If another taxpayer is entitled to claim you as a dependent, you cannot

>>> **FAST FACT**

How to Claim Exemptions

How you claim an exemption on your tax return depends on which form you file.

Form 1040EZ

If you file Form 1040EZ, the exemption amount is combined with the standard deduction and entered on line 5.

Form 1040A

If you file Form 1040A, complete lines 6a through 6d. The total number of exemptions you can claim is the total in the box on line 6d. Also, complete line 26.

Form 1040

If you file Form 1040, complete lines 6a through 6d. Also, complete line 42. ◄

---

take an exemption for yourself—even if the other taxpayer doesn't actually claim you as a dependent.

Your spouse is never considered your dependent. If you're married filing jointly, you can claim one personal exemption for yourself and one for your spouse. If you're married filing separately, you can claim one personal exemption for yourself and one for your spouse only if your spouse had no gross income, is not filing a return, and was not the dependent of another taxpayer.

If your spouse died during the past year, the tax laws provide little relief. For example, on the tax return for the year in which your spouse passed, generally, you can claim your spouse's exemption in a joint return. Similarly, if you file a separate return for the year, you may be able to claim your spouse's exemption under the rules just described in a separate return.

Finally, if you are divorced or legally separated from your spouse, on that year's return, you cannot claim your former spouse's exemption. This rule applies even if you provided all of your former spouse's support.

▶▶▶ FAST FACT

Who Qualifies for Exemptions?

Taxpayer Type	Qualify?	Notes
U.S. Citizen	☑	Any and all exemptions
U.S. Resident Alien	☑	Any and all exemptions
U.S. National	☑	Any and all exemptions
Resident of Canada	☑	Any and all exemptions
Resident of Mexico	☑	Any and all exemptions
Non-Resident Alien	☑	Only one personal exemption

Source: Internal Revenue Service

- **Exemptions for Dependents**
  You are allowed one exemption for each person you can claim as a dependent. Dependents are usually your children or elderly parents who rely on you to provide for them. Of course, another dependent would be your forty-year-old dead-beat son, who lives in the attic playing *Guitar Hero* until the neighbors call the police. The IRS allows you to claim a size-able chunk of change—$3,500—to either love or put up with him. You can claim an exemption for a dependent even if your dependent files his or her own return.
  You can claim an exemption for a qualifying child or relative only if three complicated tests (dependent taxpayer test,

joint return test, and citizen or resident test) are met. Generally, to be able to claim an exemption for a dependent, you must meet these requirements:

➤ You cannot claim any dependents if you, or your spouse if filing jointly, could be claimed as a dependent by another taxpayer.

➤ You cannot claim a married person who files a joint return as a dependent unless that joint return is only a claim for refund and there would be no tax liability for either spouse on separate returns.

➤ You cannot claim a person as a dependent unless that person is a U.S. citizen, U.S. resident alien, U.S. national, or a resident of Canada or Mexico, for some part of the year.

➤ You cannot claim a person as a dependent unless that person is your qualifying child or relative.

➤➤➤ FAST FACT

Qualifying Child and Qualifying Relative

Qualifying Child	
NUMBER	**RULE**
1	The child must be your son, daughter, stepchild, foster child, brother, sister, half brother, half sister, stepbrother, stepsister, or a descendant of any of them.
2	The child must be (a) under age nineteen at the end of the year, (b) under age twenty-four at the end of the year if a full-time student, or (c) any age if permanently and totally disabled.
3	The child must have lived with you for more than half the year.

Qualifying Child	
4	The child must not have provided more than half of his or her own support for the year.
5	If the child meets the rules to be a qualifying child of more than one person, you must be the person "entitled" to claim the child as a qualifying child *Please note: The person "entitled" to claim the child is determined by a tiebreaking system dependent upon the whether the person claiming is the parent of the child, where the child has lived the longest, and the person's AGI.*

Qualifying Relative	
NUMBER	**RULE**
1	The person cannot be your qualifying child or the qualifying child of any other taxpayer.
2	The person either (a) must be related to you in an approved way, or (b) must live with you all year as a member of your household.
3	The person's gross income for the year must be less than $3,500.
4	You must provide more than half the person's total support for the year.

Source: Internal Revenue Service ◄

Taking Advantage of Tax Credits

Here is one extra-credit course you cannot afford to pass up. It is on tax credits, one of Uncle Sam's greatest gifts to taxpayers.

What are tax credits? In Homer Simpson jargon, tax credits are the entire donut, while deductions are just a piece of the donut. A tax credit lowers your tax bill dollar for dollar. Deductions, though certainly still worth your attention, only lower your tax bill by fractions.

Here is an example: a tax credit of $1,000 slashes your tax liability by—guess what?—$1,000. Meanwhile, a $1,000 tax deduction saves you $280 on your tax bill if you are in the 28 percent income tax bracket. Again, nothing to sniff at, but not the whole donut.

So tax credits are well worth a review. Here are a few common tax credits available to taxpayers:

- **Earned Income Tax Credit**
  Earmarked for low-income earning taxpayers, the Earned Income Tax Credit (EITC) can lower your taxes substantially. To earn the credit, a taxpayer with no qualifying children must earn less than $12,880. A taxpayer with one qualifying child must earn less than $33,995. To qualify with more than one child, total earned income should be $38,646 or less. Note that the EITC is a refundable credit, meaning that you get it even if it exceeds your tax liability. For tax year 2008, a filer with one qualifying child can receive a maximum credit of $2,917. For two or more qualifying children, the maximum credit is $4,824. To file for the credit, complete Schedule EITC, which is found in IRS Publication 596.

- **Child Tax Credits**
  Under IRS rules, kids are tax credit–worthy, too. There are three primary child tax credits: child and dependent care, the child tax credit, and the child adoption credit. (Actually, there is one more credit, the additional child tax credit, which is available if you have three or more qualifying children.) As of the most recent tax year, the child tax credit is $1,000 for one qualifying child. The credit begins to phase out once an individual exceeds $75,000 in income, or a married couple filing jointly exceeds $110,000 in income.

- **Education Tax Credits**

  The two main tax credits for higher education are the Hope credit and the Lifetime Learning credit. The Hope credit is tailored for expenses incurred in the first two years of college—up to $1,800 annually, per eligible student. The Lifetime Learning credit applies to tuition costs for undergraduates, graduates, and those improving job skills through a training program. In 2002, the credit rose to 20 percent of up to $10,000 in qualified expenses, or a maximum of $2,000. Both credits phase out if income exceeds $100,000 for couples filing a joint return, or $50,000 for single filers.

>>> **FAST FACT**

Adoption Credit

You may be able to take a tax credit for qualifying expenses paid to adopt an eligible child (including a child with special needs). The credit is generally allowed for the year following the year in which the expenses are paid. In addition to the credit, certain amounts reimbursed by your employer for qualifying adoption expenses may be excludable from your gross income.

For both the credit or the exclusion, qualifying expenses include reasonable and necessary adoption fees, court costs, attorney fees, traveling expenses (including amounts spent for meals and lodging while away from home), and other expenses directly related to and for which the principal purpose is the legal adoption of an eligible child.

The credit and exclusion for qualifying adoption expenses are each subject to both a dollar limit and an income limit. ◄

Inside the Ropes:
Jesse's Challenge

Jesse had a problem.

The thirty-seven-year-old manager of a manufacturing firm moonlighted as a baseball memorabilia dealer. He had seen his once-casual hobby explode when he started a website, which allowed visitors to buy and sell rare baseball cards, hats, jerseys, and signatures among a community of baseball lovers. Within nine months, the only managing Jesse was doing was on his website.

"I never thought of this as a way to make a living," explained Jesse. "However, I must have struck a chord. I've got to say it was a dream come true."

Well, that dream quickly turned into a nightmare when the IRS stepped in. Despite Jesse's instant success, the IRS still did not see his business as . . . a business. Instead, they relegated it to "hobby" status, which made it ineligible for a business deduction.

"Well, when I read that letter, I knew right away that my tax bill would increase substantially if I couldn't prove my website was a business," recalls Jesse.

Fortunately, Jesse made a visit to his accountant. During the visit, he revealed a whole host of facts that demonstrated he had a strong case as a business owner, including evidence of a profit motive. Even though revenue was quite volatile during the website's initial inception, it had grown consistent near the end of the tax year. (It is important to note that when the IRS sees a small business that does not make profits on a regular basis, the agency tends to view it as a hobby.)

On the advice of his accountant, Jesse read the portion of the tax code dealing with businesses and profits. He discovered that while there is a perception that a business should earn a profit in three of the first five years of doing business, there is no actual tax rule that says it has to. If you do not earn a profit in three of five consecutive years, however, you must prove that your purpose and intent is to make a profit. Otherwise, your business deductions are not allowed.

With that information in hand, Jesse built a nice paper trail for the IRS, including traditional and web-based advertisements, invoices for items he purchased and sold, and copies of checks from customers.

"A few months later, I heard back from the IRS that I was in the clear," Jesse said. "It was important to me that people thought I was running a legitimate business, not just playing with baseball cards. The tax deductions are nice, but the acknowledgment of the hard work I'd put into my business concept was even better."

➤ ROUND 6

The *New* American Dream— Tax Tips for the Self-Employed

*Take care of your pennies and the pounds will
take care of themselves.*

—Andrew Carnegie

There is a humorous story about the above quote. Apparently as a ten-year-old attending Sunday school back in Scotland, Andrew Carnegie, the powerful head of U.S. Steel in the early 1900s and the son of a hardscrabble Scottish weaver; was singled out by the teacher and asked to quote a passage from the Bible.

After replying with the above, the incredulous teacher admonished the young lad. "Surely," the teacher answered, "such a passage is not in the Bible."

"It ought to be," Carnegie shot back.

Now *there* was an entrepreneur who knew the secret to running a business: take care of the little things and the big things will take care of themselves.

That is a good lesson for today's self-employed business owners. In the tax world, the pennies can really add up, in the form of the many deductions and credits available under U.S. tax laws. The trick is to know where to find them—and how to use them.

That is a tall order for the growing number of busy entrepreneurs setting up shop in the 2000s. It is no secret that self-employment, particularly in the home-based business sector, is a burgeoning trend in the United States. In one sense, thanks to the Internet and a renewed sense of entrepreneurship among Americans, self-employment is a viable and highly attractive career option. On the other hand, with a flagging economy, many individuals are finding themselves transitioning along a new career path due to layoffs and corporate downsizing. Regardless of the motivation, too often entrepreneurs leap into the small business world without fully realizing what role taxes play in their move and how their tax status will change—and change significantly.

But what if the self-employed knew how taxes impact self-employed Americans? What if small business owners knew how to place their business in the best possible position to take advantage of tax laws? And what if they knew about the wide array of deductions available to those who operate a personal business? Then they could take advantage of those tax-saving opportunities and begin saving some of those pennies—and dollars—that Carnegie was talking about.

That is the aim of this Round—to help you understand the self-employed tax picture and leverage as many of its advantages as possible. And the best way to start doing that is to learn more about taxes and the self-employed.

What Is the Self-Employment Tax?

Some say that self-employment is the new American dream, the modern incarnation of the cowboy roaming freely on the range or the fisherman casting his nets on the open sea, answering to nobody. (Except my mother, in my case. Lucky me.)

But there are more *taxing* (get it?) distractions for self-employed individuals than loving mothers. The good news is that the income tax form for self-employed individuals is the same as just about everyone else: IRS Form 1040. In addition, the self-employment tax is the same amount for wage-earners as it is for self-employed individuals. A portion is even earmarked for Social Security and Medicare.

But there are some differences. First, unlike the traditional wage-earner, the self-employed individual must voluntarily make self-employment tax payments throughout the year, instead of having them automatically deducted from his or her wages as they are paid. Second, unlike a traditional wage-earner, a self-employed person can deduct Social Security and Medicare taxes from his or her Form 1040 tax bill.

⟫⟫⟫ FAST FACT

What Is Taxable

At the end of 2008, the Social Security and Medicare tax rate for self-employed individuals was 15.3 percent. The IRS slices that rate into two categories—12.4 percent of it goes to Social Security (yes, as a self-employed taxpayer you pay both the employee and employer portions of that tax, or an extra 7.65 percent), and 2.9 percent of it goes to Medicare. Note that the employer half of the Social Security payment—otherwise known as the "self-employed tax"—is tax deductible.

And remember, only the first $102,000 of your annual income is subject to the Social Security tax. ◄

Estimating Your Tax Payments

As a group, self-employed taxpayers already know that tax planning is a year-round event. That's because they generally pay taxes on a quarterly basis, four times a year.

The self-employed pay these taxes on an estimated basis. That means estimating your tax bill if you anticipate owing Uncle Sam when you file your return. Usually this means filling out Form 1040-ES, Estimated Tax for Individuals. So if you estimate your tax liability to be $10,000 for the year, you can ship the IRS four quarterly checks of $2,500 apiece. Alternately, you can wait until the following April 15 and fork over the entire $10,000 at one time—however, this method may expose you to a penalty so it is best to stick with the quarterly check approach.

TAX TIPS

$0 in Estimated Taxes

A self-employed individual need not make any estimated tax payments if the amount due after subtracting exemptions, deductions, and credits is less than $1,000.

The IRS offers several different scenarios for you to pay estimated taxes. First, there is a "voluntary" payment mechanism where you can pay estimated taxes based on your previous year's tax bill, even though this year's tax bill may be higher. By paying under the voluntary method, the IRS allows you to pay just the minimum amount required now, and pay the rest on April 15. Voluntary payment is a good move if you have a steady flow of income and have the time and financial wherewithal to spread your tax payments out through the year.

Self-employed individuals can also make estimated tax payments even when they don't have to. Granted, this occurs only when a self-employed individual is running at a loss or an extremely low profit. But with a struggling economy, this may be the case for more taxpayers now than it has been in the past. Perhaps continuing to make estimated tax payments allows those folks to sleep better at night, knowing that April 15 will not bring a big tax burden. Alternatively, maybe these individuals are expecting a big cash crunch when the tax bill comes due. Either way, it is an option worth considering.

When deciding what method to use to pay your taxes, take your own personal characteristics into consideration. If you are the sort who cannot resist temptation, pay on a quarterly basis. That way you won't be tempted to grab some of that $10,000 and buy the new big-screen TV you noticed down at Best Buy. But if you can manage to leave your mitts off the money, you can gain some valuable interest on it by waiting to pay.

Also, if you have a new business, different tax rates apply. I advise my clients to put about 20 percent of their income aside to handle their tax burden.

 TAX TIPS

Pay or Hold?

It may be a load off your mind when you pay your taxes on an estimated basis well ahead of April 15. But Uncle Sam is not going to be paying you interest on that money like an investment account could.

If you are confident in the stock market—what goes down can go up—it may be better to hold off on paying your taxes and make a few extra bucks for yourself in the interim. If you are not so sure about exposing your tax dollars to the financial markets, you can open an interest-bearing checking account. That way, you can pull money out to pay your taxes, but keep the interest you have accrued.

Are You a Business?

How do you know if you are self-employed? The IRS has a few criteria.

In general, any commercial endeavor that attempts to make a profit is a business. That is not to say that your daughter Megan's lemonade stand is something the IRS is interested in. But if a business

---

>>> **FAST FACT**

Tax Dates

If you pay your taxes on a quarterly basis, the IRS is going to make you meet certain deadline requirements. Usually that means you will have to pay up by the 15 of April, June, and September of the current tax year, and January of the following. ◄

---

exceeds certain profit levels on an annual basis, it becomes a taxable entity. So watch out, Megan!

Once you establish a profit motive—that is, if your venture has earned any net income during three of the past five years, per the IRS's definition—you can describe yourself as a business and begin taking the appropriate deductions for what, in many cases, you used to call personal expenses.

Setting Up Your Business in a Tax-Friendly Manner

So you're done with the rat race and are finally going to open that surf shop down by the beach. Of course, you'll want to set up your business in the most tax-advantageous way possible. The first step in that process will be deciding whether to establish your business as a sole proprietorship or as a corporation.

While there are several business categories to consider, most self-employed people prefer to establish sole—or individual—proprietorships. As a sole proprietorship, you and the business are essentially interchangeable. You are the business and the business is you.

Sole proprietors prepare their taxes using IRS Form 1040, specifically on a Schedule C. As mentioned above, most sole proprietors file under their own name. Yes, you can name it "Petey Pirate's Pet Store." Just file a "doing business as" (DBA) form with your local tax assessment office or municipal documents office.

As a sole proprietor, you can either pay taxes on an estimated basis (as outlined above) or only once, on your personal income

>>>> **FAST FACT**

The IRS Rules

In most cases, establishing a profit motive is enough to determine that you are self-employed. But what specifically is the IRS looking for to confirm that you are in fact running your own business? Here is a list:

IRS Checklist to Determine Whether You Are Self-Employed	
✓	**Manner in which you carry on the activity**
✓	**Expertise of individual and his or her advisors**
✓	**Time and effort expended in carrying out the activity**
✓	**Expectations that the assets used may appreciate in value**
✓	**Success in carrying out similar or dissimilar activities**
✓	**History of income and losses with respect to the activity**
✓	**Amount of occasional profits earned**
✓	**Financial status of individual**

Source: Internal Revenue Service ◄

tax return. Your tax bill will be based on the income your business earns. For example, if Petey Pirate's Pet Store has a great year and makes $50,000, you are going to be paying taxes based upon that $50,000. But don't forget you'll be able to claim $60,000 in business expenses for Amazonian piranhas and Rhesus monkeys you bought during the year.

If you do not want to be a sole proprietor, you also have the option of establishing your business as a corporation. Unlike a sole proprietorship, in which the owner is essentially the business, a corporation is a legally recognized entity encompassing all your business's assets, debts, expenses, and revenues. If your business is starting out on larger scale than, say, a pirate pet store, and you already have a good number of employees, corporation status may be a better option because of its limited liability advantages. In other words, were the corporation to fail, its owners—i.e., shareholders—would only lose their investment. They would not be personally liable for the remaining debts of the corporation.

TAX TIPS

Fraud Watch

There is a difference between tax avoidance and tax evasion. Tax avoidance is generally the legal exploitation of the tax regime to one's own advantage. Tax evasion is the general term for efforts by people or businesses to evade the payment of taxes by illegal means. The following is a list of the most common types of self-employed fraud the IRS is likely to investigate:

Common Types of Self-Employment Tax Fraud		
	TYPE	EXAMPLE
➔	Not reporting substantial amounts of income	Video rental store owner's failure to report a portion of the daily business receipts
➔	Phony deductions on a tax return	Obvious overstatement of travel expenses, or a large deduction for charitable donations to an organization that does not actually exist
➔	Accounting discrepancies	Computer technician's failure to keep adequate records

Be forewarned about corporations, though—they are a lot more complicated than sole proprietorships, and are also subject to twice as much taxation. That's because the corporation's income is taxed two times, the second being on dividends paid out of earnings.

So What Tax Breaks Am I Entitled To?

From a tax standpoint, being self-employed is a pretty sweet deal, because there is no shortage of deductions for self-employed people to use.

Just look at the numbers: every $100 worth of deductible expenses trims $28 off your income tax bill, assuming you are in the 28 percent bracket. Even better, because you are self-employed you qualify for the self-employment tax deduction, which provides an additional $15.30 of savings from every $100 of taxable income. It is well worth your while to find every business deduction available to you.

Below is a list of some of the more common expenses self-employed taxpayers deduct each year:

Expense Type
✓ Rent/Lease Property (office, studio, etc.)
✓ Home Office
✓ Office Supplies/Equipment (computers, pencils, furniture, telephones, etc.)
✓ Insurance (health, disability, liability, automobile, etc.)
✓ Utilities (telephone and Internet service, etc.)
✓ Automobile Expenses (fuel, maintenance, etc.)
✓ Taxes (self-employment, state, local, etc.)
✓ Travel Expenses (hotels, airfare, etc.)
✓ Meals and Entertainment

Expense Type	
✓	Material/Inventory Purchased
✓	Gross Wages/Salary Paid
✓	Professional Services Paid (legal, accounting, etc.)
✓	Professional Dues and Licenses
✓	Subscriptions
✓	Postage and Delivery Charges

Now, let's look at some tax-planning strategies you might want to think about as a self-employed business owner.

- **Expensing**

  Any self-employed person would love to deduct $250,000 worth of business property right from the get-go. And thanks to the expensing provision of the tax law, he or she can!

  This provision enables you to immediately write off up to the above figure of otherwise depreciable property used by your business. Even if it is something you did not put into service until late in the tax year, you can still deduct the full cost of up to $250,000 of qualifying items. The property-type eligible only includes personal property—not real property.

  For example, say you buy $100,000 of business property with a five-year tax life. Under the tax law's half-year convention provision, your first-year depreciation deduction would be $20,000—certainly not chump change. But if you choose expensing, you can write off the entire purchase price on the current year's return.

  Alternatively, if you are thinking of deducting the entire cost of your new Chevrolet Silverado, expensing will not let you deduct $24,000 of the full cost of a car all at once. Under the "luxury car" rules, in the most recent tax year, the luxury depreciation deduction was as follows:

Year	Deductible Amount
1	$3,060
2	$4,900
3	$2,850
4	$1,775
5	$1,775

Bear in mind that this expense is a one-time opportunity. There is no carry-over into the following year if you do not take full advantage of the deduction in the year of ownership. In addition, all these figures are based on 100 percent business use. If the car is also used for personal purposes, the limits will decrease.

 TAX TIPS

SUV 1; Other Cars 0

An exception to the luxury car rules allows you to use expensing if your new business vehicle is heavier than six thousand pounds. For a car, that means six thousand pounds empty, which disqualifies almost everyone right off the bat. But for a sports utility vehicle, it is six thousand pounds including the maximum for passengers and cargo, so many SUVs can qualify.

- **Social Security**

  Believe it or not, there is a way to trim your taxable business income and create double savings. Here's how: in addition to cutting your income tax bill for the year, you can also save on Social Security and Medicare taxes. As mentioned above, self-employment income is subject to a 15.3 percent Social

Security and Medicare tax. The full tax applies to the first $102,000 of earnings from salary, wages, and net self-employment income in 2008. Every $1,000 of extra business deductions can save $153 in Social Security and Medicare taxes, as well as save on income taxes.

• Hobby Expenses

If you are not making a profit on your business in at least three years out of every five, the IRS may consider your fledgling enterprise just a hobby. That distinction prevents you from claiming a loss on your taxes, because your deductions are limited to the amount of income you report and the completion of a Schedule A, Itemized Deductions.

Consequently, your year-end planning needs to consider both where you stand on the profit-or-loss front and how you are doing on the three-out-of-five-years test. If you need to show a profit this year to avoid having your activity fall into the hobby category, your strategy may be the opposite of that outlined above. You may want to press for collection of any income you are due and delay paying expenses or buying new equipment until the following year.

• Income Deferral

The idea here is pretty straightforward: income you receive after midnight on New Year's Eve is not taxed until the following year. Regardless of whether you wind up in the same tax bracket, you win simply by delaying the tax bill an entire year.

A wage-earner cannot employ this tactic, primarily because he or she has a hard time postponing wage and salary income. Your employer is not going to hold on to your December paycheck until January, nor can you push income into the next year by not cashing your check until then. Income is taxable in the year it is "constructively received"—in other words, the year you could have had the money if you wanted it.

Say, for example, your employer offers you a choice of receiving a Christmas bonus in December or the following

January. It does not matter which option you choose—the IRS will expect you to report and pay tax on the income with your return for the year the offer was made. If there is no choice involved, and your company holds your holiday bonus money until the new year, the income would be taxed in the year you receive the check.

Now, if you are self-employed or have a part-time freelance or consulting gig in addition to you job, you have more leeway—assuming you use the cash basis of accounting. By delaying your billings until the end of December, for example, you are ensuring you will not receive those payments until the following year. Therefore, if you are dealing with a delinquent client, it might make sense to call off the dogs—at least until January. Of course, business considerations always come first. But if you have the flexibility to put off payments, doing so will save you the trouble of paying taxes on them until the next year.

On the other hand, it pays more to hurry up with expenses. Remember, you get a deduction in the year that you pay for your purchases. If your office is looking a bit bare, load up on supplies before the end of the year so you can lock those deductions in by paying for them before December 31.

Wake Up, Junior, You're Hired!

Kids spending too much time in front of the TV? As a sole proprietor, you can save money by hiring them—so long as they are under eighteen years of age. When it comes to hiring children, the IRS tends to use, well, kid gloves. There are no Social Security or federal unemployment taxes involved, and kids can shelter up to $5,400 of wage income with their available standard deduction.

Let us assume, for instance, your tax rate is 35 percent. If you are shorthanded during your business's busy season, you can save $560 by paying two of your kids $800 apiece (at $8 an hour for one hundred hours) to pitch in.

>>> **FAST FACT**

Start Me Up

Typically, business start-up costs are capital expenditures. Start-up costs include any amounts paid or incurred in connection with creating an active trade or business or investigating the creation or acquisition of an active trade or business. Organizational costs include the costs of creating a corporation.

However, you can elect to deduct up to $5,000 of business start-up and $5,000 of organizational costs paid or incurred. The $5,000 deduction is reduced by the amount your total start-up or organizational costs exceed $50,000. Any remaining costs must be amortized.

For more information, see IRS Publication 535, Business Expenses. ◄

Corporations, on the other hand, are not so kid-friendly. You can still hire children and deduct their wages on the company tax return, but the payments are subject to Social Security and federal unemployment taxes, just like wages paid to regular workers. Therefore, unless little Charlie has a real knack for corporate accounting, you are better off hiring someone who does not live at your house.

And if you do hire your child, make sure he or she actually does something. IRS auditors will ask.

Baby, You Can Drive My Car

Owning a new car can be expensive these days. As a business owner, however, you can defray some of the cost of your vehicle by deducting business-related mileage expenses. Under 2008 tax law, deduction rates are 58.5 cents per business mile, 14 cents per charitable mile, and 27 cents per moving/medical mile. There are no longer any mileage limits, either, so drive as far as you want. Just remember to keep a log of your travel miles so you can get the most out of your deduction.

The Home Office Tax Picture

There are more and more telecommuters and home businesses these days, and the home office deduction has changed over time to benefit these taxpayers. According to IRS rules, so long as you use the space regularly and exclusively for business, you get the full home office deduction. Even if you are just using the room as a quiet place in which to pay bills or handle other administrative tasks, you can take advantage of this deduction—so long as you don't do the same chores in other locations as well.

 TAX TIPS

Home Office Help

If you are not certain whether you qualify for the home office deduction, look at these tips to see how you can turn your own house into a significant cut off your tax bill:

☑	Home Office Deduction Checklist
☐	Create business cards with your home address on them.
☐	Have clients who visit your office sign a guest book.
☐	Retain receipts for the purchase of office equipment and other business-related expenses.
☐	Keep all your business invoices—with your home address prominently featured.
☐	Keep a work and time log.

Not only will these help you more easily prepare your tax return (not to mention get the deduction), but they also prove that you are running a business out of your home.

Accelerating Deductions

So you have established that you are running a home-based business. Now it's time to begin accelerating those write-offs. If you are a sole proprietor, you will be recording these deductions on Form 8829, Expenses for Business Use of Your Home.

You can begin by deducting any preparation work you did turning your garage or spare bedroom into an office. Painting, spackling, rug cleaning—any type of maintenance work intended to spruce up the place qualifies. If you attach a rider to your home insurance to add a home office, deduct that, too.

The next step is deducting all the costs linked to your infrastructure, such as telephone lines, Internet services, and utilities. Also, make sure to deduct the home office portion of the insurance on your home (considered an indirect expense by the IRS). If you rent, deduct the home office portion of your rental payments, too. See IRS Form 8829 for further instruction on how much to deduct from indirect expenses.

⫸ FAST FACT

Eat, Drink, and Be Tax Merry

The way to my heart is through my stomach. If the same is true for you, then take full advantage of the tax law's "meals and entertainment" allowances.

You can deduct half your meal and entertainment bills, as long as they are somehow business-related. The savings will buy you more than a cup of coffee, too. For example, a $100 dinner only costs $86 if you belong to the 28 percent tax bracket.

You can also deduct up to $25 on your tax bill for every gift you give to a business client per year. In other words, keep the Brett Favre bobble-head dolls coming until your client begs you to stop.

But remember to save the receipt (for meals and entertainment of $75 or more—for anything less a receipt is not necessary), and record the time, date, amount paid, and the name of the restaurant, golf course, theater, etc. Jot down a business reason for the meeting as well—the IRS may want to know why you keep taking clients down to the local watering hole. ◄

Sample IRS Form 8829

Here is a sample IRS Form 8829, Expenses for Business Use of Your Home. We completed it to help you understand how to take advantage of allowable deductions. Take a look:

Form **8829**

Department of the Treasury
Internal Revenue Service (99)

Expenses for Business Use of Your Home

▶ File only with Schedule C (Form 1040). Use a separate Form 8829 for each home you used for business during the year.

▶ See separate instructions.

OMB No. 1545-0074

2007

Attachment
Sequence No. **66**

Name(s) of proprietor(s)
Don August

Your social security number
000 : 01 : 0000

Part I Part of Your Home Used for Business

1	Area used regularly and exclusively for business, regularly for daycare, or for storage of inventory or product samples (see instructions)	1	200
2	Total area of home	2	2000
3	Divide line 1 by line 2. Enter the result as a percentage	3	10 %

For daycare facilities not used exclusively for business, go to line 4. All others go to line 7.

4	Multiply days used for daycare during year by hours used per day	4	hr.
5	Total hours available for use during the year (365 days × 24 hours) (see instructions)	5	8,760 hr.
6	Divide line 4 by line 5. Enter the result as a decimal amount	6	
7	Business percentage. For daycare facilities not used exclusively for business, multiply line 6 by line 3 (enter the result as a percentage). All others, enter the amount from line 3 ▶	7	10 %

Part II Figure Your Allowable Deduction

		(a) Direct expenses	(b) Indirect expenses		
8	Enter the amount from Schedule C, line 29, **plus** any net gain or (loss) derived from the business use of your home and shown on Schedule D or Form 4797. If more than one place of business, see instructions			8	28500 00
	See instructions for columns (a) and (b) before completing lines 9–21.				
9	Casualty losses (see instructions)	9			
10	Deductible mortgage interest (see instructions)	10	4000 00		
11	Real estate taxes (see instructions)	11	1000 00		
12	Add lines 9, 10, and 11	12	5000 00		
13	Multiply line 12, column (b) by line 7	13	600 00		
14	Add line 12, column (a) and line 13			14	500 00
15	Subtract line 14 from line 8. If zero or less, enter -0-			15	28000 00
16	Excess mortgage interest (see instructions)	16	400 00		
17	Insurance	17	300 00	1400 00	
18	Rent	18			
19	Repairs and maintenance	19	1800 00		
20	Utilities	20			
21	Other expenses (see instructions)	21	400 00		
22	Add lines 16 through 21	22	300 00	4000 00	
23	Multiply line 22, column (b) by line 7	23	400 00		
24	Carryover of operating expenses from 2006 Form 8829, line 42	24	300 00		
25	Add line 22 in column (a), line 23, and line 24			25	1000 00
26	Allowable operating expenses. Enter the **smaller** of line 15 or line 25			26	1000 00
27	Limit on excess casualty losses and depreciation. Subtract line 26 from line 15			27	27000 00
28	Excess casualty losses (see instructions)	28			
29	Depreciation of your home from Part III below	29	320 50		
30	Carryover of excess casualty losses and depreciation from 2006 Form 8829, line 43	30			
31	Add lines 28 through 30			31	320 50
32	Allowable excess casualty losses and depreciation. Enter the **smaller** of line 27 or line 31			32	320 50
33	Add lines 14, 26, and 32			33	1820 50
34	Casualty loss portion, if any, from lines 14 and 32. Carry amount to **Form 4684**, Section B			34	
35	Allowable expenses for business use of your home. Subtract line 34 from line 33. Enter here and on Schedule C, line 30. If your home was used for more than one business, see instructions ▶			35	1820 50

Part III Depreciation of Your Home

36	Enter the **smaller** of your home's adjusted basis or its fair market value (see instructions)	36	150000 00
37	Value of land included on line 36	37	25000 00
38	Basis of building. Subtract line 37 from line 36	38	125000 00
39	Business basis of building. Multiply line 38 by line 7	39	12500 00
40	Depreciation percentage (see instructions)	40	2.564 %
41	Depreciation allowable (see instructions). Multiply line 39 by line 40. Enter here and on line 29 above	41	320 50

Part IV Carryover of Unallowed Expenses to 2008

42	Operating expenses. Subtract line 26 from line 25. If less than zero, enter -0-	42	0 00
43	Excess casualty losses and depreciation. Subtract line 32 from line 31. If less than zero, enter -0-	43	0 00

For Paperwork Reduction Act Notice, see page 4 of separate instructions.   Cat. No. 13232M   Form **8829** (2007)

✆ *Printed on recycled paper*

Flying the Tax-Friendly Skies

You may have a hazy definition of the difference between business travel and recreational travel, but you can bet the IRS aims to draw a clear line between the two.

If you are self-employed, however, that line is currently drawn in your favor. If you can prove you were doing some sort of business on your visit to Key Biscayne or Honolulu, you can deduct the trip on your taxes. There is a good reason, after all, why many larger companies traditionally host their seminars and conventions in the Grand Cayman instead of Grand Rapids.

You can deduct expenses on your trip, too, such as convention or seminar fees, hotel accommodations, meals and entertainment, and travel expenses to and from your destination. If you can prove it's business related, your spouse could come and expense the trip, too.

Obviously, when you add up all these expenses, it can really make a big dent in your final tax bill. A self-employed business owner in the 30 percent tax bracket spending $10,000 to travel to Tokyo to drum up some business can have $3,000 of the trip subsidized by Uncle Sam. Pretty generous, huh?

Of course, not everything can be deducted as a business trip expense. The IRS will not be impressed by those financial advisory seminars that are held on a deep sea-fishing cruise and at golf resorts. Likewise, that quilting convention in Las Vegas is not going to qualify as business-related if you are mainly selling power tools. The IRS tends to take a dim view of trying to deduct expenses on trips that do not have anything to do with your business.

TAX TIPS

Top Ten Tax Record Keeping Tips for Small Business Owners

Having a hard time getting your business records organized? Relax. Follow these tips to get back on track:

Top Small Business Tax Record Keeping Tips	
1	Keep business and personal tax records separate.
2	Open a separate checking account for your business and keep your records accordingly.
3	Keep all records and receipts to support income and expenses claimed.
4	Use a separate credit card for your business.
5	Keep a business use mileage log for your service vehicle.
6	Avoid cash purchases that do not produce a valid receipt.
7	Reconcile your bank and credit card statements each month.
8	Highlight all long distance business calls on your personal (home) telephone bill.
9	Get a receipt for *everything*. If the expense was incurred for business purposes or in the course of producing business income, it is likely to be tax deductible.
10	Keep all records and receipts in a safe, dry location.

**Inside the Ropes:
Rusty's Nightmare**

Rusty was an over-the-road truck driver. He had been working as an independent contractor for a variety of shipping companies for the past twenty-two years. Rusty was not a rich man, but he was making ends meet while working on the road. Unfortunately, working the road wears on anyone, and Rusty was looking to settle down and move into a steadier lifestyle.

"I'm forty-five years old," explained Rusty. "I've been driving as long as I can remember. It's time for me to get a 'real' job, and park my butt in an office chair," he added with a wink.

Last year, Rusty got an offer to become a regional director of one of the shipping companies he had worked for in the past. "Yep, I was hanging up the truck driving hat and putting away the sunscreen for good," explained Rusty. "I was even going to sell my rig to finance the down payment on a house. Things were looking good."

However, the sale of the rig caught a snag when a title search by the buyer caught that the IRS had filed a $25,000 tax lien against it. It turns out Rusty, while working as an independent contractor, had neither filed a tax return nor paid estimated taxes on his anticipated tax liability for any of those twelve years.

"Yeah, there really weren't any education requirements going into trucking other than your license," stated Rusty. "No one was really stopping you every seven hundred miles to remind you to make your estimated tax payment or file your return. So, you know what? I didn't. As a result, I was in a bad place."

In response, the IRS had filed four years of returns on Rusty's behalf, showing a total tax liability of more than $140,000. The original tax liability was high due to the IRS claiming all income but not showing any expenses that Rusty incurred as an over-the-road trucker. In addition, the Substitute for Returns claimed the standard deduction as opposed to some lucrative itemized deductions, exemptions, and credits that Rusty was eligible for. Finally, penalties and interest had been tacked on and were continuing to grow.

Luckily, Rusty's change in employment tipped him off. Rusty's new employer saw this all the time with current and former truckers and ended up referring Rusty to my law firm and tax-preparation company.

"Roni Lynn Deutch and her firm explained what I needed to do—file my original tax returns," explained Rusty. "After preparing the returns, filing them with the IRS, and having them reassess the tax liabilities, it turned out I owed less than ten percent of the IRS original assessment."

To resolve the debt, Rusty sold the semi. "I got more for the truck than I owed," Rusty said. "While I did lose out on my first choice of a house, I feel much better about the whole situation. I am really starting off on a clean slate, having put my tax problems behind me. Also, I talk to truckers about taxes whenever I can, to ensure that the same thing doesn't happen to them."

➤ ROUND 7

Fight for Your Tax Savings Diploma

Education is not filling a bucket, but lighting a fire.
—William B. Yeats

How important is a college education? Well, my Aunt Ider was a steadfast believer. Every time I visited, from age five on, Aunt Ider would lecture me about how education was the fuel that drove success. Thanks to both her and my mother, I was able to get a great collegiate education, and I carried that all the way to a Master of Laws in Taxation.

Now, if Aunt Ider is not convincing enough for you, how about the greatest boxing champion of all time?

One day, Muhammad Ali was walking down the street when a college student came up to greet him. After the heavyweight boxing champ signed an autograph for him, the young fan asked Ali what he should do with his life. The student was grappling with the decision between remaining in school or going straight into the working world.

"Stay in college and get the knowledge," replied Ali. "If they can make penicillin out of moldy bread, they can make something out of you."

In his inimitable way, Ali made a good point. He knew that, all things being equal, a young person making her way through the business world could benefit much more from having a diploma than not.

Uncle Sam knows that, too. The U.S. Government offers a plethora of tax benefits to help young Americans save for college. Whether it is an education savings account that you can launch while your child is just learning to walk or a tax credit for older Americans returning to school, Uncle Sam wants to help you get your degree.

Moreover, he is using the U.S. tax code to do it.

>>> **FAST FACT**

Start Saving Early

Just had a baby? Congratulations—now is a good time to start saving for little Brent's or Brooke's college education. Check out these options to find the best way to do it:

College Saving Methods
Series EE U.S. government savings bonds
State-sponsored 529 savings plans
Education savings accounts (aka Coverdell savings accounts)
Prepaid college savings plans

Where to Start

Years ago, when the tuition bill for a four-year stay at Cal-Berkeley had a few less zeroes in it, saving for college was as simple as opening a custodial account or investing in some conservative U.S. treasury bonds.

⟫⟫⟫ FAST FACT

Parents and College Costs

Below, please find a chart outlining the results from a survey of parents concerning investing, saving, and college:

Statement	% of Respondents Agree
Tuition will be astronomically high by the time child reaches college	87%
Investments pose too great a risk for college savings	85%
Possess a conservative college savings investment plan	61%
Volatility of stock market will hurt college savings	57%
College savings plan will not be enough to send child to college	39%
Possess an aggressive college savings investment plan	35%

Source: Aegon Institutional Markets ◀

Now that the cost of a college education is rising—close to 5 percent annually—the simple method just isn't going to cut it. These days, Mom and Dad—not to mention aunts, uncles and grandparents, too—are starting earlier and investing much more aggressively to get their son Brandon into an Ivy League school down the road. This process can be a whole lot easier if you recognize—and take advantage of—every tax break you can find.

- **College 529 Plan**

  Saving for college today means starting when your kid is still in diapers. You can get an early start on saving for your baby's education fund through state-sponsored college savings plans called 529 plans.

  With a 529 plan, anyone can open up an education savings account for as little as $25 and contribute regularly while not having to pay a cent to the government. That is because in a 529 plan, earnings are tax-free and, in some cases, deductible on your state tax returns. Some states do have limits to these plans, but they tend to be generously high. Nebraska, for instance, allows future Cornhuskers to put away more than $200,000 for their college education.

  Your investment grows tax-free for as long as you remain invested in the plan. Even better, when the 529 plan makes a distribution to pay for your child's education costs, the distribution is federal tax-free, as well. Keep in mind that this tax break applies for distributions up to the year 2010.

  A 529 plan isn't just for tuition, either. You can earmark plan money for other college expenses, such as room, board, meals, and transportation. And there are no age limits—older Americans can save for college using a 529 plan as well.

  Before you get too excited, be aware that the 529 plan could present a few problems down the road. If your particular plan has limited investment options, you may not get the performance you want or need. There is usually one opportunity a year to jump from one investment class to another, so if your money is tied up in a bond fund and the market is

INVESTMENT TIP:
What to Look for in a 529 Plan

Your College 529 Plan Should Have	
WHAT?	**WHY?**
✓ **Good Investment Package**	*This means a plan with a good amount of diversity in investment, including large- and small-cap stocks and U.S. government bonds. You don't want all your eggs in one basket.*
✓ **Reasonable Fees**	*If you are paying more in fees for your 529 plan than you are for your mutual funds, that's not a good sign. Management fees that are more than 1.5 percent annually are too high. Most plans come in at less than that, including some as low as 0.5 percent.*
✓ **Little to No Commissions**	*Keep broker-sponsored 529 plans at arm's length. Up-front commissions of up to 5 percent are part of the deal—and you will be footing the cost for higher ongoing expenses.*
✓ **Good Performance**	*Check the plan's past performance record. A history of underperformance should be a big red flag. Remember that you are trying to make money here!*

running with the bulls, you might want to switch to a stock fund.

However, the benefits of a 529 plan are many, and here's a chart outlining some of the best reasons to use one:

Benefits of 529 Plans

	BENEFIT	EXPLANATION
💰	Tax Break	Earnings are tax-free with a 529 plan and withdrawals for qualified expenses are exempt from federal taxes as well.
💰	Easy	529 plans operate similar to mutual funds. You just have to choose an investment option—a large-cap fund, balanced fund, or bond fund, for example—and keep the contributions flowing.
💰	Professional Help	Some of the most prominent money managers in the country offer state 529 plans. These money managers usually take the reins of your plan, meaning you don't have to worry about the management or administration of the fund.
💰	Tax Deductible	In many states, you can deduct your plan contributions from your state taxes. The rules vary by state, however, so check with your state tax office to figure out your options.
💰	Flexible	Both state residents and non-state residents can open a 529 plan in most cases. In addition, since 2001, you can roll your plan over from one state to another with no tax consequence or penalty.
💰	Control	If your child does not use the money for school, you still have options about how it is withdrawn.
💰	Higher Limits	You can invest more in comparison to other college savings plans.
💰	Not Included in Taxable Estate	In addition to having a large contribution limit in most states, 529 plans are effective estate-planning tools for grandparents.

TAX TIPS

Child's Play

If you have to take money out of a 529 plan for non-education expenses, it is taxed at the child's rate. This is great because, while you may be in the 28 percent tax bracket, your child is probably in the 10 percent tax bracket.

- **Coverdell Savings Account**

   This is another college savings program with ample tax benefits. Often referred to in investment circles as Educational Savings Accounts (ESA), these accounts used to be known as Education IRAs. ESA plans are similar to 529 plans, except that they give you a bit more freedom in choosing ways to allocate the money saved in the accounts. For example, with an ESA plan you can take out money to pay for grade school or high school tuition in addition to college. Ever since Congress rescinded the ban on investing in both a 529 plan and ESA in the same year, many parents are now using both to boost their college savings plans.

   One drawback to the ESA is that its usefulness is limited, especially in comparison with 529 plans. You cannot contribute more than $2,000 to an account annually, and if your family's Adjusted Gross Income is more than $190,000 ($95,000 on a single return), you cannot contribute to an ESA plan at all. Of course, one loophole is to just give $2,000 to a grandparent to invest for you.

   There are also age deadlines to the ESA plans. Contributions must be must be made to the account on or before the date the student turns eighteen and must be distributed, along with the plan earnings, before age thirty. If there is a leftover balance, it can be rolled into another child's account.

>>> FAST FACT

State-by-State Comparisons of Available 529 Plans

State	Plan Name	Fund Manager	Fees	Contribution Limit	Max Annual Deduction	Tax-Free Withdrawals In-State	Tax-Free Withdrawals Out-State	Investment Options	Open to Non-Residents
Alabama	The Higher Education 529 Fund	Van Kampen	0%	0.78%–1.72%	0	Yes	Yes	14	Yes
Alaska	John Hancock Freedom 529	T. Rowe Price	0.75%	0.55%–1.23%	0	Yes, as Alaska has no state income tax	Yes, as Alaska has no state income tax	20	Yes
Alaska	T.Rowe Price College Savings Plan	T. Rowe Price	0.3%	0.49%–0.75%	0	Yes, as Alaska has no state income tax	Yes, as Alaska has no state income tax	5	Yes
Alaska	University of Alaska College Savings Plan	T. Rowe Price	0%–0.3%	0.4%–0.75%	0	Yes, as Alaska has no state income tax	Yes, as Alaska has no state income tax	6	Yes
Arizona	Arizona Family College Savings Program (CSP)	College Savings Bank	0.3%	0.49%–0.75%	0	Yes	Yes	1	Yes

State	Plan Name	Fund Manager	Fees	Contribution Limit	Max Annual Deduction	Tax-Free Withdrawals In-State	Tax-Free Withdrawals Out-State	Investment Options	Open to Non-Residents
Arizona	Fidelity Arizona College Savings Plan	Fidelity Investments	0.3%	0.47%–0.86%	0	Yes	Yes	4	Yes
Arizona	Pacific Funds 529 College Savings Plan of Arizona	Pacific Life	0%	1.1%–2.05%	0	Yes	Yes	19	Yes
Arizona	Waddell & Reed InvestEd Plan	Waddell & Reed	0.25%	0.83%–0.93%	0	Yes	Yes	4	Yes, only through Waddell & Reed advisor or a Legend advisor
Arizona	Arizona Family College Savings Program (SM&R)	Securities Management & Research	0%	0.5%–2.1%	0	Yes	Yes	10	Yes
Arkansas	The Gift College Investing Plan	Upromise, Inc.	0.87%	0%	$10,000	Yes	No	9	Yes, only through a financial advisor
California	ScholarShare College Savings Trust	TIAA-CREF	0%–0.8%	0%	0	Yes	No	5	Yes
Colorado	Stable Value Plus College Savings Plan	The Travelers Insurance Company	0.75%	0%	$12,000	Yes	Yes	1	Yes

State	Plan Name	Fund Manager	Fees	Contribution Limit	Max Annual Deduction	Tax-Free Withdrawals In-State	Tax-Free Withdrawals Out-State	Investment Options	Open to Non-Residents
Colorado	CollegeInvest Direct Portfolio College Savings Plan	Upromise Investments, Inc.	0.75%	0%	$12,000	Yes	Yes	11	Yes
Colorado	Scholars Choice College Savings Program	Legg Mason Investment Services	0.35%	0.67%–0.99%	$12,000	Yes	Yes	10	Yes
Connecticut	Connecticut Higher Education Trust	TIAA-CREF	0.01%–0.5%	0%–0.27%	0	Yes	Yes	3	Yes
D.C.	The D.C. College Savings Plan	Calvert Group	0.15%	0%–1.69%	$6,000	Yes	Yes	8	Yes
Delaware	Delaware College Investment Plan	Fidelity Investments	0.3%	0.47%–0.81%	0	Yes	Yes	4	Yes
Florida	Florida College Investment Plan	Florida Prepaid College Board	0.75%	0%	0	Yes	Yes	5	Yes
Georgia	Georgia Higher Education Savings Plan	TIAA-CREF	0%–0.78%	0%	$2,000	Yes	Yes	5	Yes
Hawaii	Tuition EDGE	Delaware Investments	0%–0.95%	0%	0	Yes	Yes	5	Yes, only through a financial advisor
Idaho	Idaho College Savings Program	TIAA-CREF	0%–0.7%	0%–0.15%	$4,000	Yes	Yes	3	Yes

State	Plan Name	Fund Manager	Fees	Contribution Limit	Max Annual Deduction	Tax-Free Withdrawals In-State	Tax-Free Withdrawals Out-State	Investment Options	Open to Non-Residents
Illinois	Bright Start College Savings Program	Oppenheimer-Funds Distributor, Inc.	0.99%	0%	$20,000	Yes	No	6	Yes
Illinois	Bright Directions College Savings Program	Union Bank and Trust Company	0.45%	0.09%–1.21%	$20,000	Yes	Yes	30	Yes
Indiana	CollegeChoice 529 Plan	JP Morgan	0.4%–0.95%	0.35%–1.49%	0	Yes	Yes	13	Yes
Iowa	College Savings Iowa	State Treasurer & Vanguard	0.62%	0%	$2,500	Yes	Yes	12	Yes
Kansas	Learning Quest Education Savings Program	American Century Investment Management, Inc.	0%–0.39%	0.12%–0.92%	$4,000	Yes	Yes	10	Yes
Kansas	Schwab 529 College Savings Plan	American Century Investment Management, Inc.	0.39%	0.58%–1.11%	$4,000	Yes	Yes	10	Yes

State	Plan Name	Fund Manager	Fees	Contribution Limit	Max Annual Deduction	Tax-Free Withdrawals In-State	Tax-Free Withdrawals Out-State	Investment Options	Open to Non-Residents
Kentucky	Kentucky Education Savings Plan Trust	TIAA-CREF	0%–0.8%	0%	0	Yes	Yes	3	Yes
Louisiana	START Savings Program	LA State Treasurer	0%	0%–0.28%	$4,800	Yes	Yes	6	No
Maine	NextGen College Investing Plan	Merrill Lynch	0%–0.5%	0.47%–1.11%	0	Yes	Yes	9	Yes
Maryland	Maryland College Investment Plan	T. Rowe Price	0.38%	0.5%–0.75%	$2,500	Yes	Yes	5	Yes
Massa-chusetts	U. Fund College Investing Plan	Fidelity Investments	0.3%	0.47%–0.63%	0	Yes	Yes	4	Yes
Michigan	Michigan Education Savings Program	TIAA-CREF	0%–0.6%	0%	$10,000	Yes	Yes	3	Yes
Minnesota	Minnesota College Savings Plan	TIAA-CREF	0%–0.65%	0%	0	Yes	Yes	3	Yes
Mississippi	Mississippi Affordable College Savings Program	TIAA-CREF	0%–0.7%	0.11%–0.15%	$20,000	Yes	No	3	Yes
Missouri	Missouri Saving for Tuition (MOST)	TIAA-CREF	0%–0.65%	0%	$16,000	Yes	Yes	3	Yes

State	Plan Name	Fund Manager	Fees	Contribution Limit	Max Annual Deduction	Tax-Free Withdrawals In-State	Tax-Free Withdrawals Out-State	Investment Options	Open to Non-Residents
Montana	Montana Family Education Savings Program	College Savings Bank	0%	0%	$6,000	Yes	Yes	1	Yes
Montana	Pacific Funds 529 College Savings Plan	Pacific Life	0%	0.95%–2.05%	$6,000	Yes	Yes	20	Yes
Nebraska	AIM College Savings Plan of Nebraska	Union Bank & AIM	0.35%	0.58%–1.91%	$1,000	Yes	Yes	22	Yes
Nebraska	State Farm College Savings Plan	State Farm	0.35%	0.87%–1.29%	$1,000	Yes	Yes	4	Yes
Nebraska	College Savings Plan of Nebraska	Union Bank & Trust	0.6%	0.05%–1.04%	$1,000	Yes	Yes	31	Yes
Nebraska	TD Waterhouse College Savings Plan	Union Bank & Trust	0.85%	0.05%–1.04%	$1,000	Yes	Yes	31	Yes
Nevada	The Vanguard 529 College Savings Plan	Vanguard	0.6%–0.79%	0%	0	Yes, as Nevada has no state income tax	Yes, as Nevada has no state income tax	20	Yes

State	Plan Name	Fund Manager	Fees	Contribution Limit	Max Annual Deduction	Tax-Free Withdrawals In-State	Tax-Free Withdrawals Out-State	Investment Options	Open to Non-Residents
Nevada	Columbia 529 Plan	Upromise, Inc.	0.3%	0.67%–1.61%	0	Yes, as Nevada has no state income tax	Yes, as Nevada has no state income tax	26	Yes
Nevada	USAA College Savings Plan	Upromise, Inc., and USAA	1.1%	0%	0	Yes, as Nevada has no state income tax	Yes, as Nevada has no state income tax	7	Yes
Nevada	Upromise College Fund	Upromise, Inc.	0.3%	0.67%–1.61%	0	Yes, as Nevada has no state income tax	Yes, as Nevada has no state income tax	11	Yes
New Hampshire	Unique College Investing Plan	Fidelity Investments	0.3%	0.47%–0.83%	0	Yes, as New Hampshire has no state income tax	Yes, as New Hampshire has no state income tax	4	Yes
New Hampshire	The Advisor College Investing Plan	Fidelity Investments	0.45%–0.55%	0.4%–1.09%	0	Yes, as New Hampshire has no state income tax	Yes, as New Hampshire has no state income tax	15	Yes

State	Plan Name	Fund Manager	Fees	Contribution Limit	Max Annual Deduction	Tax-Free Withdrawals In-State	Tax-Free Withdrawals Out-State	Investment Options	Open to Non-Residents
New Jersey	Franklin Templeton 529 College Savings Plan	Franklin Templeton Investments	0.4%	0.45%–0.85%	0	Yes	Yes	13	Yes, only through a financial advisor
New Jersey	NJ Better Educational Savings Trust (NJBEST)	Franklin Templeton Investments	0.4%	0.45%–0.84%	0	Yes	Yes	7	No, account holder or beneficiary must be NJ resident
New Mexico	The Education Plan's College Savings Program	Oppenheimer-Funds	0.25%	0.55%–0.7%	$12,000	Yes	Yes	8	Yes
New Mexico	Evergreen Investments Higher Education Savings Plan	Evergreen Investments	0.7%	0.07%–0.86%	$12,000	Yes	Yes	13	Yes
New Mexico	Scholar'sEdge	Oppenheimer-Funds, Inc.	0.25%	0.73%–1.2%	$12,000	Yes	Yes	15	Yes
New York	New York's College Savings Program (Direct Plan)	Upromise Investments, Inc. (The Vanguard Group - investment manager)	0.56%	0%	$10,000	Yes	Yes	15	Yes

State	Plan Name	Fund Manager	Fees	Contribution Limit	Max Annual Deduction	Tax-Free Withdrawals In-State	Tax-Free Withdrawals Out-State	Investment Options	Open to Non-Residents
New York	New York's College Savings Program (Advisor Plan)	Upromise Investments, Inc.	0.55%	0.25%–1.35%	$10,000	Yes	Yes	25	Yes
North Carolina	North Carolina's National College Savings Program	College Foundations, Inc.	0.1%–0.25%	0.05%–1.16%	0	Yes	Yes	12	Yes
North Dakota	College SAVE	Morgan Stanley	0.5%	1.17%–1.71%	0	Yes	Yes	7	Yes
Ohio	Putnam CollegeAdvantage Savings Plan - Advisor Sold	Putnam Investments	0.49%–0.64%	0.52%–1.35%	$2,000	Yes	Yes	19	Yes
Ohio	College Advantage Savings Plan - Direct	Ohio Tuition Trust Authority	0%–0.41%	0%–1.37%	$2,000	Yes	Yes	32	No
Oklahoma	Oklahoma College Savings Plan	TIAA-CREF	0%–0.65%	0%–0.12%	$20,000	Yes	Yes	3	Yes
Oregon	Oppenheimer Funds 529 Plan	Oppenheimer-Funds, Inc.	0.25%	0.55%–0.79%	$2,000	Yes	Yes	8	Yes, only through a financial advisor
Oregon	MFS 529 Savings Plan	MFS Investment Management	0.25%	0.7%–1.67%	$2,000	Yes	Yes	26	Yes, only through a financial advisor

State	Plan Name	Fund Manager	Fees	Contribution Limit	Max Annual Deduction	Tax-Free Withdrawals In-State	Tax-Free Withdrawals Out-State	Investment Options	Open to Non-Residents
Oregon	Oregon College Savings Plan	Oppenheimer-Funds, Inc.	0.25%	0.08%–0.79%	$2,000	Yes	Yes	12	Yes
Pennsyl-vania	TAP 529 Investment Plan	Delaware Investments	0.35%	0.45%–1.29%	0	Yes	No	9	Yes, but non-residents must incur higher cost of class shares
Rhode Island	CollegeBound Fund	Alliance Bernstein	0%	0.4%–1.37%	$1,000	Yes	Yes	16	Yes, non-residents incur higher cost
South Carolina	Future Scholar 529 College Savings Plan	BACAP Distributors	0.2%	0.1%–0.41%	$12,000	Yes	Yes	11	Yes, only through a financial advisor
South Dakota	Legg Mason Core4College 529 Plan	Legg Mason	0.53%–1.2%	0.67%–0.85%	0	Yes, as South Dakota has no state income tax.	Yes, as South Dakota has no state income tax.	17	Yes, only through a financial advisor. Also, non-residents will incur higher fees of broker sold shares.
South Dakota	CollegeAccess 529	Allianz Global Investors Direct	0.45%–0.65%	0%	0	Yes, as South Dakota has no state income tax.	Yes, as South Dakota has no state income tax.	3	Yes, only through a financial advisor. Also, non-residents will incur higher fees of broker sold shares.

State	Plan Name	Fund Manager	Fees	Contribution Limit	Max Annual Deduction	Tax-Free Withdrawals In-State	Tax-Free Withdrawals Out-State	Investment Options	Open to Non-Residents
Tennessee	Tennessee's BEST Savings Plan	TIAA-CREF	0%–0.8%	0%	0	Yes, as Tennessee has no state income tax	Yes, as Tennessee has no state income tax	3	Yes
Texas	Tomorrow's College Investment Plan	Enterprise Capital Management, Inc.	0%–0.1%	0%	0	Yes, as Texas has no state income tax	Yes, as Texas has no state income tax	16	Yes, Class A, B, and C Units are available to non-residents but must be purchased through a financial advisor. Class T and Class A Units are available only to Account Owners or Beneficiaries who are Texas residents and who purchase their Units directly from Enterprise or through a fee-based financial advisor.

State	Plan Name	Fund Manager	Fees	Contribution Limit	Max Annual Deduction	Tax-Free Withdrawals In-State	Tax-Free Withdrawals Out-State	Investment Options	Open to Non-Residents
Utah	Utah Educational Savings Plan	State Treasurer through Vanguard	0%–0.25%	0%–0.16%	$1,365	Yes	Yes	9	Yes
Vermont	Vermont Higher Education Savings Plan	TIAA-CREF	0%–0.8%	0%	0	Yes	Yes	3	Yes
Virginia	CollegeAmerica	Virginia College Savings Plan and American Funds	0.39%–0.53%	0.24%–0.74%	$2,000	Yes	Yes	21	Yes
Virginia	Virginia Education Savings Trust	Virginia Education Savings Board	0.25%	0.08%–0.31%	$2,000	Yes	Yes	10	Yes
West Virginia	Smart529 - College Savings Option	Hartford Life	0.3%	0.86%	$12,000	Yes	Yes	7	Yes
West Virginia	Smart529 Select	Hartford Life	0.55%	0.2%–0.47%	$12,000	Yes	Yes	17	Yes
West Virginia	Director SMART529	Hartford Life	0.6%	0.86%	$12,000	Yes	Yes	14	Yes
West Virginia	Cornerstone SMART529	Hartford Life	0.74%	0.72%–1.31%	$12,000	Yes	Yes	27	Yes

State	Plan Name	Fund Manager	Fees	Contribution Limit	Max Annual Deduction	Tax-Free Withdrawals In-State	Tax-Free Withdrawals Out-State	Investment Options	Open to Non-Residents
West Virginia	Leaders SMART529	Hartford Life	0.74%	0.7%–1.38%	$12,000	Yes	Yes	21	No
Wisconsin	Tomorrow's Scholar	Wells Fargo Funds Management, LLC	0.25%–0.3%	0.75%–1.17%	$3,000	Yes	Yes	10	Yes
Wisconsin	EdVest	Wells Fargo Funds Management, LLC	0.12%–0.3%	0.05%–0.95%	$3,000	Yes	Yes	13	Yes
Wyoming	College Achievement Plan	Mercury Advisors	0.9%	0.92%–1.53%	0	Yes, as Wyoming has no state income tax	Yes, as Wyoming has no state income tax	5	Yes

Source: Sallie Mae

See www.401kid.com for more information. Please be aware that these ratings are general and do not apply to each individual family's specific circumstances, as different risk profiles, states of residence, investment preferences, and financial situations may warrant different types of plans. Hence, a plan that rates an 'A' according to the 401kid methodology may not be better for everybody than plans that rate lower. It is recommended that you consult your personal financial advisor or utilize an objective evaluation tool that compares these plans specific to your own tax bracket and financial profile. Furthermore, the ratings are not solely a reflection of the plan program manager, but also of the state's 529 plan legislation, which provides for tax benefits and other advantages for residents. As these plans and the associated tax legislation change frequently, 401kid cannot be held responsible for inaccuracies and non-updated information. Please check with the websites of the specific 529 plans of interest to verify information.

ESAs are usually made available by banks, mutual funds, and brokerage companies, who manage the investments. You will not get any tax deductions by investing in one, but it is easy to switch accounts when you want.

TAX TIPS

School Tax Breaks Are in Session

If you are returning to school or have dependents attending school, here is some good news: you could be eligible for tax breaks. There are a number of entitlements you could qualify for, including:

Tax Break	Explanation
Hope Tax Credit	Maximum Hope tax credit is $1,800 per student.
Lifetime Learning Credit	Maximum Lifetime Learning tax credit is $2,000 per taxpayer—up to 20 percent of the first $10,000 in expenses.
Education Deduction	If you itemize, there is a deduction for education expenses.
Interest Deduction	If you itemize, there is a deduction for interest on borrowing for the purchase of Series EE or I bonds.
Additional Exemption	If you can claim your child as a dependent, you receive an additional $3,500.

College is not cheap, so annual tax deductions, credits, and exemptions can be a big help.

- **Prepaid College Tuition Program**

Due to the invention of 529 plans and ESAs, the predecessor of these plans—prepaid college tuition programs—have fallen behind in recent years. Nevertheless, they are still worth a look, as they offer many of the same tax benefits as the other two plans.

Prepaid tuition plans allow you to lock in tomorrow's tuition at today's prices. You pay a lump sum or series of payments, and in return the state promises to cover your student's tuition and fees at a state college or university. As with the 529 plan, prepaid tuition offers some considerable tax benefits. Gains are tax-free, for example, as long as the money is used for college. In some states you can also deduct a portion of your contribution from your state income taxes.

You have two investment options with prepaid tuition plans:

Prepaid Tuition Investment of Options	
1	Make cash payments or follow a regular schedule of payments in return for guaranteed tuition, with contracts generally running from one semester to five years.
2	Purchase a series of units or credits that represent a percentage of the average annual tuition and fees at state colleges and universities. The value of these units is adjusted each year to account for increases in tuition and fees, and you can redeem them once you child enters college.

One catch with the prepaid tuition plan is that your selection of schools will be limited to the colleges and universities located in the state whose prepaid plan you are investing in. So if you live in New York but Junior gets accepted to Harvard, you cannot use the money in a New York prepaid college plan, even if he is just moving a few hundred miles up the road to Cambridge, Massachusetts.

Financial aid poses another problem. Prepaid tuition plan participants who apply for financial aid will often see their financial need reduced dollar for dollar by the amount provided by their plan. This can put a big dent in your plan to fund half your child's education and let Uncle Sam pick up the other half.

On the plus side, however, prepaid tuition offers many of the same tax benefits as 529 plans. Under the Internal Revenue Code Section 529 (26 U.S.C. 529), each plan is categorized as a "qualified state tuition program," meaning it allows earnings to be federally tax exempt. Most states also exempt earnings from state income tax, and some allow families to deduct part or all their contribution from their state income taxes. If your child relies on a qualified state tuition account for college, and your family meets household income requirements, you can also claim the Hope tax credit on your return. The Hope credit is worth up to $1,800 each year for the first two years of college. On top of that, up to $2,000 worth of Lifetime Learning credits can be claimed in subsequent years.

- **Roth IRAs**
  In addition to offering retirement savings benefits, Roth IRAs can be used as college savings plans, too. When you take out money from a Roth IRA, the IRS will consider your contributions withdrawn first. If you withdraw more than you initially contributed, you will pay tax and penalty, though money used for tuition may be eligible for an exception to the penalty.

  Like prepaid tuition, Roth IRAs may have a negative effect on your child's financial aid opportunities, however, as Roth withdrawals will count as parental income. You will learn more about Roth IRAs in Round 8.

- **UTMA or UGMA Accounts**
  Named for the Uniform Transfers/Gifts to Minors Act, this vehicle may be an endangered species as a college savings plan option, though in decades past it was very popular and

constituted the bulwark of many families' college savings efforts. The main benefit of saving for college with a custodial account was the subsequent reduction of the family's tax bill. Up until age eighteen, the first $850 of a child's investment earnings is tax-free, and the following $850 is taxed at the child's rate (typically 10 or 15 percent). After that, the parents' rate would kick in. But essentially the child would only pay half the 20 percent capital gains tax on earnings from investments cashed in to pay for college.

UTMAs and UGMAs have fallen by the wayside in recent years as more families have turned to state-sponsored 529 plans and all their comparatively better benefits. For example, when your child becomes an adult—at either eighteen or

---

>>> **FAST FACT**

Custodial Accounts Defined

Custodial accounts are usually available through banks, savings & loans, credit unions, mutual funds, and brokerage firms. To start one, you will need your child's Social Security number and a custodian to manage the account until the minor reaches maturity. You can name yourself custodian, but if you are also the donor and die before the child comes of age, the gift will be considered part of your estate for federal estate–tax purposes. Another important point to consider about custodial accounts is that you cannot get the money back once it has been invested—even if your child doesn't want to use it for education. That's right—when your son or daughter reaches maturity as defined by your state's UGMA or UTMA law—usually eighteen or twenty-one—he or she can take off to Cancun with your carefully invested dollars instead of using them to buckle down at Ivy U. And there's not much you can do about it.

Also keep in mind that you do not need a custodial account to invest your child's money in U.S. savings bonds. Just buy the bonds in the child's name and don't name yourself co-owner, or the income will be taxed to you when the bonds are cashed. ◄

twenty-one, depending on where you live—he or she receives full legal access to the money from a UTMA or UGMA, and can spend it on whatever seems appealing. Maybe your kids will want to go to school, or maybe they will want to buy a Harley and join a motorcycle gang.

Another disadvantage to custodial accounts is that they can decrease your child's financial aid amount. Custodial accounts are actually considered a student asset and are thus assessed more harshly under financial aid formulas than parental assets like 529 plans and Coverdell ESAs.

INVESTMENT TIP:

Getting Out

If you are already in a UTMA or UGMA plan and want to get out, many 529 plans will let you roll over your custodial account into a 529 plan. Before you can complete the rollover, however, capital gains come into play. Any gains you have made in the custodial account must be recorded on your tax return. In addition, if your son decides to join the Marines, you will not be able to change the custodial account and name his little sister as the beneficiary.

Education Expenses

So you're on your way back to school to get a better set of job skills. Congratulations! And an added benefit is that your education expenses will likely provide you with a healthy tax break. If you're taking classes to improve your skills in your current occupation, your expenses are deductible as an itemized deduction.

But this deduction is limited to the amount of your qualified education expenses—along with other expenses—that surpasses 2 percent of your Adjusted Gross Income. Bear in mind that the same expenses are probably eligible for the Lifetime Learning credit as well. You are only allowed one tax break for each set of education expenses, so you will want to figure out which one will save you the most money.

The Hope Credit

This handy provision offers a tax credit of up to $1,800 for each qualifying full-time student in his or her first two years of college who attends school at least half the time.

You can claim the Hope credit for 100 percent of the first $1,200 and 50 percent of the next $1,200 of qualified expenses, including tuition, fees, and books that are purchased from the college or university the student attends. Awarded on a per-child basis, the Hope credit provides you a tax credit of up to $1,800 for every qualifying student dependent you claim on your tax return.

Filing status is also a factor in Hope credit eligibility. If you are single, your credit begins to phase out once your modified Adjusted Gross Income (AGI) exceeds $47,000; the credit is completely eliminated once your modified AGI reaches $57,000. If you are married and file jointly, the phase-out range falls between a modified AGI of $94,000 and $114,000. If you are married and file separately, you cannot claim the credit at all.

The Lifetime Learning Credit

Okay, let's say that you made it through sophomore year at Cal-Berkeley and are looking forward to starting your junior year next fall. You no longer have the Hope credit in your pocket, but now you can turn to the Lifetime Learning credit, which picks up where the Hope credit leaves off. With the Lifetime Learning credit, you can receive a credit for 20 percent of the first $10,000 you pay for any eligible student in your family—a maximum of $2,000 per tax return. You can claim the credit every year and can also apply it to prepaid expenses for the next school year.

As with the Hope credit, your modified AGI affects your benefits. If you are single, the credit begins to phase out once your modified AGI hits $47,000. Again, if you are single and your modified AGI exceeds $57,000, you do not qualify for the credit at all. If you are married and file jointly, that phase-out range falls between $94,000 and $114,000. If you are married and file separately, you cannot claim the credit.

TAX TIPS

Here's to a Lifetime of Hoping

You may be able to claim both the Hope credit and the Lifetime Learning credit if you have two kids in college at the same time: one attending his first or second year and another entering her third year or later. You cannot claim both credits for the same expenses, but you can claim a Hope credit for each qualifying student and a Lifetime Learning credit for a different student's qualifying expenses. Both credits are nonrefundable, and any credit remaining after your tax liability drops to zero is gone for good.

Additional Tax-Advantaged Ways of Saving for College

While education IRAs and state-sponsored 529 plans are probably the most popular tax-advantaged ways of saving for college, they are not the only ones. There are even more creative tax-saving college plan options out there for you to consider.

- **Give a Gift of Stocks**

  One great way to trim the family tax bill while also saving for college is to give gifts of appreciated securities.

  By giving your child stocks or mutual fund shares that have appreciated, for instance, the tax bill on the increase in value passes on to the recipient along with the gift. Say that stock you bought for $2,500 has increased in worth to $5,000 and you have a tuition bill on the way. By selling the stock, you would owe tax on the $2,500 gain. The 15 percent rate on long-term capital gains means that would cost you $375— not bad, you might say. Nevertheless, there is a way to cut the bill to zero.

  You do this by giving the shares to your college student. When the same above stock is sold, it will still be taxed, but now it is at the child's rate (assuming he is not Doogie Howser and attending college before age eighteen). If he or she falls in the 25 percent income bracket, the long-term capital gains rate would be 0 percent. That means a tax bill of $0! And don't think your student has to hold on to the stock for more than twelve months to get special capital gains treatment—with gifts of an appreciated asset, the recipient's holding period includes the time that the donor owned the property.

U.S. gift tax law permits you to give up to $12,000 each year to any number of people without the gift tax coming into play, and if you're married, that total jumps to $24,000 for each person on your gift list. Anything pricier than that and the gift tax applies. Keep in mind that the tax is imposed on the giver of the gifts, not the recipient.

As I mentioned earlier in this Round, there is no such thing as starting a college savings plan too early, especially when you have all those tax breaks and interest to accumulate. It doesn't matter if your child is still in the crib; start saving early, and Uncle Sam will pitch in to help pay for his or her college education.

- **Use the "Kiddie Tax"**

  The "kiddie tax" is a rule within the Internal Revenue Code stating that certain unearned income of a child will be taxed at the parent's marginal rate, regardless of whether the child

---

➤➤➤ FAST FACT

Bonds . . . Savings Bonds

Can you roll savings bonds into a 529 plan? Yes, and there is no tax penalty.

First, cash out the bonds and reinvest the money in the savings plan. Around tax time, file IRS Form 8815 to exclude the bond interest from income taxes. Make sure that the savings bond rollover follows all the rules and that your income does not go over the limit. Make sure to check state contribution limits as well. ◄

can be claimed as a dependent on the parent's return. However, the first $1,700 of investment income is not subject to this tax. Thus, your child could have $25,000 saved away in an account yielding 6 percent, and you won't have to worry about the tax on the interest. Your child's tax bill will be just $85 for that $1,700 of interest income if it is his or her only income. This is because the first $850 is tax-free, and the second $850 is taxed in the 10 percent bracket. That same $1,700 would yield a $595 tax if it were in the parent's 35 percent bracket. In a roundabout way, the $510 savings is the IRS's contribution to the college fund.

Considering that the "kiddie tax" disappears once a child turns eighteen, you may want to give your kids investments that defer income until that time.

U.S. savings bonds are a logical choice because income can be deferred until the bond is cashed. If that happens after the child is eighteen, the interest accrued during his or her earlier years is still taxed at the child's own rate. An even better deal happens when the parent buys the bond in his or her own name. When parents own the bonds and cash them in to pay for college tuition and fees, the interest on the bonds can be completely tax-free.

Another way to get around the "kiddie tax" is to buy growth stocks, which generally throw off little if any current income in the form of dividends. As the stock appreciates, there is no tax on that paper profit. Should the stock be sold after the child turns eighteen, the profit would be taxed in the child's bracket. If a child invests in growth-stock mutual funds instead of individual stocks, the fund will pay out capital gains distributions each year based on trading within the fund. This income would then undergo the "kiddie tax" if the child's unearned income surpasses $1,700.

Note that for income splitting to work, the child must in fact own the assets that generate income. You cannot simply give your son $1,000 if you want him to pay taxes in his bracket on $1,000 of interest income generated by a $15,000 savings account. You have to give him the $15,000 in the account. Only if you do that will the produced income be his for tax purposes.

 TAX TIPS

Claiming Dependents

If your children are under age twenty-four and you provided them with more than half their support, you can still claim them as dependents, even if they have income exceeding one exemption amount. To claim children between the ages of nineteen and twenty-three, they must be full-time students for at least five months out of the year.

- **Buy a Home for Your College Student**

    This option is not for everyone, obviously. But if you can afford to buy a home or condominium for your college student to live in near campus, it could translate to tax savings for you. That is because when your child—and his or her roommates—pay you the going rate of rent to live in your home or condo, you will report the rent as income but also get to deduct mortgage interest, property taxes, and depreciation.

    Another bonus is to hire your college student to manage the apartment (i.e., finding tenants, collect rent, and arrange for maintenance and repairs). The pay you give him is deductible from the rental income. If the rental shows a loss and you qualify for the $25,000 exception to the passive loss rules, that loss can also shelter other income. And if you can sell the property for a profit after graduation, that's just icing on the cake.

INVESTMENT TIP:
Get Some Help

It can get complicated planning to use a trust to benefit your children or grandchildren for educational purposes. It may be beneficial for you to consult a financial planner who can give you clear advice on navigating the variety of trust options available. A trust can be a useful planning tool, but your particular circumstances will determine how you go about setting one up.

Inside the Ropes:
Jordan's Ivy League Dreams

Scott is a proud parent. He and his wife Lorena invested a lot of time and energy into providing a good education and solid upbringing for each of their children. But now that his eldest son is only a few years away from high school graduation, Scott realizes the annual IRAs he had been investing in for college savings are not going to meet his son's higher education needs.

"My son Jordan got my good looks, but more important, his mother's brain," explained Scott. "He is potentially Ivy League material, which is going to cost a little bit more than I had originally planned."

Scott is a golf club professional and instructor, and he heard from one of his students about 529 college savings plans. The student told him about the terrific tax breaks and the expanding assortment of investment options that the major mutual fund companies sponsoring these plans were offering. Scott wanted in on the action.

Scott's view of 529 plans became even more positive after a meeting with his financial advisor. He intended to stay in control of the 529 and keep all the rights to himself.

"I'd heard stories about prepaid tuition plans where the child got the money and didn't use it for college," says Scott. "Instead the kid opened a skateboard shop. Although I'm not worried so much about that for Jordan— not much of a skateboarder, really—I do remember my college days. I really don't want Jordan pulling money out of this plan to purchase a tap for a kegerator."

His financial advisor also pointed out to Scott that 529 plans were a great hands-off way of investing for college funds. "Hey, I'm no Warren Buffet," adds Scott. "I like to know what's going on, but I don't want to be picking stocks or anything like that. I loved the fact that I won't get a 1099 until I take proceeds out of the plan."

He also liked that he could stash a lot of money into the plans right off the bat. "That way I could put more in so we could catch up," Scott explains. "The grandparents got involved, too, and pretty soon we had a nice nest egg for Jordan."

➤ ROUND 8

Answer the Bell: Keep the IRS Out of Your Investment Portfolio

There's only one kind of tax that would please everybody—one that nobody but the other guy has to pay.

—Earl Wilson

It saddens me when clients walk in the door and tell me they are in trouble with the IRS.

Why? Because they took money out of their 401(k) plans or Individual Retirement Accounts (IRA) to keep their homes out of foreclosure or to pay off hefty car loans—and the tax guys are on them like a Doberman on a rib-eye steak.

Due to today's shaky economic conditions, people are getting caught in a vicious double bind. You cannot take money from your 401(k) without incurring a big tax penalty (more on that later in this Round); nevertheless, people are so desperate for cash these days that they either overlook that fact or ignore it altogether.

What I like to do with these clients is to walk them through the tax and investment process—an exercise I would like to do here in Round 8.

 TAX TIPS

When Losing Wins

Capital losses can be written off against ordinary income up to $3,000 per year.

It's an important exercise. After all, there are fewer places you can save more money on your taxes than in the investment world.

Why? Lots of reasons. The most important one is that the relationship between Wall Street and Congress has always been a tug-of-war over the amount of money made by investors on Wall Street and the amount of that sum that Uncle Sam deserves in taxes.

Each side has its battle lines drawn. Wall Street would prefer that as little as possible of its investors' earnings be taxed. Congress is constantly asking investors to dig into their pocketbooks and ante up some of the proceeds from their portfolio gains.

Just a case of some high-level give-and-take? Perhaps—but that's the way it has been for decades.

⟫⟫⟫ FAST FACT

The Skinny on Holding Periods

A holding period is the length of time you own an investment like a stock, bond, or mutual fund. The IRS uses holding periods as a timeline or benchmark to figure out what you tax liability is, if any. ◀

While those two entities agree to disagree, what can you, the investor, do to hang on to your investment proceeds tighter than a barnacle on the hull of a boat?

The answer is that you can do plenty. First, you should know the lay of the land, namely, the types of investment taxes, such as dividend, capital gains, and interest income tax, and how they work. Second, once you know what the stakes are, it is up to you—and your tax preparer, if you have one—to craft a tax strategy that keeps more of your money in your pocket.

➤➤➤ FAST FACT

What Is Not Taxed

Not every investment of yours is taxable in the eyes of the IRS. At the top of the list of nontaxable investment-related income are life insurance proceeds due to the death of the insured and municipal bond interest. ◀

Let's get started doing just that.

Your Investments and How They Are Taxed

Taxes can be owed on a wide variety of investments, from Portuguese debentures to South African gold futures. But do not be confused by the diversity of investment options. Primarily, tax-related events occur on the purchase and sale of U.S. stocks, bonds, mutual funds, and other investments. They also happen when you invest in tax-deferred retirement vehicles, such as individual retirement accounts and 401(k) plans. In addition, your house—which may be your biggest investment—is also affected by the tax code.

By and large, investment income is taxable in three areas: dividends, capital gains, and (investment) interest.

- **Dividends**

  Dividends are not exactly free money—they are taxable—but they are the next best thing. Dividends are income distributions from a company's profits to its shareholders. Investors have the option of receiving the dividend in the form of a check, or they can have the proceeds automatically reinvested in a dividend reinvestment plan (DRIP).

- **Capital Gains and Losses**

  Capital gains are a bit more confusing. Each time you sell an investment security such as a stock, bond, or piece of real

---

 TAX TIPS

A Last-Minute Tactic That Could Save You Big Bucks

If you sell capital assets (such as stocks, mutual fund shares, real estate, and bonds) during the year, you will have a gain or loss on each transaction. Near the end of the year, say in October or November, review all your sales of capital assets and see if you have a net loss or gain from all your transactions.

If you have a large net loss, consider cashing in some investments that are currently showing large paper gains. The losses you already have will offset your gains, thus, in effect, allowing you to realize capital gains while avoiding the tax you would otherwise pay.

If you have a large net gain, congratulations! After popping open some champagne, consider the tax consequences. In this case, do the exact opposite of the above: sell some assets currently showing a large paper loss at the same time as the sale of your gain. The result is the same: Your losses will offset your gains and reduce your tax bill.

Now, don't just follow this advice blindly. Remember that the tax consequences are just the icing on the cake. The meat and potatoes are the investments that comprise your lifelong investment portfolio.

TAX TIPS

Last-Minute Sales

Because it takes several days to settle a stock or other investment trade between the time you order the sale to the time you get your money, sales during the last few days of the year often straddle year-end. Some can even spill over into the next tax year—a big no-no if you are trying to generate a capital loss for that tax year.

However, as far as the IRS is concerned, a gain or loss should be reported on the return for the year the trade occurs, regardless of when settlement takes place. That means profits and losses taken as late as the closing bell on New Year's Eve go on the current year's return.

estate at a profit, you generate a capital gain. When you sell at a loss, a capital loss is generated.

With a capital gain, the tax rate is determined by the holding period of the asset (short-term capital gain versus long-term capital gain) and the tax bracket of the individual.

Tax Rate for Capital Gain (2008–2010)							
CAPITAL GAIN TYPE	HOLDING PERIOD	TAX BRACKET					
		10%	15%	25%	28%	33%	35%
Long-Term	> 12 months	0%	0%	15%	15%	15%	15%
Short-Term	≤ 12 months	10%	15%	25%	28%	33%	35%

Source: Internal Revenue Service

Thus, for holding periods of more than twelve months (with long-term capital gains), the rate is now 15 percent for those in the 25, 28, and 35 percent tax brackets and 0 percent for those in the other brackets. But for holding periods of twelve months or less (with short-term capital gains), the capital gain is the same as ordinary income.

The good news? With a capital loss, long-term and short-term losses can be written off dollar for dollar against any capital gain.

- **Interest**

Interest is the amount of money you earn on a bond investment, bank account, certificate of deposit (CD), etc. Interest earned from your investments, like treasury bonds or money market investments, are considered taxable at your marginal tax rate.

Most people don't take the time to understand how interest is treated by the IRS because they think that only mortgage interest is deductible. And that's true—but it's not the complete truth. You see, the law still allows investors to deduct interest on loans used to make investments. That interest is deductible depending on the amount of your investment income. When totaling up your investment income to see where your limit lies, you typically cannot count capital gains that get special treatment under the law. There is a reason for that and

 TAX TIPS

Installment Sales

Uncle Sam's version of installment plans, installment sales let you hold off reporting taxable income from a sale until you receive the proceeds. Be careful, though. You cannot use the installment method to defer recognition of income from the sale of publicly traded stocks and bonds. However, it is available to individuals who sell a vacation home, for example, or rental property on an installment note. If the buyer will pay you over a number of years, you can report the income as you get it rather than all at once in the year of the sale.

TAX TIPS

Bonjour, Foreign Tax Credit

Is a foreign tax credit on your docket? Generally, you may claim a tax credit or an itemized deduction for taxes paid to foreign countries, and you do not need to live or work in that country to do so. The taxes paid to foreign countries include taxes on foreign investments.

Thus, you may be eligible, for example, if you own shares in a mutual fund that invests in foreign securities. If you are, you have two options: you can treat foreign taxes paid on your behalf as an itemized deduction or claim a credit.

As you learned earlier in this book, credits are usually worth more because they offset your tax liability dollar for dollar, whereas an itemized deduction simply reduces the amount of income on which you pay tax.

it involves the best and brightest up there in Washington. You see, Congress doesn't want to let you deduct investment interest in a higher bracket if your gains are being taxed at only 15 or 20 percent. You have the option of including your capital gains in investment income, but then you can't take advantage of the lower capital gains rates. It gets confusing, I know, especially when the geniuses in D.C. are on the case.

Creating an Investment Tax-Planning Strategy

In the past year, everyone has taken a beating in the stock market. With a volatile economy and ever-increasing prices on such staples as fuel and food, the stock market has generally reflected a cautious approach toward the worldwide economy. However, if you play your cards right, you should be able to continue to use investments to fund your wealth. To do so, you need to take into account all the risks, both positive and negative.

The goal of any investment plan is to minimize your loss and maximize your gain. The goal of your investment *tax* plan is to minimize the tax liability you owe for your net gains. In other words, take all the investment trades you made from January 1 to December 31, add their value as of year-end, and you will have your net gain and loss. Then count up all your gains and losses for the year and write off the losses. If your losses in the stock market totaled $11,000 for the year and your gains totaled $10,000, you can write off $1,000 in losses.

In tax planning, just as in investing, timing is everything. So the idea is to separate your investment losses and stick Uncle Sam with a piece of the bill. If, for example, you have capital gains on investments where you have earned a profit, selling another security you own for a loss may offset those gains. You can do so by selling your investments at a loss before the end of the tax year to give your trade a chance to settle before the year runs out, thus timing your sale to fully maximize your tax advantage.

The idea is to cut your losses by December 31, particularly when your gains are higher. That move will net you a tidy deduction for your investment loss, plus you pay any taxes owed at a much lower rate.

The Importance of Holding Periods

As I mentioned earlier in this Round, the amount of tax you owe on a given investment is based on the length of time you've owned it. In tax lingo, that is called a "holding period." The actual gain or loss is determined by comparing the asset's basis with its selling price—the holding period helps determine the rate at which the gain is taxed—not the actual gain or loss itself. The IRS doesn't calculate holding periods starting January 1 of a given year; it starts the clock when you buy an investment. For instance, if you purchased a hundred shares of Yahoo! on May 1 and sold it all the following April 30, that is a short-term taxable event. If you sell the stock on May 2 of the following year, the IRS considers that a long-term gain or loss and will tax the sale at a lower tax rate.

The Importance of Wash Sales

Ever hear of "wash sales"? No? Well, they have nothing to do with the Maytag repairman. To the IRS, a wash rule means that you have sold a stock to lock in a capital loss, then you go right back into the market and buy the same stock again. The wash sale period for any loss consists of sixty-one calendar days—thirty days before the sale, the day of the sale, and thirty days following the sale.

Note that wash sales are not illegal—they are just not allowed. The loss is actually added to the basis of the newly acquired shares. Finally, the rules also cover contracts or options to acquire stock.

Types of Investment Tax Categories

I know, I know. This tax and investment stuff can feel like a root canal without Novocain. However, as I have been saying all along, Congress—and by extension the IRS—wants it that way. The more confused you are, the more money they get because of the errors they are counting on you to make. So far, we have had to grind our way through it. But let's now turn to an easier tax and investment topic— how taxes are treated in the primary investment asset classes.

- **Stocks**

  Good stock tax management depends on your ability to keep track of all your trades, particularly when you buy the stock of the same company at different times and at different prices. When you decide to sell some of the stock, being able to identify which shares to part with will permit you to control the tax consequences of the deal.

  That's why it's important to know the cost basis of all your stock transactions. The cost basis, in brief, is your investment in the property, the amount you will compare to the sales proceeds to determine the size of your gain or loss. The higher you can prove your basis to be, the less gain there is to be taxed . . . and the lower your tax bill.

- ### Mutual Funds

  Mutual funds are treated a bit differently than stocks in that they are taxed in three ways: (1) sale of shares, (2) capital gains distributions, and (3) dividend distributions.

  Just like a stock transaction, you must pay capital gains taxes on any profit that you made when you sell shares of a mutual fund. In addition, like a stock, you can declare a loss on the investment if the shares decreased in value. The amount of gain or loss is determined by the difference between the sale price and the basis of the fund shares.

  Mutual fund investors are also taxed on dividends and capital gains. Dividend distributions are triggered by the interest and dividends earned from the investments that comprise the fund portfolio. *Psst*—don't forget that dividends should be reported as income on your 1040.

  Capital gains distributions are a tad different. They come from gains from the sale of shares that the fund itself made during the year. Capital gains are taxed as capital gains, often at lower rates than your marginal tax rate.

- ### Municipal Bonds

  Uncle Sam usually keeps his mitts off money earned from municipal bond investments. Municipal bonds typically provide a lower interest rate than fully taxable bonds, and certainly cannot match the gains from stocks and stock mutual funds.

  It would be nice if municipal bond investing were as easy as that—but it's not. Although interest from municipal bonds is not subject to federal income tax, the IRS does not ignore the gain or loss that results when you sell the bonds. If you sell a bond for more than your basis, the profit is a capital gain; if you sell it for less, it is a deductible capital loss.

- ### Life Insurance

  Once a virtual afterthought at the Wall Street dot.com party during the late 1990s, life insurance is in big demand these days. Thanks to recent changes by Congress to boost its appeal, some elements of stocks and bonds were merged into life insurance options. Policies that combine investments with insurance—including whole life, universal life, and single-premium life policies—enjoy tax-favored status.

Perhaps the best part of insurance as investments from a tax point of view is that proceeds from the cash value of your insurance policy escape the clutches of Uncle Sam.

- **Annuities**
A stronger investment-insurance hybrid, annuities also have big tax advantages. With annuities, you are guaranteed that your heirs will receive at least as much as you have invested

---

⯈⯈⯈ FAST FACT

Taxes and Insurance

Make no mistake, life insurance policies offer some great tax advantages. For example, you don't have to pay any taxes on your life insurance until you cash in the policy. Moreover, when you pass away, the proceeds go to your beneficiary without incurring any federal income tax. ◀

 TAX TIPS

Borrow at Will

If you are strapped for cash, you can always borrow against the cash value of your life insurance policy tax-free—and you never have to pay it back! If there is an outstanding loan at the time of death, it just comes out of the proceeds paid to your beneficiary. Note that you do have to pay interest on the loan, though.

TAX TIPS

Cash-Out at Your Own Risk

If you cash in an annuity before retirement, watch out. For starters, most contracts impose surrender charges during the first several years. Any earnings pulled out of the annuity are taxable, and if you are under age 59½, you will be hit with a 10 percent penalty tax.

---

in the annuity, even if your investments have lost money. But that's just window dressing. The real attraction of an annuity is that earnings accumulate tax-free until you begin to withdraw the funds.

Annuities come in two basic flavors: fixed and variable. With a fixed annuity, your investment earns interest at a rate set by the insurance company, a rate that can change periodically in line with market interest rates. A variable annuity gives you investment options much like a family of mutual funds. The insurance company offers you the choice of several funds—stock, bond, money market, etc.—and your return depends on the success of the investments you choose.

Unlike bank CDs and mutual funds, however, the annuity contract serves as an impenetrable wrapper that keeps the tax collector's hands off your earnings. No tax is due until you pull funds out of the contract—presumably during retirement—either in a lump sum or by annuitizing the contract and having the company make payments to you for life.

Such tax-deferred growth gives funds invested in an annuity the same advantage as cash stashed in an individual retirement account. Unlike an IRA, though, you cannot deduct amounts put into an annuity.

Deduct Those Expenses

Are investment-related expenses tax deductible? You bet.

Everything from the cost of calling your broker to the service charges you pay for your dividend redistribution plan is tax deductible. In fact, many costs associated with helping you with the investments that produce taxable income are tax deductible.

Here is a short list of what you can deduct:

Deductible Expenses
☑ Cost of investment magazines, newsletters, books
☑ Cost of meetings, trips, calls to financial advisor/stockbroker
☑ Cost of dividend redistribution plan
☑ Investment fees
☑ Custodial/trust administration fees
☑ Online trading account management fees

And just to cover all our bases, here's a short list of what is not deductible:

Nondeductible Expenses
☒ Online trading fees
☒ Commissions
☒ Expenses related to municipal bonds

However, trading fees, commissions, and expenses related to municipal bonds do reduce the sales proceeds of the security.

Taxes and Your Retirement Plan

Ahh, retirement. Leisurely days at the beach or on the golf course. Cocktails on the deck while the grill heats up. Long, carefree trips to exotic shores.

Sounds great, right?

It is—but you may not enjoy your golden years as much if you don't take advantage of tax-free and tax-deferred investments.

The beauty of these investment vehicles is that you don't have to pay taxes right away on things like individual retirement accounts and 401(k) plans. Instead, your money appreciates over time, tax-free. You only pay taxes on it when you take it out.

Then there are tax-free investments like the Roth IRA, where withdrawals are completely tax-free as long as you are 59½ years old and the account is at least five years old.

With the landscape rich with such investment vehicles, let's look at what they are and how they work.

INVESTMENT TIP:
Five Rules of Investment Success

Hey, I'm the Tax Lady—not the investment lady. But I do have a good understanding of investment tenets that work, mostly from my own portfolio and those investment portfolios I have worked on for tax purposes.

Here are five good rules for success—learn them, live them, love them, and profit from them.

	Rule	Description
1	Start Early	There is no substitute for getting a good start on your financial future. All the studies on the subject conclude that the earlier you get going with your investments, the more money you will have in retirement. That's because the earlier you start, the earlier compound interest goes to work for you.

	Rule	Description
2	**Max Out**	If you have a 401(k) or other employer-sponsored plan, know that it provides a multitude of benefits for investors. One of the most beneficial is the plan's tax-advantaged status. In short, the more you contribute to your 401(k) every year, the less you will pay in taxes to Uncle Sam. Then there's the obvious advantage of maxing out and investing the legal limit in your 401(k): the more money you invest, the more your company might match, and the faster you will become a 401(k) millionaire.
3	**Learning Is Everything**	The value of good investment research is priceless. And the value of knowing enough about your investments to become the master of your financial future is priceless, too. Read all you can on finance and investments, and make sure you read every word of the 401(k) packets, brochures, and memoranda that come from your employer each year. The payoff for spending an hour or two a week boning up on the ways of Wall Street are potentially huge, particularly as investments are starting to expand and go global. Do not be left behind.
4	**Be Aggressive**	Prudence is the proper course if you're an airplane pilot or a brain surgeon. But it is a drawback for investors—especially younger ones. Studies show that to beat inflation and make your money grow faster, a good chunk of your plan should be earmarked for higher-performing stock funds. That's not to say that you should be reckless; there's no rule that says you have to put money into stocks because your buddy in accounting did. But if you stick to conservative investments like bonds or, worse, bank savings accounts, your chances of becoming financially secure are diminished.

	Rule	Description
5	**Keep the Money Working**	The IRS can take up to 20 percent of your retirement plan assets away from you if you elect to take a lump sum payout when you leave a job. If that's not grim news, consider this: they will also tax you on the gains your money has earned while participating in the plan, and *then* penalize you 10 percent for the early withdrawal. And your state will get a slice of the pie, too—usually at 1 to 9 percent. That means you're looking at almost a 40 percent loss on that early withdrawal—if not higher. That's why keeping your money working in your retirement plan is not just your best option, it's your only option.

- **Individual Retirement Accounts (IRAs)**

  Contributing to any kind of IRA is a good idea, even if you cannot deduct your contributions. That's because the earnings in the account grow tax-free until you withdraw them. With a traditional IRA, you may be able to deduct your contributions, too. (In the following statistics, numbers are current as of 2008.)

  ➤ If you are single and have an employer-maintained retirement plan, there is good news. You can deduct the full amount of your traditional IRA contributions—up to $5,000—if your Adjusted Gross Income (AGI) is less than $53,000. You can deduct a portion of your contributions if your AGI is between $53,000 and $63,000. If your AGI is $63,000 or more, you cannot deduct any contributions. If you do not participate in an employer-maintained plan, you can deduct all your contributions, no matter how high your AGI is.

➤ If you're married and filing a joint return, the rules are a bit more complicated. If neither you nor your spouse invests in an employer-maintained retirement plan, your traditional IRA contributions are fully deductible. If you participate in such a plan, your contributions are fully deductible if your AGI is less than $85,000, partly deductible if your AGI is between $85,000 and $105,000, and nondeductible if your AGI is $105,000 or more. If your spouse participates in an employer-maintained plan but you do not, your traditional IRA contributions are fully deductible if your AGI is less than $150,000, partly deductible if your AGI is between $150,000 and $160,000, and nondeductible if your AGI is $160,000 or more.

When you hit age 70½, the IRS insists that you begin withdrawing from your traditional IRA. But the first mandatory distribution—the one for the year you turn 70½—can be put off until as late as the following April 1. Holding off trims your taxable income and your tax bill in the current year, but you must double up in the second year. In addition to the withdrawal made by April 1, another has to be made by December 31. If the resulting boost in taxable income shoves you into a higher tax bracket, your income-deferral strategy could backfire. Note that withdrawals from a traditional IRA are taxable

---

TAX TIPS

A Caveat

Cash taken out of a traditional IRA is, by and large, taxable. Smart move? Wait until year-end to take a withdrawal from your IRA. By holding off until after January 1, you can make Uncle Sam wait an extra year before he gets his share.

unless you made nondeductible contributions, in which case a portion of the withdrawal will be nontaxable.

- ## Roth IRAs

Another nice option is the Roth IRA. Contributions to a Roth IRA are not deductible, but qualified withdrawals from a Roth IRA are nontaxable.

With Roth IRAs, earnings are nontaxable when withdrawn, provided you meet the holding requirements. Also, the original contribution can be withdrawn at any time, tax- and penalty-free. Another advantage is that unlike traditional IRAs, the IRS does not require you to take a distribution from a Roth IRA when you reach age 70½.

Roth IRAs are not without some restrictions, however. As with traditional IRAs, distributions of earnings are taxable and subject to a 10 percent penalty if taken out prematurely. With a Roth, you must leave the earnings in for five years.

If you are eligible for both a deductible traditional IRA and a Roth IRA, your choice can be a difficult one. The $5,000 maximum contribution, however, can be split in any fashion you choose between a traditional or Roth IRA. You may need to balance your need for current deductions with your desire for tax-free retirement income.

- ## 401(k) Plans

These are what Wall Street types call "defined contribution" plans—meaning it is up to you to contribute money toward your retirement.

Like most investments, the more you know about 401(k)s, the better your retirement will be. For example, there is a limit on how much you can sock away in a 401(k) each year, but the limit is far above the IRA cap. For 2008, the cap was $15,500. However, workers age fifty and older by the end of the year will be allowed to make "catch up" contributions above and beyond the set dollar limitations. For 2008, the catch up amount was $5,000, setting a $20,500 contribution ceiling for a worker age fifty and older.

Clearly, Congress wants to encourage us to save for our retirements. Your personal limit depends on your salary and what percentage the company permits you to put into the retirement plan. Most firms allow contributions of between 2 and 15 percent of compensation.

▶▶▶ FAST FACT

Match Game

The big advantage of 401(k) plans is that many employers match a portion of the funds you contribute to your plan. Translated, this means free money. ◀

A 401(k) counts as a "company retirement plan" for IRS purposes. Thus, it does squeeze some of your rights to deduct traditional IRA contributions. However, by steering part of your salary into a 401(k), you may be able to boost the size of your allowable IRA deduction. Because 401(k) contributions reduce your taxable salary, they may pull your AGI down to a level that permits IRA deductions.

In return for long-term tax-deferred benefits, the IRS wants you take a hands-off approach to your 401(k) plan, making it very difficult to cash out before you retire. You may be able to get at your money early if you face financial hardship, though you have to be in pretty bad shape to qualify. Basically, you have to prove an immediate and heavy financial need—for example, an inability to pay medical bills, cover a down payment on a home, or avoid being evicted—to qualify for a hardship withdrawal. You also have to show that you do not have any other source for the cash, that your savings are depleted, and that you are unable to borrow from a bank. The IRS imposes other restrictions, too, and it is also up to your company to decide whether or not to permit hardship withdrawals and, if so, under what circumstances.

Even if your plan provides for such withdrawals, you are not home free. Hardship withdrawals made before age 59½ are subject to a 10 percent early distribution penalty. The money will also be taxed in your top bracket. The most you can pull out for hardship expenses is the total of your personal contributions to the account; you are not allowed to touch company deposits or earnings.

TAX TIPS

Leave the Job, Take the 401(k)

You can withdraw your funds from your 401(k), but, again, if it is before the year you reach age 59½ (fifty-five in qualified plans), you have to worry about the 10 percent early withdrawal penalty. There is a reprieve—the penalty is waived for the following reasons:

- Death
- Disability
- Part of a series of roughly equal payments based on your life expectancy or the joint life expectancy of you and a beneficiary
- Deductible medical expenses that exceed 7.5 percent of your Adjusted Gross Income

- **403(b) Plans**
  The Internal Revenue Code defines a 403(b) plan as a defined-contribution retirement plan available only to employees of private organizations that are tax-exempt under IRC 501(c)(3) and to educational organizations of a state, political subdivision of a state, or an agency or instrumentality of a state.

  Typically, eligible employers include nonprofit and nonpolitical religious, charitable, scientific, educational, and other public interest–oriented organizations such as private schools, colleges, universities, research institutions, and teaching hospitals. The term *qualified* is reserved for plans regulated by IRC sections 401(a) or 403(a).

The big tax advantage of 403(b) plans is the same benefit you garner from 401(k) plans: amounts contributed (other than employee after-tax contributions) and the "inside" (pre-retirement) buildup of earnings are not subject to federal income taxes until withdrawn.

In addition, like 401(k) plans, 403(b) plan participants can change the rate of contributions whenever they want. And that's not all—contributions to 403(b) plans can consist of employee elective deferrals, employer contributions, and after-tax employee contributions.

▶▶▶ FAST FACT

Match Game, Part II

As is the case with 401(k) plans, companies that provide 403(b) plans can offer matching contributions. Especially if the plan is the employer's only retirement plan, the match can be quite generous when compared to most private-sector 401(k) plans. ◀

- ### Company Pension and Profit-Sharing Plans
  If you work for a company that offers a company pension or, better yet, an employee profit sharing plan, lucky you—not a lot of companies do that any more. But if you have either one, note the tax implications. For instance, the same 10 percent penalty that hits early withdrawals from IRAs applies if you receive money from a company plan early. Although "early" is defined by the law as before you reach age 59½, an exception to the penalty means that most employees can take penalty-free payouts starting the year they reach age fifty-five. The age fifty-five exception applies if you get the payout because you

leave the job—which, of course, is usually the case. The penalty stretches to age 59½ only for withdrawals while you are still on the job. (Note that the exception applies in the year you reach age fifty-five; you do not have to be fifty-five when you leave the job and get the money as long as that birthday comes by December 31.)

The IRS is not being totally evil here—they actually want you to have money in your golden years so you don't have to work anymore. Consequently, the 10 percent penalty is designed to encourage you to roll over early payouts into an IRA—and not spend the money. Such a rollover lets you dodge the 10 percent penalty—as well as the tax—but once inside the IRA, the money is still tied up until you are at least 59½.

Buying a Home—The Stealth Investment

Ask people what their biggest investment holding is and they might mention their retirement fund or company-sponsored pension plan. And they might even be right.

 TAX TIPS

Leave the Job, Take the Pension

As with 401(k) plans, there are other exceptions to the early withdrawal penalty for pensions. At any age, it does not apply if due to:

- Death
- Disability
- Part of a series of roughly equal payments based on your life expectancy or the joint life expectancy of you and a beneficiary
- Deductible medical expenses that exceed 7.5 percent of your Adjusted Gross Income

>>> **FAST FACT**

Tax Haven

Owning a home is one of the best things you can do to reduce your taxes. Congress, in its infinite wisdom, wants Americans to own homes. That's why you can deduct many home-related expenses—including points, yearly mortgage interest, and real estate taxes—every year. Even in the face of great financial turmoil, Congress will do everything it can to encourage and reward home ownership. With that built-in advantage, it is the investment that keeps on giving, year in and year out. ◄

But for many of us, the homes we own represent our greatest investments. Homes, like stocks and mutual funds, can go up or down in value. That said, home ownership is a grand slam investment-wise, as homes historically appreciate in value and offer great tax advantages, too. Here are the key points on home ownership and taxes.

- **Mortgage Interest Paid**

  As you plan your year-end tax moves, be sure you are up to date with your payments on mortgage and home-equity loans that carry deductible interest. You may be able to beef up your home-mortgage deduction by making your December payment before year-end, even if it is not due until the following January.

- **Points on Home Mortgages**

  Points paid on a mortgage to buy your principal residence remain fully deductible in the year paid, assuming the points amount to prepaid interest, which they usually do. If you plan to settle on a home near the end of the year, closing the deal and paying the points by New Year's Eve can give you a big deduction on the tax return you file the following spring. Note that deducting points in the year of purchase is an election

TAX TIPS

Make It Right

If you make a payment on your mortgage or home-equity loan late in the year, the interest portion might not be included on the Form 1098 your lender sends you and the IRS to show how much interest was paid during the year. Watch this point carefully. If you mail the check by December 31, you get the deduction in the current year even if the lender does not register the payment until the following year. However, you will need to attach a statement to your tax return explaining the discrepancy between the Form 1098 and the amount you are deducting.

▶▶▶ FAST FACT

Tax Break on Home Sale

Single taxpayers may exclude up to $250,000 of gain from the sale of a principal or main residence. Married taxpayers filing jointly may exclude up to $500,000. This exclusion is available every two years. Any loss on the sale of a personal residence is not deductible.

To be considered the principal or main residence, the taxpayer must live in and own the home for two of the five years before the sale date. However, these periods do not have to be consecutive. ◀

and not a requirement. Amortizing points over the life of a loan is sometimes the wise tax choice. An example would be if the taxpayer purchases the home late in the year and even with the points does not have enough deductions to itemize.

- **Home-Equity Credit**
  The special status of home-equity debt offers great tax-saving opportunities. If you can exchange nondeductible personal

borrowing for deductible home-equity borrowing, you get Uncle Sam's help paying the interest on your debts. This makes home-equity lines of credit the debt of choice for millions of homeowners. These loans offer a line of credit—which you can usually tap in to simply by writing checks—secured by your home.

In addition to preserving the deductibility of interest charged, these loans often carry lower interest rates than unsecured borrowing. That makes a home-equity line of credit a powerful tool. Beyond considering this source for your future borrowing needs, you may want to tap a home-equity line to pay off higher-priced debt, such as credit cards, auto loans, and student loans.

For example, trading $10,000 of 18 percent nondeductible debt for $10,000 of 7 percent deductible debt would slice the after-tax carrying costs from $1,800 to $504 a year for a taxpayer in the 28 percent bracket.

INVESTMENT TIP:
Be Smart, Dummy

Although the tax law encourages consumers to borrow against their homes, a word of caution is necessary. To qualify for the tax deduction, these loans must be secured by your home, which means that if you find yourself unable to repay, your home is at stake. Also, many individuals who tap in to home-equity lines of credit do so through accessing over-inflated values on their homes. Finally, if the equity line of credit is used for something other than the home (i.e., to pay off credit cards) and the home subsequently drops in value and the loan gets cancelled, the cancelled loan will be treated as income—cancellation of debt income.

Thus, the home-equity line of credit has gotten a bad name of late, and has been under intense scrutiny by Congress. I mean, just look at how many people are walking away from their homes. So don't let the siren song of deductible interest pull you into a deal if you don't fully understand the risk and terms of that deal.

TAX TIPS

The Early Bird Gets the Tax Break

Buying your home early in the year will increase the mortgage interest and property taxes that you may be able to deduct—just ask Justin from the beginning of Round 5.

Mortgage interest and points are deductible as itemized deductions on Schedule A. If you buy your home later in the year, your itemized deductions may be less than your standard deduction. In that case, you are better off with the standard deduction and should amortize the points over the life of the loan.

- **Rental Property**

  As long as you actively manage a parcel of property and your Adjusted Gross Income is under $100,000, you can deduct up to $25,000 of rental losses against other income. That $25,000 allowance is phased out as your AGI moves between $100,000 and $150,000.

  Any excess losses fall into the category of "passive losses," which cannot currently be deducted unless you have "passive income" (royalties, rental income, etc.) to offset. On the other hand, another exception allows certain real estate professionals—those who spend at least half their time and a minimum of 750 hours a year tending to their real estate—to deduct their losses.

  As part of their end-of-year tax planning, owners of rental property can pull down their taxable income by scheduling and paying for repairs on their units before year-end. Be sure, too, that you are up to date on paying other deductible expenses, such as property taxes, mortgage interest, and insurance premiums. These costs will trim taxable rental income or increase your loss.

- ## Vacation Home

Got a vacation home? If yes, hopefully you have been able to tend to your fishing hole or comb your beach lately.

However, have you fully tapped in to the advantage that your vacation home offers you tax-wise? IRS rules state that if you use the vacation home for more than fourteen days, or greater than 10 percent of the number of days it is rented, the house is considered a personal residence. Thus, overuse limits your rental-expense deductions to the amount of rental income. In other words: no tax loss to offset other income.

To get this tax advantage, you will have to limit your personal use. This will permit you to pass the fourteen-day test and have your house considered a rental property. Qualifying it as a rental property lets you deduct losses under the $25,000 rule, and if you actively manage the place and your AGI is below $100,000, you won't be tripped up by the passive-loss rules.

But here's the reality check—you have to actually rent the place out! That means finding families who may want to claim part of your fishing hole or beach at different parts of the year. But if $25,000 isn't enough to help you stomach that thought, then I do not know what would be.

Inside the Ropes:
Crossing the 401(k) Threshold

Newlyweds Richard and Leah were excited. After months of house hunting, they had finally found the perfect property. The only problem was that the house cost $50,000 more than they were planning to spend.

"We knew we could get half from our parents, but that still left us $25,000 short," says Leah. "A friend at work told me I could get the rest by borrowing from my 401(k) plan, something I had not considered."

After talking with their company benefits representative, Richard and Leah discovered that they could tap in to their respective accounts early without being burned by the 10 percent penalty that normally comes with the IRS's "hardship rule" concerning taking money from retirement accounts before you retire.

"At first, it still looked like we were road-blocked," said Richard. "Basically, I could borrow no more than half of my account value, up to a maximum loan of $5,000."

"That was $7,500 for me," Leah added. "However, both of our companies provided an exception that let us borrow more for the purchase of a primary residence. And that is exactly what we planned to do."

Although the exception permitted them to borrow more, it did not relieve them of their obligation to repay the loan after five years to ensure that they wouldn't be hit with the 10 percent penalty. So, after talking it over with their companies' 401(k) advisors, Leah and Richard both took out $12,500 from their respective 401(k) accounts. Then they each set up repayment plans in which half of their future contributions would pay down the amount borrowed, ensuring that they would be paid off well in advance of the five-year mark.

"Although I couldn't carry Leah across the threshold immediately after our wedding, I was excited when I was finally able to do so," Richard said. "Even then, it was a bit difficult, as Leah was four months pregnant at the time."

➤ ROUND 9

The Main Event—*Now* You're Ready to Rumble!

Good fortune is what happens when opportunity meets with preparation.

—Thomas Edison

Much like the first time you tee up to golf, the task in front of you—preparing your taxes—will be very intimidating if you've never done it before. The bulk of that intimidation is likely to be a direct result of failing to prepare, but the task can be just as daunting for someone who has practiced and prepared, but has used bad habits all along. In fact, for this individual, the situation may be even bleaker, as he or she is confidently careening down a path of failure.

So let me reiterate a message I've been sending throughout this book: if you do not prepare, you will not perform. If you prepare poorly, you will perform poorly. And in either case, not performing and performing poorly lead to the same thing—a big bill from the IRS.

This is no different for Tiger Woods. Repeatedly, Tiger has explained that his success is due to patience and practice. "I've busted my butt on the range for hours on end and made changes to get to . . . where I'm able to compete at the highest level in major championships," he has said.

He has also made changes when confronted by poor habits. As you may know, in the middle of his stunning career, Tiger had the audacity to completely re-vamp his golf swing. "People thought it was asinine for me to change my swing after I won the Masters by twelve shots," explained Woods. "Why would you want to change that? Well, I thought I could become better. If I play my best, I'm pretty tough to beat. I'd like to play my best more frequently, and that's the whole idea. That's why you make changes."

The first eight Rounds of this book were designed to show you how to do that. Think of them as practice rounds, where you begin to understand how you can improve your game—your tax game. You organize yourself, learn the tax code, figure out tax deductions, and prepare a tax plan that covers key issues like family, home, finances, business, and education.

But this Round is the one that counts. All the long work of practice, preparation, and planning come to this one point in the year, in early spring. If you prepare yourself adequately, the execution becomes less intimidating. It also becomes less difficult, since you have organized yourself, planned, and taken advantage of all the potential deductions, exemptions, and credits out there for you. In this Round, I am going to help you pull all that information together and file your taxes. In short, it is time to win the game—time to save big bucks on your taxes.

This is the part of my job that I really love. I guess that's why they call me the Tax Lady.

What to Do on Tax Day

Now, let's take this step by step, okay?

The first item on your tax-preparation "to do" is to make sure you have all your ducks in a row, so to speak. To that end, it is a good idea to have a checklist of all the items you are going to need to complete your taxes. Not only will such a list make organizing your tax paperwork much easier, it will also save you multiple trips back and forth between your home and your tax specialist's office—or from your bedroom to your office.

Your list should look something like this:

Tax-Preparation Checklist
Personal Data
☐ Name(s) and Social Security number(s)
☐ Name(s) and individual taxpayer identification number(s)
☐ Childcare provider(s)—name, address, taxpayer identification number
☐ Alimony—name and Social Security number of individual paid
Employment/Income Data
☐ Form W-2 (wages and salary)
☐ Form 1099-G (unemployment compensation, state and local tax refunds)
☐ Form 1099-Misc (royalties, other income)
☐ Form 1099-C (cancelled debt)
☐ Form 1099-R (annuities and pensions)
☐ Form RRB-1099 (Social Security—RR1 benefits)
☐ Schedule K-1 (partnership, S corporation, trust income)
☐ W-2G (gambling/lottery winnings)
☐ Jury duty pay received
☐ Prizes/awards
☐ Scholarships/fellowships/grants
☐ Alimony received

Tax-Preparation Checklist

Self-Employment Data

☐ Form 1099-Misc (non-employee compensation)/own records

☐ Schedule K-1 (partnership SE income)

☐ Receipts/own records for business-related expenses

☐ Receipts/own records for farm-related expenses

☐ Payment records for employment and other business taxes paid

Homeowner/Renter Data

☐ Residential address(es) for this year

☐ Form 1098 (mortgage/second mortgage interest paid)

☐ Form 1099-S (sale of home or other real estate)

☐ Form 1099-Misc (rent)

☐ Real estate taxes paid

☐ Receipts/own records of rent paid during the tax year

☐ Receipts/own records of moving expenses

Financial Assets/Income Data

☐ Form 1099-INT & 1099-OID (interest income)

☐ Form 1099-DIV (dividend income statements)

☐ Form 1099-B (proceeds from broker transactions)

☐ Form 1099-R (retirement plan distribution)

☐ Form 1099-SA (distributions from medical savings accounts)

Financial Liabilities

☐ Form 1098-E (student loan interest paid)

☐ Form 1098-T (qualified tuition)

☐ Early withdrawal penalties (CDs, IRAs, etc.)

Tax-Preparation Checklist

Automobiles

- ☐ Receipts/own records of personal property taxes paid
- ☐ Automobile loans/leases (account numbers and car value)

Expenses

- ☐ Form 1099-Q (qualified education program expenses)
- ☐ Medical savings accounts (name, account number, etc.)
- ☐ Receipts/own records for medical expenses
- ☐ Receipts/own records of investment expenses
- ☐ Receipts/own records for job-hunting expenses
- ☐ Receipts/own records of non-reimbursed expenses for job
- ☐ Receipts/own records for job-related education expenses
- ☐ Receipts/own records of non-reimbursed expenses for volunteer work
- ☐ Receipts/own records of gifts to charity
- ☐ Receipts/own records for adoption expenses
- ☐ Receipts/own records for alimony paid
- ☐ Receipts/own records for tax return preparation expenses and fees
- ☐ Travel log

Miscellaneous Tax Documents

- ☐ Receipts/other records for federal, state, and local estimated taxes paid
- ☐ Receipts/other records for IRA, Keogh, retirement plan contributions
- ☐ Records documenting casualty/theft losses
- ☐ Records for other deductible expenditures
- ☐ Records for other revenue or sales of property that may be taxable

TAX TIPS

Key Tax Forms

Having the following tax forms at the ready is a good idea:

Form	Title	Description
1040	U.S. Individual Income Tax Return	The most commonly used tax form (covered in Round 4). The 1040 reports all types of income. You must use this form if your taxable income is $100,000 or more, you itemize your deductions, or you received nontaxable dividends.
1040A	U.S. Individual Income Tax Return (Abbreviated)	A condensed version of Form 1040 that can be filed if you meet certain requirements, including having a taxable income of under $100,000 that comes only from certain sources, not itemizing your deductions, and not owing any employment taxes on wages you paid to a household employee.
1040EZ	U.S. Individual Income Tax Return for Single and Joint Filers with No Dependents	The simplest IRS tax form, 1040EZ is limited to those taxpayers who meet certain requirements, including having a taxable income of under $50,000, no dependents, and a filing status that is single or married filing jointly.
W-2	Wage, Salary, and Taxes	Must be filed by employers for each employee from whom income, Social Security, or Medicare taxes have been withheld.

Form	Title	Description
W-4	Employee's Withholding Allowance Certificate	You should complete this form with your employer so that the correct amount of federal income tax will be withheld from your pay.
1099-DIV	Dividends and Distributions	For mutual fund investors, the 1099-DIV reports the type of distribution you received from your mutual fund. It also includes any dividends, capital gain distributions, foreign tax paid, nontaxable distributions, and federal income tax withheld.
1099-R	Distributions from Retirement	Reports all distributions from retirement accounts during the year, except fund exchanges and transfers of assets.
1099-MISC	Miscellaneous	Reports income from any source that does not have a specialized form. Often used by the self-employed or independent contractors.
1099-B	Proceeds from Broker and Barter Exchange Transactions	A form mailed to shareholders that reports proceeds from the sale of shares through fund redemptions or exchanges from non-money market accounts.

Source: Internal Revenue Service

If you lack these or any other forms that you think you will need to complete your tax return, you can download the forms—other than the W-2 and 1099—directly at www.irs.gov.

Keep It Quiet

In my mind, the physical act of doing your tax returns can be as
. . . well . . . *taxing* as the mental part. That is why it's a good idea
to be as comfortable as possible when you start preparing your tax
return.

If you are doing your taxes on your own, try getting away from
the usual household interruptions. You do not need kids screaming,
cell phones ringing, and the television blaring while you're trying
to fill out your tax forms. Pick a quiet room, like a home office or a
corner of your bedroom, and set up shop there. Put a DO NOT DISTURB
sign on the door if you have to—make it clear to one and all that
you are off duty for a while and do not want any interruptions. Have
a big mug of coffee or tea on hand, with a sandwich or snack available to keep your energy up.

For me? I, unfortunately, have to turn off the Giants game,
unplug the telephone, and really get focused. That means no day-
dreaming about surfing, no drop-ins by my siblings, and absolutely
no talk about the law firm. Unplugging from your day job is universal—even when you're the Tax Lady.

Filing a Clean Tax Return: Strategies You Can Use

Okay, so now you are safely tucked away in a quiet nook, checklist
and cappuccino in hand. The house is quiet and you have all your
paperwork at your fingertips. If you are working on a computer,
bookmark a handy tax-planning website (like, dare I say, www.rdtc.
com, for example). If not, keep a copy of this book or another tax
reference guide nearby as well. The point is to have some kind of
help available to consult if you hit a sticking point.

TAX TIPS

Before You Get Started

Here are some helpful hints to remember before even starting your return:

Hint	Description
Use a Computer	Anyone who has ever tried to read a doctor's handwriting on a prescription can appreciate how much easier it is to read a cleanly presented, computer-generated document instead. IRS staffers are no different. They have to be able to read a great deal of information on each tax return, and a sloppily written return will only slow them down—and increase your chances of having your return incorrectly processed.
Be Exact	When the IRS sees a tax return with numbers that are all rounded off and lots of zeroes, as opposed to accurately presented (ex: $10,000 vs. $9,999.57), that is a big red flag that the taxpayer is estimating the numbers. This could increase your chance of being audited. Rounding is acceptable, so long as you limit your rounding to the "change" (i.e., the $0.57 in $9,999.57).
Maintain Good Records	Record keeping was covered in Round 2, but it bears repeating that good document management is vital around tax time. So make sure to hang on to copies of all tax documents you will use to prepare your return.

As you complete your tax forms, cross-reference your allowable deductions and credits with a pre-made list that includes those you believe you are entitled to. That way you have a backup system and reduce your chance of missing out on a money-saver. Use a good, dependable calculator to tally all your numbers, and always double-check every number you intend to include on your taxes.

TAX TIPS

Form 1040

Form **1040**	Department of the Treasury—Internal Revenue Service **U.S. Individual Income Tax Return** 2008	(99)	IRS Use Only—Do not write or staple in this space.

For the year Jan. 1–Dec. 31, 2008, or other tax year beginning , 2008, ending , 20

OMB No. 1545-0074

Label (See instructions on page 14.) Use the IRS label. Otherwise, please print or type.

Your first name and initial | Last name | Your social security number

If a joint return, spouse's first name and initial | Last name | Spouse's social security number

Home address (number and street). If you have a P.O. box, see page 14. | Apt. no.

▲ You **must** enter your SSN(s) above. ▲

City, town or post office, state, and ZIP code. If you have a foreign address, see page 14.

Checking a box below will not change your tax or refund.

Presidential Election Campaign ▶ Check here if you, or your spouse if filing jointly, want $3 to go to this fund (see page 14) ▶ ☐ You ☐ Spouse

Filing Status
Check only one box.

1 ☐ Single
2 ☐ Married filing jointly (even if only one had income)
3 ☐ Married filing separately. Enter spouse's SSN above and full name here. ▶
4 ☐ Head of household (with qualifying person). (See page 15.) If the qualifying person is a child but not your dependent, enter this child's name here. ▶
5 ☐ Qualifying widow(er) with dependent child (see page 16)

Exemptions

6a ☐ **Yourself.** If someone can claim you as a dependent, **do not** check box 6a
b ☐ **Spouse**

Boxes checked on 6a and 6b
No. of children on 6c who:
• lived with you
• did not live with you due to divorce or separation (see page 18)
Dependents on 6c not entered above
Add numbers on lines above ▶

c **Dependents:**

(1) First name Last name	(2) Dependent's social security number	(3) Dependent's relationship to you	(4) ✓ if qualifying child for child tax credit (see page 17)
			☐
			☐
			☐
			☐

If more than four dependents, see page 17.

d Total number of exemptions claimed

Income

Attach Form(s) W-2 here. Also attach Forms W-2G and 1099-R if tax was withheld.

If you did not get a W-2, see page 21.

Enclose, but do not attach, any payment. Also, please use Form 1040-V.

7	Wages, salaries, tips, etc. Attach Form(s) W-2	7	
8a	**Taxable** interest. Attach Schedule B if required	8a	
b	Tax-exempt interest. **Do not** include on line 8a	8b	
9a	Ordinary dividends. Attach Schedule B if required	9a	
b	Qualified dividends (see page 21)	9b	
10	Taxable refunds, credits, or offsets of state and local income taxes (see page 22)	10	
11	Alimony received	11	
12	Business income or (loss). Attach Schedule C or C-EZ	12	
13	Capital gain or (loss). Attach Schedule D if required. If not required, check here ▶ ☐	13	
14	Other gains or (losses). Attach Form 4797	14	
15a	IRA distributions 15a	b Taxable amount (see page 23)	15b	
16a	Pensions and annuities 16a	b Taxable amount (see page 24)	16b	
17	Rental real estate, royalties, partnerships, S corporations, trusts, etc. Attach Schedule E	17	
18	Farm income or (loss). Attach Schedule F	18	
19	Unemployment compensation	19	
20a	Social security benefits 20a	b Taxable amount (see page 26)	20b	
21	Other income. List type and amount (see page 28)	21	
22	Add the amounts in the far right column for lines 7 through 21. This is your **total income** ▶	22	

Adjusted Gross Income

23	Educator expenses (see page 28)	23	
24	Certain business expenses of reservists, performing artists, and fee-basis government officials. Attach Form 2106 or 2106-EZ	24	
25	Health savings account deduction. Attach Form 8889	25	
26	Moving expenses. Attach Form 3903	26	
27	One-half of self-employment tax. Attach Schedule SE	27	
28	Self-employed SEP, SIMPLE, and qualified plans	28	
29	Self-employed health insurance deduction (see page 29)	29	
30	Penalty on early withdrawal of savings	30	
31a	Alimony paid b Recipient's SSN ▶	31a	
32	IRA deduction (see page 30)	32	
33	Student loan interest deduction (see page 33)	33	
34	Tuition and fees deduction. Attach Form 8917	34	
35	Domestic production activities deduction. Attach Form 8903	35	
36	Add lines 23 through 31a and 32 through 35	36	
37	Subtract line 36 from line 22. This is your **adjusted gross income** ▶	37	

For Disclosure, Privacy Act, and Paperwork Reduction Act Notice, see page 88.   Cat. No. 11320B   Form **1040** (2008)

Form 1040 (2008)			Page **2**

Tax and Credits

	38	Amount from line 37 (adjusted gross income)	38	
	39a	Check { You were born before January 2, 1944, ☐ Blind. } Total boxes		
		if: { Spouse was born before January 2, 1944, ☐ Blind. } checked ▶ 39a		
	b	If your spouse itemizes on a separate return or you were a dual-status alien, see page 34 and check here ▶ 39b ☐		
	c	Check if standard deduction includes real estate taxes or disaster loss (see page 34) ▶ 39c ☐		

Standard Deduction for—

- People who checked any box on line 39a, 39b, or 39c or who can be claimed as a dependent, see page 34.
- All others:

Single or Married filing separately, $5,450

Married filing jointly or Qualifying widow(er), $10,900

Head of household, $8,000

	40	Itemized deductions (from Schedule A) **or** your **standard deduction** (see left margin) .	40	
	41	Subtract line 40 from line 38	41	
	42	If line 38 is over $119,975, or you provided housing to a Midwestern displaced individual, see page 36. Otherwise, multiply $3,500 by the total number of exemptions claimed on line 6d .	42	
	43	**Taxable income.** Subtract line 42 from line 41. If line 42 is more than line 41, enter -0-	43	
	44	**Tax** (see page 36). Check if any tax is from: **a** ☐ Form(s) 8814 **b** ☐ Form 4972	44	
	45	**Alternative minimum tax** (see page 39). Attach Form 6251	45	
	46	Add lines 44 and 45 . . . . ▶	46	
	47	Foreign tax credit. Attach Form 1116 if required	47	
	48	Credit for child and dependent care expenses. Attach Form 2441	48	
	49	Credit for the elderly or the disabled. Attach Schedule R . .	49	
	50	Education credits. Attach Form 8863	50	
	51	Retirement savings contributions credit. Attach Form 8880 .	51	
	52	Child tax credit (see page 42). Attach Form 8901 if required .	52	
	53	Credits from Form: **a** ☐ 8396 **b** ☐ 8839 **c** ☐ 5695	53	
	54	Other credits from Form: **a** ☐ 3800 **b** ☐ 8801 **c** ☐	54	
	55	Add lines 47 through 54. These are your **total credits**	55	
	56	Subtract line 55 from line 46. If line 55 is more than line 46, enter -0- . . . . ▶	56	

Other Taxes

	57	Self-employment tax. Attach Schedule SE	57	
	58	Unreported social security and Medicare tax from Form: **a** ☐ 4137 **b** ☐ 8919	58	
	59	Additional tax on IRAs, other qualified retirement plans, etc. Attach Form 5329 if required .	59	
	60	Additional taxes: **a** ☐ AEIC payments **b** ☐ Household employment taxes. Attach Schedule H	60	
	61	Add lines 56 through 60. This is your **total tax** . . . . ▶	61	

Payments

If you have a qualifying child, attach Schedule EIC.

	62	Federal income tax withheld from Forms W-2 and 1099 . .	62	
	63	2008 estimated tax payments and amount applied from 2007 return	63	
	64a	**Earned income credit (EIC)**	64a	
	b	Nontaxable combat pay election 64b		
	65	Excess social security and tier 1 RRTA tax withheld (see page 61)	65	
	66	Additional child tax credit. Attach Form 8812	66	
	67	Amount paid with request for extension to file (see page 61)	67	
	68	Credits from Form: **a** ☐ 2439 **b** ☐ 4136 **c** ☐ 8801 **d** ☐ 8885	68	
	69	First-time homebuyer credit. Attach Form 5405	69	
	70	Recovery rebate credit (see worksheet on pages 62 and 63) .	70	
	71	Add lines 62 through 70. These are your **total payments** . . . . ▶	71	

Refund

Direct deposit? See page 63 and fill in 73b, 73c, and 73d, or Form 8888.

	72	If line 71 is more than line 61, subtract line 61 from line 71. This is the amount you **overpaid**	72	
	73a	Amount of line 72 you want **refunded to you.** If Form 8888 is attached, check here ▶ ☐	73a	
▶	b	Routing number [ ] ▶ **c** Type: ☐ Checking ☐ Savings		
▶	d	Account number [ ]		
	74	Amount of line 72 you want **applied to your 2009 estimated tax** ▶ 74		

Amount You Owe

	75	**Amount you owe.** Subtract line 71 from line 61. For details on how to pay, see page 65 ▶	75	
	76	Estimated tax penalty (see page 65) 76		

Third Party Designee

Do you want to allow another person to discuss this return with the IRS (see page 66)? ☐ **Yes.** Complete the following. ☐ **No**

Designee's name ▶   Phone no. ▶ ( )   Personal identification number (PIN) ▶

Sign Here

Joint return? See page 15.

Keep a copy for your records.

Under penalties of perjury, I declare that I have examined this return and accompanying schedules and statements, and to the best of my knowledge and belief, they are true, correct, and complete. Declaration of preparer (other than taxpayer) is based on all information of which preparer has any knowledge.

Your signature	Date	Your occupation	Daytime phone number
			( )
Spouse's signature. If a joint return, **both** must sign.	Date	Spouse's occupation	

Paid Preparer's Use Only

Preparer's signature ▶		Date	Check if self-employed ☐	Preparer's SSN or PTIN
Firm's name (or yours if self-employed), address, and ZIP code ▶			EIN	
			Phone no.	( )

Form **1040** (2008)

✪ *Printed on recycled paper*

Source: Internal Revenue Service

Cover Your Tracks

When you finish your taxes, run through your return again to make sure there's nothing you missed. Don't forget to review these key items before sending your taxes off:

Item	Reminder
Signature	Did you sign the return? Yes, this seems like an obvious point, but the IRS says that unsigned tax returns are one of the most common taxpayer mistakes.
Filing Status	The wrong tax category could cost you plenty in deductions and credits. Also, make sure you only check off one filing status category. Listing more than one could get your return disallowed.
Social Security Number	Another area where many taxpayers err. Without your Social Security number—or with the wrong one—the IRS will not process your return. Also, add your Social Security number to each page of your tax return so that if a page gets lost, the IRS will know where it goes.
Allowable Exemptions	Make sure you include the right number of exemptions on your tax form. At $3,500 for each exemption, that is one tax savings you do not want to miss.
Tax Forms	If you are adding additional IRS forms to your 1040 or 1040A, make sure they are included in the correct order. Again, this might appear to be a minor point, but delivering the forms in sequential order makes it easier for IRS staffers to read—and much easier for you to get the deductions you have coming without mistakes being made.

Item	Reminder
Who's on Your Check?	Many Americans who owe Uncle Sam make their checks payable to the Internal Revenue Service. Actually, checks should be made payable to the United States Treasury. Also, include as much information on your check as possible, like your name, address, telephone number, e-mail address, and Social Security number. Do not staple the check to your return because they are handled separately when the IRS gets them.

How Should You Pay?

The good news is you finished your taxes with a minimum fuss. The bad news finds you reaching for your pocketbook to cut a check to Uncle Sam for taxes owed. The silver lining, in this instance, is that there are more ways to pay your tax bill than by check alone. Personal checks, money orders, credit cards, and direct debit from your bank account are all accepted methods of paying your taxes.

Here is a snapshot of each:

Payment Type	Advice
Personal Checks	Most people pay by check, especially those who file the old-fashioned way. If this is your preferred payment method, make sure to sign the check and include your Social Security number on the front. Put the tax year and "Form 1040" on your check as well.
Bank Account Debit	Online filers are big fans of direct debit. It is easy and quick, and you get a confirmation notice from the bank letting you know that proceeds from your checking or savings account have been used to pay your taxes. A bonus: if you want to file early, but don't want to pay early, notify your tax preparer or indicate in your tax-preparation software that you want the payment to be deducted from your bank account on April 15.

Payment Type	Advice
Credit Card	American Express, MasterCard, Visa, and Discover cardholders can use their plastic to cover their tax tabs. Charge your taxes by calling 1-800-2PAY-TAX or 1-888-PAY-1040. Or you can pay over the Internet at www.officialpayments.com or www.pay1040.com. A bonus—you may also earn some reward points (a minus—you may incur service charges).
ATM or Debit Card	You can pay by ATM or debit card by calling 1-866-4PAY-TAX or 1-866-213-0675. Pay over the Internet at www.officialpaymentsdebit.com or www.incometaxpayments.com. A caveat—you will have to pay a $2.95 surcharge.

 T A X   T I P S

Install It

If you cannot pay what you owe to the IRS, you can apply to pay via an Installment Agreement. However, this is pending IRS review and approval. You can apply by completing IRS Form 9465 at the same time you file your return.

If you get the thumbs-up from Uncle Sam, you will have to make monthly payments to the IRS based on an agreed-upon figure. There is a fee if the IRS approves the Installment Agreement: $105. However, the fee is reduced to $52 if you make your payments by electronic funds withdrawal, or $43 if you fall under poverty levels set by the IRS (see IRS Form 13844, Application for Reduced User Fee for Installment Agreements, for more information).

Note that if you are already paying the IRS via an Installment Agreement because you owed taxes in previous years and you have not completely paid off those previous years, you won't be able to start a new plan until the bill is paid. Since penalties and interests do come in to play, a bank line of credit or loan may be a smarter financial option than the Installment Agreement.

>>> **FAST FACT**

Watch the Fees

If you pay your taxes by credit card, your card company will likely charge you a "convenience fee" of up to $50. ◄

Sending Your Tax Return to the IRS

Back in the days when pencil-pushing accountants walked the earth, the best way to send your tax return to the IRS was by mailing it— first class, preferably.

While you can certainly still do that, filing your taxes electronically through the Internet is now a fast, safe, and dependable option. Why go the e-route? Filing electronically makes sure your return cannot be lost in the mail—you will get an acknowledgment that the IRS received your forms—and should get you your refund a few weeks faster than if you use the mail.

According to the IRS, 57.8 percent of Americans filed their taxes electronically in the most recent tax year. There is much to be said for doing so. As mentioned above, the completed tax return, absent of messy pencil markings and illegible script, is much cleaner-looking. The prevalence of online calculators has also helped eliminate tax calculations scribbled on the backs of barroom napkins. And hey, the fewer errors you make, the more deductions you get and the more of your own money you keep.

>>> **FAST FACT**

Who Takes Credit?

The IRS has authorized two companies to accept credit and debit card payments: Official Payments Corporation and Link2Gov Corporation. ◄

If you file your taxes electronically, you will also likely get your refund check sooner, as computer-generated tax forms are easier—and less mistake-prone—for the IRS to process.

Most online tax accounting software packages offer direct access to the IRS via electronic filing—for example, visit RDTC.com. But note that the IRS does not accept e-file delivery of tax returns directly. You have to use a third party (like, hypothetically, Roni Deutch Tax Center) or your local accountant to electronically deliver your taxes to Uncle Sam.

If e-filing sounds like a good deal to you, here are the various ways you can do it:

E-Filing Options	
METHOD	**DESCRIPTION**
Authorized Tax Professional	Professional tax preparers—like Roni Deutch Tax Center—are authorized by the U.S. government to e-file your tax returns.
Online/Computerized Tax-Preparation Software	You can file your taxes yourself if you use some of the more prominent tax software packages available on the market.

And guess what: you can e-file your state taxes just like your federal taxes. Make sure to check your state tax office for requirements, but all states with income taxes now permit them to be filed electronically. You may want to check with your state tax office to see if their other options are even more convenient for you, though.

The Sting of Rejection

If for some reason the IRS rejects your e-filed tax return, what you do next depends on the reason your return was rejected. If the return was rejected because you misspelled a name or made a mistake in a Social Security number or birth date, you can fix these errors and resubmit the return to the IRS. Other errors will cause you to have to file a paper return. Refer to your reject error messages for specific re-filing instructions.

Also, be sure to check your e-file status. If you filed before the April 15 deadline, you have until April 20 to re-submit. If you do not feel you can quickly fix the problem that caused the reject, you should file a paper return just to be safe. Print and attach a copy of your rejection message to your return. If you print this rejection message and mail it along with your return, the IRS will consider your return filed on time, so long as the rejection message indicates that the attempt to e-file was before the due date. You also need to write TIMELY FILED REJECTED ELECTRONIC RETURN across the top of your paper Form 1040, 1040A, or 1040EZ.

►►► FAST FACT

Rejection Notice

If your e-filed return was rejected by the IRS, your return deadline for e-filing corrections is April 20. If you cannot correct your return electronically, you must print and mail your return to the IRS within ten days of the rejection notice. ◄

Snail Mail Is Okay, Too

If you are old-school, and online delivery of your taxes makes you skittish, go ahead and send your tax returns by registered mail. You can also send them by certified mail, although it is highly unlikely your taxes will get lost in the mail. But certified only cost a few bucks extra, and if that ensures your return is delivered and delivered on time, then it's worth twice the price.

Besides, even if your return is misplaced or destroyed, chances are good that the IRS will believe that you filed on time if you have a copy of the signed and dated return. If you have a refund coming, remember, there is no penalty for filing late anyway.

T A X   T I P S

More than Peace of Mind

If you owe a big chunk of money to the IRS, using certified mail is a good idea. The penalties for late filing rise with the amount of tax owed with your return, so the more money potentially at stake, the more valuable the peace of mind you get by using certified mail. In addition, a recent change means a receipt from a private delivery service, such as FedEx or UPS, will be accepted by the IRS as proof that your return was filed on time.

Express Line

The IRS has authorized the following express delivery firms to handle delivery of tax returns:

Company	Services
Airborne Express	Overnight air express, next afternoon, second-day service
DHL Worldwide Express	Same day, USA overnight
FedEx	Priority overnight, standard overnight, two-day delivery
UPS	Next-day air, next-day air saver, second-day air, second-day air AM, worldwide express, worldwide express plus
USPS	All

It's April 15 and You Forgot to File

Don't worry. The world is not going to end. Many people fail to prepare and file their tax returns by April 15.

However, just because there are a lot of people in your boat, doesn't mean it isn't sinking. So, please take the following steps to ensure you stay afloat and don't fall victim to drowning in tax debt or being attacked by sharks, err, the IRS:

- File your tax returns immediately. Remember, you might not owe, and tax refunds expire in three years.
- Pay what you can right away.
- Get a bank loan to pay what you owe.
- Enter into a formal Installment Agreement with the IRS (requires IRS approval, filing of IRS Form 9465, and a fee). This will allow you to pay off the rest of what you owe over time.

It is important that you take direct action to rectify this situation—the stakes can get high in a hurry. If you neglect to file your return or forget to file for an extension by April 15, you may receive a "failure to file" penalty ($100 or 100 percent of the amount due, whichever is less)—plus compounded daily interest on taxes due will accrue starting from April 15.

If you do not file on time, you will be responsible for monthly payments plus interest on the remainder due. Remember, the IRS

 TAX TIPS

Send What You Can, Even If It's Nothing

If you can't pay Uncle Sam what you owe by April 15, go ahead and file your tax return and pay whatever you can. The IRS will bill you for the rest. You will owe interest on the balance, and you may owe a late payment penalty.

As you will learn in Round 10, it is important that you file your return as soon as possible, even if you can't pay anything then, because doing so establishes the earliest possible expiration date for the IRS to collect the amount you owe. If the IRS fails to collect the principal balance, interest, or penalties on a debt by its expiration date, the debt disappears.

may garnish your paycheck, levy your bank account, or even put liens on your property to get their money.

Filing for an Extension

If, after all your preparation and hard work, you still can't manage to finish your taxes on time, don't despair. Uncle Sam believes in second chances, so you can always file an extension.

In fact, you can get an automatic six-month extension (until October 15) and avoid a late filing penalty by filing IRS Form 4868. Extensions should be filed whether you have a balance due or are expecting a refund. Here are the rules of the road when it comes to filing an extension:

Extension Filing Checklist
☐ File IRS Form 4868, Application for Automatic Extension of Time to File, on or before April 15.
☐ File a separate extension for your state income tax return.
☐ Pay at least 90 percent of the tax due on your return (through withholding, estimated tax payments, or a lump sum payment) before April 15.
☐ To avoid interest, pay 100 percent of the tax due before April 15.
☐ Save the remaining tax due (by reducing spending or increasing savings) over the next six months.
☐ Prepare your return.
☐ File your return and pay the balance due by no later than October 15.

An extension will be granted even if the balance due is not paid in full, but your extension request must be postmarked on or before midnight, April 15.

TAX TIPS

Pay Up

While filing Form 4868 gives you more time to file, it does not give you more time to pay. To avoid a late payment penalty, you must pay 90 percent of your taxes by April 15.

Filing an Amended Return

Americans are so busy these days that losing car keys and forgetting to water the plants are just unfortunate byproducts of our chaotic lives. And we can be just as forgetful about our taxes. Fortunately, that's why the U.S. tax code has the amended return.

Known formally as Form 1040X, the amended return allows us to right some wrongs on our completed—and mailed—tax returns. So if you forgot a key deduction or missed that education tax credit, you are not completely out of luck.

According to the IRS, their service center will usually correct errors in math, or request forms (such as W-2s) or schedules you left out. In these instances, you do not need to amend your return, but must simply provide the requested information.

That said, you do need to file an amended return if any of the following were reported incorrectly:

- Filing status
- Total income
- Deductions
- Credits

Changes requiring an amended return include:

- Failure to report some income
- Errors in computing deductions or credits

- Claiming additional exemptions, deductions, or credits
- Change in filing status

You should also file an amended return if you made a mathematical error calculating an entry on a form or on a worksheet that is not attached to your return that changes your tax liability.

Amending Your Return

The IRS is pretty clear about the steps to take in filing an amended return. You will need to file an amended return and include copies of any schedules that have been changed or any W-2s you did not include with your original return. Also include forms and schedules for any new credits or deductions not claimed on the original return. You do not need to send a copy of your original Form 1040EZ, 1040A, or 1040.

The form must be filed within three years from the date you filed the original return or within two years from the date you paid the tax, whichever is later. You cannot send an amended tax return electronically. An amended return must be filed on a paper Form 1040X, Amended U.S. Individual Income Tax Return.

Form 1040X is not very complicated. It is designed with three columns. Column A is used to show the figures from the original return. Column C is used to show the correct figures. The difference between the figures in Columns A and C is shown in Column B. On the back of the form, you need to explain the specific changes being made on the return and the reason for each change. If the changes involve another schedule or form, attach it to Form 1040X. Be sure to enter the year of the return you are amending.

To check the status of an amended return, contact the IRS assistance line at 1-800-829-1040. Amended/corrected returns are processed as quickly as possible, but could take twelve weeks or longer.

>>> **FAST FACT**

State Tax Tip

Just because you had to file an amended return with the IRS doesn't mean you have to file an amended state tax return, too. Generally you only have to file an amended state return if the changes to your federal return affect your state tax liability. Some states require you to report the changes within a specified time after filing the federal amended return. ◄

Special Filing Situations

Not all Americans live in the U.S., so the IRS compensates our overseas citizens with some special tax filing breaks.

For instance, if you live abroad but are a U.S. citizen, you get an automatic two-month extension to complete and file your return. That goes for any citizen living outside the U.S. or Puerto Rico and for our U.S. military men and women.

As some unscrupulous types sought to take advantage of this situation in years past by skipping the country for a few days around April 15, you will need to prove to the IRS where you live and why you live there. There is no special form to fill out—U.S. citizens living abroad use the same tax forms they would use if they lived in New York or Iowa.

>>> **FAST FACT**

Common Refund Delays

The most common causes of tax refund delay according to the IRS include math errors, an address change after filing the return, a name on the tax return that doesn't match Social Security records, failure to sign the return, and not sending the necessary attachments, such as W-2s or schedules.

Any of these gaffes could cause your refund to be delayed by an additional eight weeks. ◄

TAX TIPS

Some Common Tax Return Mistakes

Top Eight Tax Return Mistakes	
1	**Incorrect Identification Numbers/Names for Dependents** Put in a child's name that is not recognized or the wrong Social Security number and the IRS may not provide an exemption or may not recognize a full child tax credit or earned income credit. This will also delay processing.
2	**Primary Social Security Number Is Incorrect/Illegible** This very common error causes processing problems and slows things up.
3	**Earned Income Tax Credit Calculated Incorrectly** Many taxpayers are entitled to this unique credit, which can increase the amount of your refund, but knowing whether you qualify and getting the proper amount can be tricky.
4	**Child Tax Credit Calculated Incorrectly** Parents of children under eighteen may qualify for a credit of up to $1,000 per child, but it is not always easy to tell how much applies to you.
5	**Taxable Amount of Social Security Calculated Incorrectly** For retirees, it is often difficult to tell how much of your Social Security is subject to tax.
6	**Refund Amount/Amount Owed Calculated Incorrectly** Math errors and misunderstanding the tax tables are extremely common.

Top Eight Tax Return Mistakes	
7	**Prompting IRS Recalculation Using Single-Filing Status** Your tax bill depends on your filing status. Pick another status when you should have chosen "single" and you will owe more.
8	**Failing to Sign the Return** It happens all the time.

Inside the Ropes: Claudia's Hurrah

Claudia always paid her bills on time. But when the fifty-two-year-old self-employed benefits consultant found her business slumping after a year when a tough economy held sway, she realized she would not have enough cash on hand to pay her tax bill.

"It felt like I had been punched in the stomach when I realized that I'd be a few grand short of what I needed to pay up," says Claudia. "Once the shock wore off, I had to begin thinking about how I could raise the money."

After doing some research, Claudia discovered she had a few options: pay the bill by credit card, apply for an installment payment plan with the IRS, or dip in to her home equity line of credit. "I didn't want to raid my retirement account because the tax penalties were too high," she explains. "And, while I considered using the credit card, I didn't want that heavy an interest rate load at this point in my life. The installment plan looked promising, until I found out there was a $105 processing fee and that there would be interest and penalties."

That left her $50,000 bank line of credit, which she had secured a few years before, at 4.5 percent interest. "I'd originally gotten it to finish our basement," she adds. "Once we did that, I paid it right off." All Claudia had to do was write a check against her line of credit and mail it off to the IRS—and then begin working hard to pay off the debt.

"I wasn't thrilled about having to borrow against the equity on my home," Claudia says. "But in the end, it was the best option for me."

Not every taxpayer has the luxury of cutting a check and paying the IRS in a single lump sum payment. In our next Round, we will explore some of the additional options Claudia may have been able to pursue, given her financial situation.

➤ ROUND 10

Boom! Eliminating Tax Debt . . .
Or Surviving an IRS Audit

If the IRS took a thousand taxpayers at random and purposefully sent each an incorrect notice that they owed an extra $92.35 in taxes and interest, more than two-thirds would probably just send in a check without investigating it any further.

—Anonymous

Humorist Dave Barry summed up taxpayer attitudes toward dealing with the IRS when he wrote, "All that happens is, you take your financial records to the IRS office and they put you into a tank filled with giant, stinging leeches. Many taxpayers are pleasantly surprised to find that they die within hours."

Although he was speaking about an IRS audit, dealing with IRS tax debt is not any more pleasant. It may in fact be a little more painful. Well, one thing I am *not* going to tell you in this Round is that dealing with the IRS is all gumdrops and sunshine. Because, well, it's not. Instead, I'm going to explain the basic frameworks of the two situations you don't want to find yourself in—tax debt or a tax audit.

And this is not because I think that's where you're headed. Heck no! Especially if you have been adopting some of the advice contained in the previous Rounds. However, you might be reading this book because you are already behind the eight ball when it comes to tax debt or a tax audit. Alternatively, this might be a good time to scare you, to make you appreciate the stakes at hand. If that's what it takes to get you to develop better tax habits, then so be it. Either way, I have great advice for you.

What Is Tax Debt?

IRS tax debt is just like any other type of debt. It occurs when a taxpayer does not pay enough to account for his or her tax liability. This can happen because the taxpayer failed to withhold enough taxes from his or her paycheck, didn't make large enough estimated tax payments throughout the year, and/or could not pay the difference by the due date of the return. Once the IRS processes the return and assesses the balance due, the taxpayer will owe the IRS back taxes. Bummer!

So, you ask, why can't the taxpayer just pay the taxes? Well, there is nothing barring a taxpayer from paying the taxes, except for the fact that he or she usually cannot afford it.

As I said, tax debt is just like any other debt. Granted, it might accumulate due to some ignorance on the part of the taxpayer, however it typically goes unpaid because the individual just cannot afford to pay it off or even pay it down. This could be due to any hardship the individual is facing—e.g., losing a job, losing a loved one, experiencing a medical emergency, going through substance abuse, or going through a divorce.

Not to mention the fact that the IRS is not generally high on people's list of priorities for payment. More than likely, people are going to purchase food, fuel, clothing, medicine, or self-medication before they decide to perform their annual civic duty and pay their taxes.

>>> **FAST FACT**

Stealth Tax Debt

There are two additional ways a tax debt can be assessed against a taxpayer:

- **Under/Unreported Income**
  Back taxes can be assessed against a filed and paid federal income tax return when the return failed to account for all income earned during the previous year. This means that the taxpayer prepared, filed, and paid his or her federal income tax return, but failed to include all of the income he or she earned throughout the year. Remember that the IRS receives records from all employers and financial institutions showing all amounts paid to taxpayers throughout the year, so if the IRS records do not match what the taxpayer claimed on the return, the taxpayer may face an unreported or underreported income issue. If the taxpayer does not promptly account for the disparity in records, the IRS can amend the taxpayer's filed return to account for the unreported or underreported income, and then assess additional taxes. If those additional taxes go unpaid, they become back taxes.

- **Substitute for Returns**
  Back taxes can occur even if a taxpayer does not file a tax return. If a taxpayer fails to file a tax return, the IRS may file a return on his or her behalf. Isn't that nice of them? These are called Substitute for Returns. The IRS will often prepare the return in a light least favorable to the taxpayer—e.g., filing status of single, no additional exemptions, claiming the standard deduction, etc. Often, the substitute return reflects a much higher tax than what the taxpayer would have been assessed if he or she had filed his or her own return. Once that tax is assessed and remains unpaid, it becomes back taxes. ◄

>>> **FAST FACT**

IRS Enforcement Over the Years

Below is a chart detailing the amounts IRS Collections has amassed over the years:

Fiscal Year	Amount
2004	$25.7 billion
2005	$26.6 billion
2006	$28.2 billion
2007	$31.8 billion

Source: Internal Revenue Service ◄

Sometimes the IRS is slow to come after those who owe back taxes. This is not to say that the IRS doesn't come down on those with tax debt, though. No, as you will learn in the next section, when they come down, they come down *hard*. However, they are not consistent. In fact, it often takes a while before a defaulting taxpayer even gets on the IRS's radar. Consequently, tax debts accumulate and grow rapidly without being much of a distraction to an already distracted individual.

If you have high cholesterol, slowly but surely, the cholesterol continues to coat the blood vessels, eventually slowing the blood flow and leading to debilitating pain, and maybe even death. Tax debts can act the same way, eventually leading to personal, professional, and financial pain.

IRS Collections

Congress gives the IRS authority as the ultimate collection agency in order to protect the federal government and to collect back taxes.

This means the IRS has almost unfettered power to inundate taxpayers with telephone calls, visits to home and work, and can use unmatched enforced-collection techniques.

In general, the IRS can engage in collection activity after giving the client a series of notices. The IRS has to wait thirty days from the date of the Final Notice to engage in any type of collection activity. During this period, the individual taxpayer is given every opportunity to fully pay his tax liability, resolve it—see forms of tax debt resolution below—or find a forum to disagree with the alleged balances due or proposed collection activity.

After the thirty days have passed, the IRS can sic their dogs on someone who owes them money. This is done through a variety of methods. Each is discussed in further detail on the following pages:

⫸ FAST FACT

Failure-to-Pay Penalty

The Failure-to-Pay Penalty is 0.5 percent per month for each month there is a balance due—up to 25 percent. Keep in mind that filing an extension does not give you an extension of time to pay. In order to avoid being assessed the Failure-to-Pay Penalty, you must:

- File a valid extension
- Pay 90 percent of the tax due by the return due date (April 15)
- File the return by the extended due date
- Pay any amounts due with the return

If you fail to meet any of these four requirements, the Failure-to-Pay Penalty will be assessed from the original due date (April 15).

The Internal Revenue Service has three years after the return is filed to assess the Failure-to-Pay Penalty. ⫷

- **Federal Tax Levy**

  This action redirects income or liquid assets (money within a bank account) from a taxpayer to the IRS on behalf of the federal government. For income, it acts as a garnishment on wages—an involuntary deduction—taking a portion of the taxpayer's income and applying it directly to his or her federal tax debt. For liquid assets like a bank account, it freezes the account and then distributes the entire account balance directly to the IRS for federal back taxes. A bank levy can be applied to any type of bank account—checking, savings, money market, even the contents of a safe deposit box.

  The IRS can actually use levies on forms of income other than wages. Social Security, pensions, and some forms of retirement income can all be subject to levies. In addition, accounts payable and unpaid contracts of the self-employed can be completely seized.

  Levies on bank accounts are one-time events. However, they wipe out the entire contents of a bank account. Alternatively, levies on income are typically continuous events, remaining on the wages or benefit until the tax debt is paid in full or resolved.

  In the most recently completed tax year, 3.75 million levies were issued. Yikes!

 TAX TIPS

Multiple Withdrawals

While levies on bank accounts are one-time events, that doesn't mean that the IRS is prevented from issuing bank levies multiple times. No, oftentimes the IRS follows up one bank levy with another, in order to account for any additional funds placed into the account by the taxpayer. The IRS can levy your bank account on any day of the month—even during the holidays.

- ## Federal Tax Lien

  A lien is a lock on your property. It keeps you from selling or refinancing until your IRS tax debt is paid in full. A tax lien is different from a wage garnishment or bank levy in that it does not actively collect income from the taxpayer. Rather, a tax lien is much more passive. It acts to protect the federal government only when the taxpayer elects to sell property—personal or real. However, it can affect a taxpayer's credit or the ability to be flexible in the sale of valuable assets.

  The value of the lien is equal to the amount of the back tax liability. Upon the sale of the property, the proceeds of the sale are first given to senior lienholders (individuals or financial institutions who secured a debt owed to them through claim to the property before the IRS), the IRS, then junior lienholders (individuals or financial institutions who secured a debt owed to them through claim to the property after the IRS), and then the individual property owner (the seller).

  A lien is typically not released unless the back tax liability is paid in full, expires, or is compromised through some of the forms of back tax resolution—like the acceptance of an Offer in Compromise—that you will learn about later.

  In the most recently completed tax year, 683,659 liens were issued.

- ## Seizure of Property

  Occasionally, the IRS will seize the private property of a taxpayer in order to satisfy a tax debt. Typically this is done when the taxpayer has sizeable tax debts and equally sizeable assets. Assets that can be seized—in addition to income and account balances—include real estate, automobiles, artwork, jewelry, equipment, machinery, etc.

  Upon seizure, the IRS and the U.S. Department of Treasury will attempt to sell the property. If it is subject to foreclosure sale, this may be done via auction.

  In the most recently completed tax year, there were 676 property seizures.

- **Private Debt Collectors**

In addition to the above collection techniques, Congress recently privatized a portion of tax debt collection. Private debt-collection agencies have now been charged with collecting unpaid taxes from taxpayers the IRS has failed to collect from or had previously deemed unworthy of collection (i.e., old tax debt or tax debt less than $10,000). Now taxpayers with even the smallest balances may be contacted by private debt collectors. In the most recently completed tax year, private debt collection agencies collected $1.686 million.

As part of the private debt collector hand-over, Congress has told the IRS to provide private debt-collection agencies with taxpayers' private information (including the name, Social Security number, address, and phone number of taxpayers and their spouses) to ensure that collection efforts are maximized. The IRS's private debt collectors will contact taxpayers to collect balances owed and to inform taxpayers of their need to file delinquent tax returns. If the taxpayers are uncooperative, the private debt collector can then forward the taxpayer back to the IRS to engage in enforced collections.

- **Automated Collection Service**

Typically, the IRS engages in enforced collections through a centralized office called the Automated Collection System (ACS), a large, computer-driven system that attempts to collect on past-due tax liabilities. This branch of the IRS is the first contact most taxpayers have with the IRS after receiving a past-due tax bill. ACS is responsible for sending out nearly all the various collection letters and legal notices required to collect delinquent tax liabilities.

However, ACS is not a fully automated system. It is staffed with a large number of tax collection professionals whose efforts are focused on collecting your past-due liability. A large portion of these tax collectors work in call centers across the nation. Yet no individual ACS representative is ever assigned to a particular taxpayer's account or back tax liability. Instead, ACS passively enters into forms of tax resolution that are proposed by taxpayers. In some ways, it makes dealing with an IRS tax debt even more difficult, as there is no continuity and very little consistency when dealing with ACS to get enforced collections to stop—unless you are willing to pay your tax debt in full.

➤➤➤ FAST FACT

Revenue Officers: The Bounty Hunters of the IRS

In addition to ACS, the IRS employs a substantial number of elite tax collection professionals called Revenue Officers (ROs). Generally, Revenue Officers are assigned to cases within their local area that have been flagged by the IRS for one reason or another. This could be due to a variety of factors, including the taxpayer repeatedly not filing tax returns, repeatedly underreporting income, having substantial balances due, having substantial assets/income, etc. For whatever reason, the IRS has determined that it can receive more effective compliance and collection from this taxpayer by having a local RO assigned to his or her case.

ROs have broad authority to conduct investigations and take all legal action necessary to collect past-due taxes. They have the right to thoroughly investigate the personal and business affairs of the taxpayer they are assigned. They also have the ability to contact the friends, family, business associates, and anyone else who may have information relevant to the collection of the taxpayer's tax liability. Most ROs will not hesitate to show up at a taxpayer's home or place of business.

Furthermore, ROs can take any enforced collection action authorized by law. These collection actions may include garnishing wages, levying bank accounts, filing tax liens, and seizing assets. ◄

Forms of Tax Debt Resolution

It may be obvious, but the fastest way to resolve IRS tax debt is to just pay it in full. Paying in full means, in addition to the debt itself, paying the interest and penalties that have accrued since the debt was originally assessed. The penalties and interest can quickly add up to thousands of dollars, since they are constantly accruing.

Assuming, however, that you can't whip out your checkbook and pay your balance due in a single lump sum, don't fret. The IRS really wants your money, so they give you a variety of different ways to resolve the tax liability. While some are more attractive than others, they are offered based on a very similar set of criteria of income, expenses, and assets.

 TAX TIPS

Conquer Compliance

Before the IRS is willing to enter into any form of tax debt resolution, the taxpayer must be compliant with all filing requirements and IRS regulations. What this means is that the taxpayer must file all necessary returns. Typically, this includes returns from the last six years where the taxpayer's total income exceeded the filing requirement. It doesn't matter if you owe additional taxes that you cannot pay, because whatever is owed can be added to your existing debt and wrapped up into a single form of tax debt resolution.

Therefore, even if you are not ready to enter into any of the below resolution types, you can still start the resolution process by filing your missing tax returns.

- **Installment Agreement**

  If a taxpayer can afford to pay his or her IRS back taxes, but not in one lump sum payment, then he or she might be interested in an Installment Agreement with the IRS. An Installment Agreement is a monthly payment plan to the IRS based upon how much the taxpayer owes and how much he or she can afford to pay. It is similar to any car loan or credit card debt. However, instead of the size of the payment being based upon the size of the debt, it is actually based upon what the individual can afford to pay. Because of this, it typically requires a disclosure of the taxpayer's and his or her spouse's financial information, including current income, expenses, and assets.

- **Streamlined Installment Agreement**
A Streamlined Installment Agreement (SIA) is based upon the taxpayer's back tax liability amount. A taxpayer is eligible for the SIA if his or her back tax liability is less than or equal to $25,000 and the amount of the payment will pay the back tax liability in full within five years or before the tax liability expires.

    In order to determine the amount of the SIA, the IRS will normally divide the amount of the tax debt by sixty months. However, the number of months can change if the IRS has less time to collect the liability. The IRS also factors in an additional amount for interest and penalties that will continue to accrue on the balance due.

- **Currently-Not-Collectible Status**
If a taxpayer is experiencing a financial hardship and cannot afford to pay anything toward his or her IRS back taxes, then Currently-Not-Collectible status might be an option. This will place a protective shield around the taxpayer, his or her income, and his or her assets. The shield notifies the IRS that

 TAX TIPS

SIA Confidential

To establish an SIA, the taxpayer does not typically need to provide the IRS with detailed financial information. That is because the monthly payment is not calculated based upon what the taxpayer can afford, but what is currently owed.

the taxpayer cannot presently afford to pay anything to the IRS and is currently in dire financial straits, and that even the smallest levy could completely devastate the taxpayer financially. Currently-Not-Collectible status protects him or her from being levied. For many taxpayers with tax debt in our struggling economy, Currently-Not-Collectible status is a good way to keep afloat.

The bad part about Currently-Not-Collectible status is that, as with an Installment Agreement, it will require the disclosure of financial information. The taxpayer must prove that his or her monthly income is exceeded by his or her monthly necessary living expenses. The IRS will also regularly review the taxpayer's financial situation—typically on an annual basis based upon information provided by banks, employers, and other relevant third party reporting companies—to see whether it has improved significantly enough to handle a monthly or full payment. This is why Currently-Not-Collectible is considered only a temporary form of resolution. In addition, being designated as Currently-Not-Collectible does not stop interest and penalties from accumulating on the tax debt. Moreover, it will likely result in a federal tax lien being placed on any valuable property that the taxpayer owns or will own while in the status.

- **Offer in Compromise**

  If a taxpayer cannot afford to pay back taxes at all, he or she may qualify for an Offer in Compromise. This requires the disclosure of extensive financial information in order to prove to the IRS that it could not collect the full amount of back taxes the taxpayer currently owes. Specifically, an Offer in Compromise requires proving to the IRS that it could not collect the taxpayer's full back taxes over four or five years, even if the IRS forced the sale of all assets that he or she currently owns and collected all the monthly income he or she had left over after all necessary living expenses were paid.

TAX TIPS

Collection Statute Expiration Date

After going over all those payment options, I've got some news for you: you may not need to do anything to resolve your back taxes.

Huh?

This is because the IRS only has ten years to collect back taxes from the date on which they were assessed. Just like many other liabilities, tax debts come with a statute of limitations for collections. The date is established ten years from the debt assessment. It is called the Collection Statute Expiration Date (CSED). So, if you know that you have back taxes or unpaid taxes from 1997 or before, the IRS may not be able to collect those taxes anymore.

However, there are events that can occur that will extend this time-frame, such as bankruptcy. To ensure that your back taxes have expired, you may want to hire a tax professional to review your tax account with the IRS on your behalf. A tax professional can contact the IRS to find out whether you still have back taxes, the amount due, and date on which they expire.

But don't think it's going to be easy to go ten years owing the IRS without being bothered. The IRS has an insatiable appetite for owed back taxes and if they catch a whiff of you owing, watch out. Think, "Lions and tigers and bears, oh my!" but with an IRS twist: "Notices and levies and liens, oh my!"

This is accomplished by proving to the IRS that a theoretical amount—called the Reasonable Collection Potential (RCP)—does not exceed your IRS tax debt. Your RCP is based on the following things:

Offer in Compromise Reasonable Collection Potential		
	ITEM	DESCRIPTION
1	Gross Monthly Income	From all sources, including Social Security, disability, unemployment, and assistance from family and friends; includes income from all household members
2	Allowable Monthly Expenses	Necessary for health, welfare, and the production of income; some types have caps based on geographical location and size of household; some are prorated based on the income of non-liable household members
3	Asset Value	The current fair market value of any account, investment, property, etc.
4	Asset Liabilities	The current loan balance, if any, on accounts, investments, property, etc.
5	Dissipated Assets	Valuable assets transferred out of your ownership or income spent after accruing a tax liability; asset or income could have been used to pay tax liability
6	Retired Debt	Monthly allowable expense that will expire during the period under consideration (e.g., car payment will expire within the four- or five-year Offer in Compromise window)

To calculate your RCP, take your gross monthly income and subtract the allowable monthly expenses from it. If that amount is positive, multiply it by forty-eight months. If it is negative, disregard it. Next, add the difference between the asset value and asset liabilities on each separate account, investment, and parcel of property. Then, add the value of any dissipated asset. Finally, add the value of any retired debt (number of months without the expiring monthly payment × the amount of the expiring monthly payment). If your tax debt exceeds that calculated amount, then you qualify for an Offer in Compromise.

If the Offer in Compromise is accepted, it acts as a settlement of the outstanding tax debt. This means the debt is extinguished in exchange for the payment amount equal to the calculated RCP. As you can imagine, your RCP can be quite large, so some taxpayers find it difficult to pay it in one lump sum payment. Thus, the IRS offers a second type of Offer in Compromise—Short-Term Periodic Payment—in which the RCP can be paid off over two years. In exchange, the IRS requires that sixty months be used in the calculation above, as opposed to forty-eight for the regular Offer in Compromise (lump sum payment). This is just to squeeze a little more blood from the turnip.

- **Bankruptcy**
Finally, back taxes can be resolved by filing for bankruptcy. There are a number of factors that must be considered before back taxes can be discharged in this way, however. First, you

---

⟫⟫⟫ FAST FACT

Currently-Not-Collectible Status as a Permanent Form of Tax Debt Resolution

According to the IRS, Currently-Not-Collectible status is a temporary protected status, designed to give taxpayers the ability to get back onto their feet financially, so that they can start making payments on their tax debt.

Well, the reality is that many taxpayers' financial situations do not improve. Instead, they remain the same—or get worse. In those cases, the taxpayer's debt remains in a Currently-Not-Collectible status indefinitely—and could very well remain there until after the Collection Statute Expiration Date passes. When that happens, the tax debt, interest, and penalties are extinguished, the tax debt has been permanently resolved, and any federal tax lien is released. So much for "temporary." ⟪

TAX TIPS

Additional Methods of Addressing Tax Debt

In addition to the main forms of tax debt resolution, the IRS offers the following programs for addressing tax debt:

Alternative Tax Debt Actions	
NAME	**EXPLANATION**
Innocent Spouse Relief	This form of tax debt resolution is available to those individuals whose spouses filed a joint tax return on their behalf, though the individual had no knowledge of the actions taken that caused the IRS tax liability.
Injured Spouse Relief	Individuals use this relief to receive their overpayment refund from the IRS when it had been applied to a spouse's back tax liability and where the individual can prove that the spouse's tax liability is separately held—i.e., not the result of a joint tax return, prior to marriage, etc.
Penalty/ Interest Abatement	Individuals use this relief to stop and reduce penalties and/or interest on an IRS tax liability when the liability arose due to erroneous IRS instruction or guidance and/or reasonable cause.
Lien Subordination	Individuals use this relief when purchasing, selling, or refinancing a parcel of property in order to pay down and/or address IRS tax liability.
Release of Federal Tax Lien	Individuals use this relief to remove federal tax liens on parcels of personal or real property when the IRS back tax liability expired or had been paid in full.
Collection Due Process Hearing	This is a hearing offered by the IRS Office of Appeals for taxpayers to dispute IRS collection activity—i.e. levies, liens, seizures, etc.

need to qualify for bankruptcy. Second, you need to properly file the bankruptcy. Third, you need to examine the age and type of back taxes. In general, recently assessed federal income back taxes cannot be discharged in bankruptcy, and neither can business-related federal payroll back taxes.

Typically, filing for bankruptcy involves more debt that just tax debt. So, if you are considering filing bankruptcy, you should speak with a bankruptcy attorney regarding whether the IRS back taxes can be discharged in a bankruptcy, among the other liabilities you may be trying to eliminate.

Avoiding Tax Debt

We touched upon avoiding tax debt earlier in this book. However, now seems like a reasonable time to quickly remind you of what you need to do to avoid unwittingly walking into the minefield of IRS collections.

Below are ten things you can do to ensure that you will never have to experience a tax debt owed to the IRS, the most powerful and aggressive collection agency in the world.

	Top Ten Ways to Avoid Tax Debt
1	Use **correct withholdings**—complete a Form W-4 and claim the correct number of exemptions.
2	If self-employed, make your monthly/quarterly **estimated tax payments**. Base them upon a three-year average of your business's gross earnings, unless you anticipate higher earnings this year.
3	If you employ workers, make your monthly **payroll tax deposits.**
4	**Marry wisely**—do not marry someone with tax debt problems or bad financial habits; if you do, make sure you or a third-party tax professional is in charge.
5	**Understand investment consequences**. If you have many financial vehicles, understand that most transactions involving them will have taxable events.

Top Ten Ways to Avoid Tax Debt	
6	**File your tax returns**. Even if you don't think you owe, file the returns and find out for sure (you may even end up with a refund).
7	**Report all income on your return**. Most audits and tax debt are due to unreported and/or underreported income.
8	Purchase within your means when it comes to a home—if you end up walking away from your home, you could still be on the hook for **cancellation of debt income**.
9	**Borrow from your bank or family**—it's better than owing the IRS. Get a low-interest loan to pay the balance due on the return, and make adjustments for next year.
10	**If facing a crisis**—personal, professional, financial, medical, etc.—make sure to have a third-party professional overlooking your tax plan.

I Have Tax Debt and/or Am Facing IRS Collections—Do I Need Help?

Yes.

I say this in all seriousness. If you have an IRS tax debt, it more than likely means that you got tripped up by one of the ten items listed above. If that's the case, then it is probably in your best interest to work with a professional to get back on the right track.

Resolving tax debt and/or stopping IRS collections involves the same procedure. Below, please find those steps:

Steps for Resolving Tax Debt/IRS Collections	
1	Get into compliance
2	Confirm compliance, tax debt, and collection statute expiration date
3	Gather all income, expense, asset, and liability information/documentation

Steps for Resolving Tax Debt/IRS Collections	
4	Complete financial statement(s)
5	Enter negotiations with IRS, timely providing requested documentation
6	Confirm acceptance/request facsimile communicating release of levy
7	Abide by all terms of resolution type (payments, compliance, etc.)

First, you must file all missing, necessary returns. The IRS wants you to commit to basic compliance before playing ball concerning your debt or the levy on your bank account or wages. There really is no negotiating away that basic obligation.

After confirming your tax debt, you will need to complete a financial statement. A financial statement can go onto one of three forms, depending upon who has the tax debt and what type of resolution he or she is seeking. The IRS Form 433-F, Collection Information Statement, is used by individual taxpayers seeking an Installment Agreement or Currently-Not-Collectible status. For an Offer in Compromise, you must complete an IRS Form 433-A, Collection Information Statement for Wage-Earners or Self-Employed, or an IRS Form 433-B, Collection Information Statement for Businesses. All three forms request very similar information. All forms also identify the items that will require documentation—which you will need anyway to accurately complete the forms.

 T A X   T I P S

Use the 433-A and 433-B

While these forms are more thorough, they are also more flexible. They can be used for Installment Agreements and Currently-Not-Collectible status, in addition to the Offer in Compromise. The Form 433-F cannot be used for an Offer in Compromise.

Next comes the negotiation. For Installment Agreements and Currently-Not-Collectible status, that involves contacting the IRS via telephone and going through a lengthy negotiation/interview where the IRS agent asks the taxpayer or representative a series of questions regarding the information contained on the aforementioned forms.

The Offer in Compromise process is a little more formal. It requires filling out IRS Form 656, Offer in Compromise, in addition to the financial statement. Both must be formally submitted. Then, over a couple of months, the IRS engages in a fishing expedition of sorts concerning the terms on the financial statement. It may also challenge the RCP determination, asserting that for one reason or another you do have the ability to pay your tax debt in full over the next four to five years. You will be given an opportunity to overcome the IRS objections through additional submittal and/or argument.

Assuming your negotiation is successful, you will be notified in writing. The letter will provide all the terms of your resolution type and direct you as to where and when you are to make your payment—if any. At this time, you should contact the IRS and request that any release of levy or lien occur immediately. For levies on wages, make sure that you provide the IRS with your employer's fax number. For levies on bank accounts, provide your bank's fax number.

If your negotiation is unsuccessful, you will probably be notified first via telephone, which will then—sometimes—be followed by something in writing. Either way, you will have thirty days to appeal the decision. You must first go back through the party who rejected your proposed resolution and request reconsideration. Only after reconsideration is denied can you forward a request to the IRS Office of Appeals.

Once there, the Office of Appeals will engage in an abbreviated version of the same form of negotiation described above. Here, unless the proposed resolution is definitely not in the best interests of the government, you will find a more willing partner for compromise. However, if you are not able to work it out, and the Office of Appeals sustains the rejection, you will have to go back to square one and start all over.

Now, could you do all this? Yes. But that doesn't mean you will be able to do it well, especially on your first try. And, of course, what I've just outlined is a simplistic overview of a very complicated process. As you can imagine, there is a lot of nuance to how negotiations are handled. When it comes to resolving IRS collections and tax debt, you want it done fast, but you also want the best deal possible. You can only accomplish both by working with an experienced, skilled tax professional. And that's the bottom line.

What Is a Tax Audit?

Here is how one of my former clients described the process.

Imagine yourself, driving along the road, minding your own business. You've got a thousand things on your mind—who is picking up the kids after soccer practice, whether the boss liked your presentation, what you're going to have for dinner, what to get your husband/wife for your anniversary, etc.—when all of a sudden you see the red lights flashing in your rearview mirror and the sound of a siren overtakes the tunes on the radio. At that point, your heart is about to leap through your chest. You know you probably screwed up, and now the law is coming to get you.

So you pull over to the side of the road. You turn down the radio. Your mind its battling itself, asking, "Do I have proof of insurance in the glove compartment?" while also thinking, "Man, I bet I could lose this guy if I gunned it right before he got to the window."

You continue to sit in your car, as the officer remains in his. Your palms begin to sweat and you feel light-headed. You begin double-checking your seatbelt—two, three, ten times—to make sure it is securely latched. You contemplate your breath—"If I'm chewing gum, will that make him think I'm trying to cover up for booze?" You then begin to wonder if this is going to take so long that you'll miss the first quarter of the game, which makes you begin to get angry. Then you are confused, because you realize you have never seen a police officer on this stretch of the highway and you know that you always slow down here because of the upcoming bend in the road. And that blue car next to you was at least going ten MPH faster than you. "So do I have a taillight out?" you wonder. At that point, you begin to pray. "Please, God. I promise to always drive five miles under the speed limit—even on I-80—if you let me off with a warning. I will even go to church next week. Please?"

Finally, the officer makes his way out of his car and proceeds toward the driver's side window. You roll down the window and make the obligatory opening remark: "What seems to be the problem, officer?"

This is a pretty apt analogy for an IRS audit. They leave you uneasy and unsure. You are often second-guessing everything you did on your tax return, leaving no stone unturned in your mind. It is not always readily apparent why yours is being singled out from the millions of other tax returns. You are distracted and prevented from focusing on the other events going on in your life—work, family, friends, leisure.

>>> **FAST FACT**

IRS Enforcement Over the Years

Below is a chart detailing the amounts IRS Examinations (the audit bureau) have collected over the years:

Fiscal Year	Amount
2004	$14.7 billion
2005	$17.7 billion
2006	$17.2 billion
2007	$23.5 billion

Source: Internal Revenue Service ◄

However, the real drama is usually due to the range of possibilities for how it can be conducted. In the above example, the best result would probably be getting off with a warning for some minor traffic violation. But, from there, the consequences continue to worsen—first to a citation and a fine, then to a search of your vehicle for contraband, and finally to the back of the officer's car for some extra questioning down at the station.

The severity of audits is similar. Some are conducted via mail through the exchange of documents. Not too scary. But it gets worse. An audit can be conducted by the IRS on the business premises of the taxpayer. Alternatively, taxpayers can be called in to meet with the IRS, and asked to bring a pile of documents and an appetite for explaining themselves.

It is here, in the field or office audit, that you are ripe for some interrogation. In these audits, the IRS goes through an extensive accounting of what you claimed and wants you to explain it through documentation—receipts, statements, invoices, etc. There may even be questions about the legitimacy of some claimed income, expenses, or even your entire business operation. And here, there typically is no good cop–bad cop—just an unrelenting auditor.

Well, let me stop there. Instead of continuing to paint the dire picture of the audit, now I'm going to give you some good news. First, the majority of audits are conducted solely through the mail. Second, the IRS targets particular types of taxpayers, income, deductions, and credits when it comes to auditing. Third, there are behaviors that you can avoid that typically trigger audits. And, finally, if you have properly prepared yourself, through organization and storage of appropriate documentation, you should have nothing to worry about.

Therefore, while I am not denying that an audit can be painful, I am saying there is a way to approach it methodically and intelligently. So, sit back, grab a cocktail, and start reading. The bulk of the rest of this Round is devoted to explaining the types of tax audits, identifying tax audit "red flags," explaining how to avoid a tax audit, and detailing what to do if you are audited. Cheers!

>>> **FAST FACT**

A Necessary Evil

Audits are part of the IRS's day-to-day operations. The IRS is practically a business, charged with collecting taxes for the federal government and, right now, they are about $305 billion short. The audit allows this business to accomplish its goal of reducing that discrepancy. Moreover, the money collected because of audits will be used to pay for all the wonderful social programs and services the federal government affords us. How thoughtful! «

>>> **FAST FACT**

Chances of Getting Audited—Individuals Without Business Income

Below, please find statistics from the most recently completed tax year (2007). For purposes of this chart, total positive income is the sum of all positive amounts of income claimed on an individual tax return, excluding business or self-employment income. It does not include any income losses.

Total Positive Income Range	# Returns	# Audited	% Audited
$0 to $200,000	76,729,589	297,545	0.4%
$200,001 to $1,000,000	2,482,382	48,944	2.0%
$1,000,000 +	339,138	31,382	9.3%

Source: Internal Revenue Service «

Audit Types

The IRS has several types of audits, each with its own rules and rhythms. Let's take a look.

- **Correspondence Audit**

  Perhaps the most common and the simplest type of audit, here the IRS asks you to document an item on your return by a specified date. This is usually a routine test for compliance with certain items on your return. You will have to dig out your receipts or other documents, make a photocopy for the IRS, and mail them in with a copy of the audit request . . . and then keep your fingers crossed that it does not turn into one of the other two types of audits.

- **Field Audit**

  A field audit is the one that people fear most. These types of audits are typically associated with businesses. I guess the one piece of good news in a field audit is that you are allowed to decide when and where to schedule the meeting. I recommend picking a neutral location—preferably in your accountant's or attorney's office, since they probably know more about tax laws than you do, and they can provide the best possible assistance. A neutral site also prevents the IRS agent from prejudging your income level based on a first impression

 TAX TIPS

III Communication

As you can imagine, correspondence audits present a challenge—communication. Due to the fact that the audit is conducted through the mail, it can be difficult to explain something on your tax return. So, if you have an unusual situation, it may best be explain yourself face-to-face. This can be done by contacting the individual assigned to your correspondence audit and setting up an appointment to meet him or her.

But remember—choosing to meet them face-to-face is solely your option. If you have second thoughts (or get cold feet), feel free to cancel the appointment at any time.

of your home, office, or business—an impression that is generally not to your advantage.

- **Office Audit**

  Here you meet at your friendly neighborhood IRS office. You should send them copies of proof in advance of the appointment to try to resolve the issue without actually going to the office. This is usually an easy process unless discrepancies or errors prompt the IRS to dig deeper into your return.

What Can Trigger a Tax Audit?

First, let's get the obvious red flags out of the way—the ones that common sense tells us to avoid. For instance, if you live in a Malibu beach house, but list your occupation on your tax form as "crossing

---

>>> **FAST FACT**

The Audit from Hell

In addition to the above audits, occasionally the IRS conducts even more intensive audits for research purposes. The most grueling was the Taxpayer Compliance Measurement Program (TCMP) audit. This audit last took place in 1988, and involved a line-by-line review in which taxpayers were required to substantiate every single item of income, deductions, credits, and exemptions on their returns. In 2001, a "kindlier, gentler" form of this audit was resurrected, called the National Research Program audit. For the most part, it involved little to no IRS contact. Only fifty thousand returns were selected for the audit. Of those, two thousand were selected for a line-by-line audit—called a "calibration audit"—however, taxpayers were not required to substantiate each item. This was repeated again in 2006.

Although, as of 2008, the IRS was not using either form of these "audits from hell," it is important to know that they are out there and could be implemented again in the future. ◄

---

guard," you are probably going to set off some alarms when the IRS gets your return. If you take deductions for every purchase or expense you have incurred over the course of a year, you are asking for trouble. If you claim that 80 percent of your income went to charity, the IRS might beat a path to your door.

Being, of course, a decent person who does not do those sorts of things, what you should focus on are the things the IRS looks at when weighing an audit. Here is a list of a dozen characteristics that can trigger an audit:

Tax Audit Red Flags
Large income
Majority of income is not wages
Unreported income—e.g., investment earnings
Home-based business income and/or deductions
Non-cash charitable deductions
Excessive business meal and entertainment deductions
Excessive business automobile usage
"Hobby" or passive income losses
Large casualty losses
Claiming the Earned Income Tax Credit
Failing to submit the Alternative Minimum Tax schedule
Careless errors—incorrect Social Security numbers, misspellings, math errors, etc. (usually this will just earn you an IRS Correction Notice [CP 2000])

Here are a few specific deductions or taxpayer attributes that may also trigger a red flag from the IRS, along with a few suggestions for how you can properly substantiate or avoid them.

- **Charitable Contributions**
  Many taxpayers make large contributions to charities in relation to their income. If you fall into this category, keep a log of your donations, noting the date, the organization, and the amount of the contribution. Whenever possible, you should pay with a check, even for small amounts. Amounts over $250 that you contribute at one time require a written receipt from the organization, though many organizations will issue receipts for any amount given. In the event of an audit, the IRS will expect to see the name and address of the organization, the date of the donation, and a description of the property donated, when the total non-cash contributions exceed $500. You will also need to report the original cost of the property, the fair market value (FMV) for the property on the date of the donation, and how the FMV was determined. The larger the donation, the more documentation the IRS will require.

- **Home Office and Other Employee Business Expenses**
  The IRS looks very carefully at taxpayers who take a deduction for a home office. If you fall into this category, you need to be sure you meet the proper qualifications. Make sure the

---

 TAX TIPS

Car Trouble

The IRS is always on the lookout for automobile donation abuses. Any sign of excessive valuation of your car could bring a possible audit. If you take a deduction for more than the value of the car you donated, you could be hit with a penalty of up to 40 percent of the unpaid tax.

measurements of your office and of your home are correct, and, therefore, that the correct percentage ratio is used. Also, keep all utility bills with your tax records for the year and any other receipts that apply. In the event that you move, take a picture of your previous home office and keep the photo with your tax records as well. Accurate record keeping for other employee business expenses should ensure a pain-free audit.

- **Self-Employed**
  If you are self-employed or filing a Schedule C, you should take special care to keep all receipts for deductions for meals, travel, and entertainment, because the IRS often finds abuses in this area. Most self-employed individuals have large deductions for mileage, and, therefore, the IRS expects to see complete records kept to verify this deduction. Unusual deductions should have the proper documentation to show that the expense was reasonable and ordinary. Also, make sure to keep your credit card statements online—that way they are easy to get to when you need them.

- **Hefty Income**
  Generally, as your income increases, so does your chance of an IRS tax audit. In the most recent tax year, individuals earning more than $200,000 were five times more likely to be audited than individuals earning less than $200,000. Moreover, individuals earning more than $1,000,000 were more

---

▶▶▶ **FAST FACT**

Thank You, Sir, May I Have Another?

An audit is actually a two-way street—it can result in either more taxes paid or less. Obviously you don't hear about many audits coming out in the tax-payer's favor, but if you over-claimed income or under-claimed a deduction or credit, you may in fact end up with a refund at the end of an audit. ◀

than twenty-three times more likely to be audited than an individual earning less than $200,000.

- **Unreported Income**

  Unreported taxable income can be trouble, too. The IRS discovers unreported taxable income when its computers match the taxable income you reported on your tax return with data collected from financial institutions and employers, among others. For example, if you failed to report the interest earned on your bank savings account, the IRS will typically catch you when it matches the bank's interest payment records against your tax return. In addition, the IRS has discovered that not all taxpayers report alimony receipts as taxable income. Consequently, the IRS now matches tax deductions for alimony payments by one former spouse with the taxable alimony income reported by the other.

- **Earned Income Tax Credit**

  Returns claiming the Earned Income Tax Credit also catch IRS eyes. The credit was designed as a tax break for lower-

 TAX TIPS

Avoid a Big "DIF"

Once your tax return arrives at the IRS, agency computers compare it against the national Discriminate Information Function (DIF) system average. The IRS calculates the DIF score by using a closely guarded formula—think "Original Recipe" Kentucky Fried Chicken. Tax returns with the highest DIF scores are scrutinized by IRS tax examiners who determine which tax returns provide the best chance for collecting additional taxes, interest, and tax penalties. While the DIF score formula is not known, some of the red flags highlighted here in Round 10 are things thought to be a part of the formula for that score that you can avoid.

income wage-earners, and its complexity often results in legitimate mistakes on returns. Some filers, however, have been caught making false claims to increase the payment the credit provides. In the most recent tax year, individuals claiming the credit whose total positive income exceeded $25,000 had a 9.7 percent chance of being audited.

⟫⟫⟫ FAST FACT

To Live and Be Audited in L.A.

According to recent IRS statistics, metropolitan Los Angeles is the most active auditing region in the U.S. This is because L.A. audits are not decided by some software program at IRS headquarters, but by flesh-and-blood bureau officials. (Take that, Dodgers and Lakers fans!) ⟪

Avoiding an IRS Tax Audit

While, historically, the IRS rarely has audited more than 2 percent of all tax returns filed, there has been grumbling out of Washington demanding more—specifically of self-employed individuals and small business owners. In addition, depending upon the different types of income, deductions, and credits claimed by the taxpayer, your chances of being audited can increase dramatically.

However, there are certain steps you can take to minimize those odds even further. Here are a few proven methods of avoiding a nasty letter from Uncle Sam.

- **Keep Organized Records**
  Yes, maintaining orderly financial records has been a recurring theme in this book. Avoiding an audit is just one good reason why. If you keep good tax records, you will prepare good tax returns, and good tax returns avoid the red flags that may trigger audits. Back in the early 1970s, when actors Jack Klugman and Tony Randall were hamming it up to

great effect on *The Odd Couple*, a particularly funny episode revolved around Oscar's sloppy tax habits. Receipts written on footballs, IOUs on tavern napkins, and receipts scribbled on the back of dirty shirts were just a few examples of Mr. Madison's disorganized system. They say that humor is rooted in truth, and that episode may be a good example of that. You see, the IRS is no different from anyone else. They appreciate tidy, organized records, and tend to view sloppy ones with skepticism, if not contempt. The lesson? Keep a clean tax file and minimize scrutiny from the IRS. Keep a messy one and suffer the consequences.

 TAX TIPS

Childcare Issues

If you are audited because of your childcare expenses, you will need to produce the receipts to verify the claim. However, those receipts do not need to be included with your tax return.

- **File When Ready**

  If you are not prepared to file your return by April 15, then don't. It's better to file an accurate return late than to file an error-filled return on time. If you're not ready, just file an extension. You can file a six-month extension and not run the risk of penalty—so long as 90 percent of your taxes due were paid on time.

- **Big Deduction? Use a Stapler**

  If you have made a large contribution to charity or had a big medical deduction during the tax year, attach a copy of the receipt to your tax return. You can also include a clear, brief statement explaining an extraordinary contribution or deduction—just write STMT next to the item on the return, and attach the statement to the return. That should satisfy any questions IRS reviewers might have.

- **Prepare Your Tax Return by Computer**

  A neat, computer-prepared return looks more official to the IRS classifiers and fits the IRS bias favoring computer processing. All professional tax preparers now use computers. In addition, even if you are a surfboarding tax attorney (like yours truly), you want to be professional-looking when it comes to presenting your return to the IRS.

- **No Round Numbers**

  Do not use round numbers for deductions—for example, $5,000 or $7,000 instead of $4,978.31 or $7,012.45. That's a sign that you are estimating things rather than keeping good records.

- **Watch All Documentation**

  Be especially careful that the information provided on any W-2 forms you receive from employers, and 1099s or 1098s you receive as an independent contractor or from banks, mutual funds, brokerages, retirement plans, or any other source, are accurately reflected on your return. If there is an error, get it fixed. What's the big deal? The IRS computer matches these figures with the figures on your return, and it will question any mismatch—or missing figures.

- **Double-Check Your Math**

  Poor arithmetic is the most common error turned up by the IRS. If you are doing your own return with a calculator, after you have done all the computations, start at the amount of your refund (or tax you owe) and work backward to check your work. This means you will add back your payments, subtract your other taxes, and add back your credits to see whether you arrive at the same tax amount. Continue in this vein for the rest of the return.

>>> **FAST FACT**

Fuzzy Math

Here are the most common math errors by type in the most recently completed tax year:

Type of Error	Number	Percentage
Tax calculation	924,054	23.8%
Exemption number/amount	770,637	19.8%
Earned Income Tax Credit	540,768	13.9%
Standard/itemized deduction	419,290	10.8%
Adjusted Gross Income/taxable income amount	297,858	7.7%
Child Tax Credit	255,186	6.6%
Refund/amount due	225,904	5.8%
Other credits	112,422	2.9%
Filing status	109,121	2.8%
Withholding or excess Social Security payments	102,084	2.6%
Adjustments to income	65,110	1.7%
Other	63,071	1.6%

Source: Internal Revenue Service ◄

- **Sign Your Return**

  Make sure you have filled out all the information required. For example, it is common to omit the Social Security number of an ex-spouse from a return, but you are required to supply it if you are paying alimony. Make sure your return is complete.

TAX TIPS

Don't Double Dip

And not just your chips! Be extremely careful not to claim the same deduction twice, like claiming an expense on Schedule A, C, and/or E. You only get to claim it once, so do not make the IRS point that out to you.

TAX TIPS

Multiple Audits

If you are audited one year with a refund or no change, it decreases your odds of being audited in subsequent years. In fact, if you are audited on the same items two years in a row with no additional taxes due, the IRS manual specifically recommends that they not audit you on the same items for the third year.

Help, I'm Being Audited!

This is one letter you do not want to receive:

Internal Revenue Service
Small Business and Self-Employed
4330 Watt Ave.
SA1106-SC
Sacramento CA 95821

Department of the Treasury

Taxpayer Identification Number:
111-11-1111
Form:
1040
Tax Period(s):
200612

Date: April 7, 2008
Thomas A. Anderson
101 Main Street, Sacramento, CA 95816

Response Date:
April 14, 2008.
Person to Contact:
Agent Smith
Contact Hours:
8:30 - 4:00
Contact Telephone Number:
916-555-5555
Contact Fax Number:
916-555-5556
Employee Identification Number:
22-22222

Dear Thomas A. Anderson

Your federal return for the period(s) shown above has been selected for examination.

What You Need To Do

Please call me on or before the response date listed at the top of this letter. I can be contacted at the telephone number and times provided above.

What We Will Discuss

During our telephone conversation, we will discuss:

- Items on your return that I will be examining.
- Types of documentation I will ask you to provide.
- The examination process.
- Any concerns or questions you may have.
- The date, time and agenda for our first meeting.

The issues listed below are the preliminary items identified for examination. During the course of the examination, it may be necessary to expand or contract the list of items. If this should occur, I will advise you of the change.

- Home mortgage Interest and
  points From Form 1098

Letter 2205-A (Rev. 7-2006)
Catalog Number 37456E

Someone May Represent You

You may have someone represent you during any part of this examination. If you want someone to represent you, please provide me with a completed Form 2848, *Power of Attorney and Declaration of Representative*, at our first appointment.

If you prefer, you may mail or fax the form to me prior to our first appointment. You can get this form from our office, or from our web site at www.irs.gov, or by calling 1-800-829-3676. If you decide that you wish to get representation after the examination has started, we will delay further examination activity until you can secure representation.

Your Rights As A Taxpayer

We have enclosed Publication 1, *Your Rights as a Taxpayer*, and Notice 609, *Privacy Act Notice*. We encourage you to read the Declaration of Taxpayer Rights found in Publication 1. This publication discusses general rules and procedures we follow in examinations. It explains what happens before, during, and after an examination, and provides additional sources of information.

Thank you for your cooperation, and I look forward to hearing from you on or before the response date.

Sincerely

Internal Revenue Agent

Enclosures:
Publication 1
Notice 609
Information Document Request

Letter 2205-A (Rev. 7-2006)
Catalog Number 37456E

Over the years, letters of that sort from the IRS have been the cause for more ulcers and migraines than just about anything else in this great country of ours. It is not the end of the world, but it is important to react quickly and follow these steps:

	Ten Steps to Take if You Receive an Audit
1	Do not panic
2	Thoroughly review the notification to see what is needed and when
3	Call your tax professional for advice and/or representation
4	Organize the documents you need to respond to the audit
5	Do not rush a reply—wait until you have finalized what you want to communicate to the IRS, and ask for an extension if necessary
6	Identify weak areas in your return—or prior years' returns
7	Be honest during the audit
8	Only proffer answers, information, documentation, and explanations upon request
9	Dress and act professionally—check your emotions at the door
10	Organize your documentation in an accessible and easy-to-understand manner

Okay, so you've received an audit letter from the IRS. Take a deep breath and prepare for the battle. The size of that battle is, of course, dependent upon the items the IRS is challenging and whether or not you have done a good job documenting your income and expenses throughout the year. It is also important to remember that the IRS is not out to get you—they do not want to destroy you or ruin your life—although that is not always easy to see. They are only doing their job, and they just want an accurate record of your tax liabilities. If you have filed a truthful tax return and can back up your deductions, you have nothing to worry about.

If it is merely a correspondence audit, and you feel confident about the claimed income, expense, or deduction and have documentation support, then simply provide a letter explaining the item and attach a copy of the documentation. That should be enough to clarify the issue for the IRS. You will then receive a letter confirming that the issue has been sufficiently addressed, and that there is no change.

Internal Revenue Service
Small Business and Self Employed

Department of the Treasury
4330 Watt. Ave.
Sacramento, CA 95821

Date: July 2, 2008
Thomas A. Anderson
101 Main Street, Sacramento, CA 95816

Taxpayer Identification Number:
  111-11-1111
Tax Year:
  200612
Form Number:
  1040/30
Person to Contact:
  Agent Smith
Employee Identification Number:
  22-22222
Contact Telephone Number:
  916-555-5555

Dear Mr. and Mrs. Thomas A. Anderson

I have completed the examination of your tax return for the year(s) shown above. I am pleased to inform you I'm proposing no change to your tax return. As indicated in the enclosed Form 4549-A, *Income Tax Discrepancy Adjustments (Examination No Change Report),* my findings are subject to the Area Director's approval. We will send you a final letter when we finish processing your file.

If you have any questions, please call or write me at the telephone number or address shown above. If you write, please include your telephone number, the best time for me to call in case I need to contact you, and a copy of this letter.

Thank you for your cooperation.

Sincerely,

Examining Officer

Enclosures:
Form 4549-A

Letter 3401 (Rev. 8-2007)
Catalog Number 30903E

Now, if it is an office or field audit, or a correspondence audit where you do not have appropriate support documentation, you should immediately contact a tax professional. If you hired a competent professional to prepare your return or assist in your tax plan, that is the person to go to. Meet with him or her as soon as possible to create a response to the IRS. While it is important for you to let the IRS know you have received their letter, there is no sense rushing to meet with them before you and your advisor have put together a plan of action.

 TAX TIPS

The Right to Reschedule

Although the audit letter may provide a time and place to meet, you are not legally obligated to sign off on this suggested meeting time and place. In fact, you have the right to reschedule the audit to make it more convenient for you. However, make sure you or your advisor actually contacts the IRS to reschedule.

If you moved out of state after you filed the tax return(s) in question by the IRS, you can ask the agency to move the meeting to an IRS office closer to your new digs. However, if you have a tax professional you like and trust who resides in your old community, he or she can attend the meeting with the IRS in your stead. By law, you do not have to be present at an audit meeting if you have a tax professional representing you.

You may not have needed a tax professional to prepare your taxes, but you will appreciate having one by your side during an audit. Letting a professional take the reins will take the responsibility off your shoulders and help you avoid making any expensive gaffes.

TAX TIPS

Mistakes to Avoid

If you decide to handle your IRS letter or audit on your own, be aware of these common mistakes:

Ten Things Not to Do When Audited by the IRS	
1	Fail to respond to the initial correspondence/letter
2	Fail to take the initial encounter seriously
3	Respond to the inquiry after the initial due date without asking for an extension
4	Partially answer an inquiry without addressing all issues
5	Appear at a field or office audit unprepared, without all requested documentation
6	Fail to consult with a tax professional before responding to or participating in the audit
7	Fail to consult with a tax professional before signing an agreement with the IRS
8	Underestimate the IRS's capacity to uncover discrepancies
9	Let emotions get in the way of your defense
10	Fail to double-check your own or the IRS's figures that make up the audit

Any of the above mistakes can cost you time and money. Moreover, penalties and interest can cost much more than professional assistance.

>>> **FAST FACT**

Taxpayer's Bill of Rights

In your interactions with the IRS, you have specific rights, too:

- **Representation**
  You may consult with and be represented by a tax adviser, attorney, or other tax professional when dealing with the IRS. The IRS must clearly inform you in IRS Publication 1, Your Rights as a Taxpayer, of the right to be represented by an accountant, attorney, or other tax professional. Once you have chosen a representative, the IRS may not interview you alone, unless consent is given. You may give a written power of attorney to a lawyer, CPA, or enrolled agent to represent you at an IRS tax audit. You do not have to attend the IRS tax examination unless the IRS issues you an administrative summons, which does not happen often.

- **Recording Conferences with the IRS**
  You may record an IRS interview at your own expense if you give ten days' notice; likewise, the IRS may record a conference if you are informed ten days in advance.

- **Interruption of an IRS Tax Audit**
  You can suspend an IRS tax audit in progress at any time to consult with your professional advisor. ◄

At the audit itself, you will have something like a lawyer-client relationship working for you. If an IRS agent asks your tax professional the questions, you will gain two advantages. First, you will avoid revealing more information than you meant to in answering the questions, and second, your tax professional can table any questions by answering that he or she will need to consult with you for a complete answer. That can buy you more time.

TAX TIPS

Do Your Homework

The IRS has been known to make a mistake or two over the years. Thus, when you receive an audit notice, review it carefully and look for the following items:

- **Has the Notice Been Sent to the Correct Person?**
  A divorce can result in an audit letter being sent to the wrong spouse, or the notice could be for somebody else with your name.

- **Has the Statute of Limitations Expired?**
  In most cases the IRS must begin an audit within three years of the due date of your return for the year being examined, or the date on which you actually mailed your return for the year—whichever date is later.

- **Can the Query Be Handled by Mail?**
  In the case of correspondence audits, you can easily handle the process by answering the IRS's question, providing the appropriate back-up documentation, and mailing it off.

When you show up for your audit, bring the documents and/or records that were specified in the audit notice. Do not bring anything that is not related, because you don't have to and you don't want to give the IRS auditor an opportunity to uncover another issue. If your auditor wants more data, ask him or her to put it in writing. That way you have a record of what has been requested of you in case you appeal your decision or go to tax court.

At the end of the meeting, the IRS auditor will sum up any discrepancies on your tax return. After the auditor informally advises you of any tax adjustments needed on the tax return, a formal report is filed.

If you owe money, you can write a check right then and there. If you owe a lot of money and cannot pay right away, you can work out a resolution of the tax debt with the IRS, as I discussed earlier in this Round. Do not be afraid to ask for some time to come up with a payment. The IRS wants your money, so they will accommodate you in most cases.

➤➤➤ FAST FACT

Audit Trends

Here are some interesting numbers on IRS audits from the most recent tax year:

Individual Income Tax Returns	Number	Percentage
Filed	134,542,879	N/A
Audited	1,384,563	1.029%
Field Audited	449,215	0.334%

Source: Internal Revenue Service ◀

Should You Appeal Your Audit?

You can if you want to, but there are advantages and disadvantages to doing so.

The first advantage is that the entire appeal process is free, unless you hire a tax professional. In addition, if you appeal, you are also buying time to pay the taxes you owe from the audit. Though interest and penalties accumulate on the amount due if you wait, they are cancelled—along with your tax bill—if you win on appeal.

On the negative side, the IRS appeals officer may find new issues that did not come up in the original audit, which will become fair game. Remember, you will now have to go through the process of explaining your financial existence to another IRS employee. Ignoring how intrusive this is to your personal, professional, and financial life, each time this happens, it gives the IRS the opportunity to examine any activities you conduct that are just a little suspicious. There might be a legitimate explanation for everything you do, but just having to explain it at all can be nerve-wracking.

If you do appeal, the IRS Office of Appeals will handle your case. The office operates autonomously from the IRS's audit bureau, and usually likes to avoid going to tax court if it can. So, settlement is typically on the front burner. You can get the process rolling by writing a protest letter and sending it to your local IRS district office—as well as your Congressman and senator. When you appeal, make a Freedom of Information Act request for the auditor's records. Lastly, bring a tax attorney into the appeals process. You are going to need someone knowledgeable on your side of the table. After all, you wouldn't go to court without a lawyer, would you?

▶▶▶ FAST FACT

Mass Appeal

If you do not win your audit appeal, you can always go to tax court. The fee for doing so is only $60, and lawyers are allowed to argue your case. Of course, the IRS will have lawyers to argue its case, too. The U.S. tax court is the end of the line for audit appeals—the judge's ruling is final. ◀

 ### Inside the Ropes:
The Audacity of an Audit

Christina did not intend to mislead the IRS on her tax returns—she just didn't know any better.

The forty-three-year-old website designer had recently gone into business on her own, from an office in an unused room above her garage. "I wasn't tax savvy or anything, although I did try to read up on self-employment and taxes. A lot of it just went over my head, though."

So when she received a notice from the IRS that she was to be audited for her tax return for her first year of business, she was thunderstruck. "I couldn't believe it—I'd never been in trouble in my whole life!"

Christina immediately contacted her tax preparer, Samantha, who asked her to bring the letter over to discuss the audit. "I wasn't thrilled about this whole process, but I thought I should at least notify my tax preparer," she says. "She'd done thousands of tax returns over the years and knew what she was talking about. It was good to have a pro in my corner—especially one I already knew."

Samantha saw right away what the problem was. Christina had taken two trips to web design seminars during the tax year in question—one to Marco Island, Florida, and the other to Las Vegas, Nevada. The IRS wanted documentation that those trips were really for business and not for pleasure.

"Samantha had me go back and dig up the credit card receipts for the two seminars I attended and make copies of them. She also had me make copies of the trip itinerary, hotel bills, and airline receipts. She attached all of the copies to a typewritten letter from her office explaining the deduction. She also enclosed a 'power of attorney' form and asked that all future correspondence be sent to her as well. That ensured that she would be notified if there were any additional bumps in the road. I guess that did the trick, because a few weeks later I received another notice telling me that everything was okay."

Christina did learn a lesson from the experience. "As a small business owner, especially one with a home office, I guess I'm a little more vulnerable to a tax audit," she says. "So, on the advice of my tax pro, Samantha, I've begun a filing system with all my business-related expenses and accompanying receipts. I have also started using a business credit card for business purchases and expenses, which makes it easier to build a paper trail. I guess I'm just going to have to hang on to every receipt I can in case I get audited again."

➤ ROUND 11

Help in the Ring: Should You Hire a Tax Trainer?

An expert is someone who has succeeded in making decisions and judgments simpler through knowing what to pay attention to and what to ignore.
—Edward de Bono, British physician

In the mid-1920s, General Electric (GE) was having problems with a huge electrical generator at their facilities in Schenectady, New York. Their team of engineers had spent countless weeks trying to figure out what was causing the problem and were at their wits' end. They had made little progress in even limiting the problem to a particular component of the generator and were about to conclude that the problem was unresolvable.

On a whim, GE's president decided to contact Charles Steinmetz, the famous electrical engineer and inventor and retired former GE employee, noted for his research on alternating current.

GE's president asked Mr. Steinmetz to assist GE's engineers on the problem and help them solve it—to act as a consultant, which was very uncommon in those days. Mr. Steinmetz agreed to come out of retirement to provide assistance—so long as he was compensated for his services. GE promptly agreed.

Mr. Steinmetz arrived and examined the system. Initially, Steinmetz himself found the problem difficult to diagnose. So he asked for and received complete autonomy—with the machine and its design drawings. After a couple of days spent tinkering with and testing various parts of the system, he emerged from his solitary confinement and claimed that he had solved the problem.

When the generator was examined by GE's engineers, they found that Steinmetz had placed a chalk-marked X on the side of the generator's casing, along with a note instructing them to cut it open and replace a specific piece of the machinery driving the generator. GE's engineers quickly followed the instructions, and were amazed to find that the generator functioned properly, and at peak efficiency, once that defective piece was replaced. When asked, Steinmetz declined to proffer an explanation of how he knew where the defect was located. Instead, he left GE and seemingly faded back into a life of retirement.

Some time thereafter, GE received an invoice from the engineer—for $1,000. At that time, $1,000 was an unheard-of sum. Incredulous, GE protested the bill, and challenged Steinmetz to itemize it for the services he rendered. Steinmetz obliged. His invoice read:

1. Making one chalk-mark X: $1
2. Knowing where to place it: $999

Ah, the benefits and costs of hiring a professional. Luckily for you, professionals in the tax industry are not as stingy or expensive (okay, some are) as Mr. Steinmetz. Instead, they will show you the ropes and teach you how to step into the ring against the IRS on your own. I mean, look at what you are reading—a tax guide by the Tax Lady, chock-full of advice and helpful hints for beating Uncle Sam at his own game.

However, tips and advice are one thing—mentorship, guidance, and, ultimately, control are another. That's what this Round is all about—finding the right balance when it comes to getting assistance with preparing your tax return and establishing your tax plan. In this Round, I am going to let you know whether your situation merits assistance, what options are out there for you, and what to look for if and when you decide to go with a professional.

Where Do You Stand?

Before you choose between teaming up with a professional tax preparer or going it alone, take some personal inventory. After all, emotions play a major role in any plan involving your money. Building your own financial security is no different. So, ask yourself if you have qualms about handling your own taxes. Do you shudder at the thought of crunching numbers, or are you pumped about the prospect of diving headlong into those tax forms? Do you eagerly peruse the Internet looking for tax advice? Just how much time are you willing to put into your taxes? Answering these questions will help you decide whether to start calling up some tax-preparation professionals.

Moreover, remember that the IRS code is intentionally complicated—almost as if Congress and the IRS don't *want* you to figure out your tax situation. So, being strategic with your different sources of income and getting all the exemptions, deductions, and credits available to you is tough to do—even with this book in your hand. Hiring a tax professional to identify what tax breaks you have and how close you are to accruing additional tax breaks may be your best course of action.

Finally, in the go-go information age, time is a big factor as well. Essentially what you are buying from a tax professional—apart from his or her expertise—is time. A tax professional has the time to scour the world for the best tax-saving opportunities to fit your financial situation. And all the time your tax professional works is time *you* can spend doing more important things. After all, even the most basic tax returns take some time. According to the IRS, the average taxpayer needs 24.2 hours to complete his or her tax return. And if your return is more complicated—like if you use a Schedule C (for business) or a Schedule E (for rental properties)—then it takes an average of fifty-two hours to complete your taxes. Sound like a fun weekend?

So . . . are you ready to rumble . . . *on your own*? That's the question you need to ask yourself before you consider hiring a tax professional.

On Your Own Two Feet

Let's examine why going solo might be the best option for you:

Ten Reasons You Might Want to Do Your Own Taxes	
1	You work for only one employer who gives you a W-2 tax form each year.
2	You earned less than $1,500 in taxable interest in 2008.
3	You rent your residence and do not own a home or vacation property.
4	You do not have kids or other dependents.
5	You do not have any complex investments such as a partnership, a trust, or extensive stock holdings.
6	You know your itemized deductions will not exceed the standard deduction.
7	Your only source of income is Social Security, and you earned less than $32,000 in 2008.
8	You are an accountant, attorney, or tax professional.
9	You will be completing a 1040A or 1040EZ.
10	You are comfortable doing computations by calculator or by hand, or using tax software on your computer or online.

The above list covers many of the best reasons for doing your own taxes. The ones I focus on when I talk to my clients are wages—specifically, if you earn your income solely from wages. If so, chances are your taxes are pretty basic and easy enough for you to complete. Also, if you take the standard deduction, if you only have a handful of itemized deductions, or if you use the 1040EZ or 1040A short form, you should be in good shape to handle your own taxes.

If that is your situation, then the benefits of doing your own taxes are out there. For starters, you do not have to pay someone to perform a task that you yourself can complete. Also, you get to learn more about the tax return and all the possible treasures—exemptions, deductions, and credits—it contains. This can help you create your plan of attack for next year, and knowledge is always a point in your favor. It also forces you to think about your universal financial situation. Yes, "universal financial situation" sounds slightly intimidating, but it is better to confront your financial reality than to be hit by a financial train wreck because you weren't prepared.

And I cannot overstress how time is a commodity. While this typically cuts the other way, sometimes people know what they are doing, have a streamlined financial situation, and are organized. In such situations, they can get their taxes done in just an hour or so. If they file online, they can get a tax refund in a week or two. That's not bad in my book! Getting anything accomplished on your own time, in your own home, and avoiding having to drive down to an office to be on somebody else's time can be an attractive benefit. Finally, by preparing your taxes yourself, you also get the satisfaction of a job well done—so long as you don't make a mistake and either overpay or incur the wrath of the IRS Audit Unit.

So, if you like numbers, have the time, and can navigate your way through IRS tax laws, then maybe doing your own taxes is a good idea.

Cost of Preparing Your Own Tax Return

Cost alone can be the most attractive benefit for doing taxes on your own. Heck, what do you want me to say—the cover of this book says that I am going to save you "big bucks on your taxes." Well, last time I checked, $1 in tax savings is the same as $1 in tax-preparation savings. So, of course, it is going to be cheaper to prepare your return yourself—so long as you don't make a mistake and either overpay or incur the wrath of the IRS Audit Unit. (Wait, is there an echo in here?)

▶▶▶ FAST FACT

Professional Luxury

According to the National Society of Accountants, in 2007, the average fee for a federal return with itemized deductions and a state return was $205. ◀

The cheapest way to prepare your taxes on your own involves paper, an old #2 pencil, and an abacus. (If you don't know what an abacus is then you probably didn't get that joke, and if you do, it's time to upgrade to a calculator.) You will also want to turn back to Rounds 4, 5, and 9 before you get started. Then sit back, relax, and have fun with erasing, broken pencil tips, and the potential of spilling coffee on your almost-completed return.

As you can see, I am not big on turning back the clock to the Stone Age when it comes to tax preparation. Being a fan of rugged individualism does not mean I recommend or endorse tackling your tax return and the IRS with your bare hands; that would be like choosing the slingshot over the high-powered rifle as an elephant stampede comes bearing down on you. It just would not make any sense. What I'm saying is, don't turn your back on technology when it comes to taxes.

After all, technology is here to stay. This is especially true in the tax-preparation world, where ever-more-complex IRS regulations and a dizzying array of forms and paperwork make using computer programs and the Internet a natural for Americans. Not that tax-planning or preparation software is a tough sell to taxpayers.

Remember, this is the country where terms like *instant messaging* and *cyberspace* have become part of our national lexicon, right up there with baseball, hot dogs, apple pie, and Chevrolet.

Handling your taxes online, with one of the myriad tax-preparation software packages available on the market, can be a big help. Many of the benefits of software technology—better organization, quicker response times, easier and more readily available data storage, and, yes, speed—are at the top of the list of desirable items that professional tax preparers want at their disposal. So, why not you?

 T A X   T I P S

Taking the Online Plunge

If you are still hesitant about using the Internet, you can at least upgrade from the paper-and-pencil route by using an electronic PDF of IRS Forms 1040, 1040A, or 1040EZ. They are available at www.irs.gov.

Alternately, you can go to a professional tax-preparation company's website—how about, for example, www.rdtc.com—and select the "online" option. You will go through a tax-preparation wizard, which will collect your personal, income, and expense information, and complete both your federal and state tax returns. You will only pay a small fee, and the tax-preparation office can easily e-file your form once it is complete.

Most tax-preparation software and online options are inexpensive and easy to use. Consequently, in a cultural environment where America's seven-year-olds can download music and make their own digital films on their families' home computers, not taking the time to at least examine the tax-preparation technology solutions on the market is an oversight to say the least.

So, while you are welcome to use the old #2 pencil and abacus for your taxes, you will be missing out. These days, when every deduction counts and lost paperwork can cost you money, using a computer to handle your tax preparation is not really a luxury—it's becoming a necessity.

 TAX TIPS

Do Your Taxes Online for Free

The IRS offers online filing for free. In 2007, those earning less than $54,000 in Adjusted Gross Income were eligible for the Free File program.
With Free File, you can:

- File your taxes any hour of the day or night
- Benefit from Free File's automatic checks for accuracy
- Receive a quick confirmation within forty-eight hours that your return was received
- Know that your return is safe and secure
- Get your refund in as little as ten days if you use direct deposit

Free File is also available in Spanish. More than 4.8 million people used the program for their 2007 returns. For more information, visit www.irs.gov.

So, who should use tax-preparation or planning software? The same individuals who can or should prepare their returns on their own—though there are a few caveats, which we will explore later in this Round. Preparing and filing taxes online is for people who have a basic understanding of the process (not all tax software options are educational in nature—some are more execution-oriented). Also, the easier your tax situation, the easier it is to handle your taxes online or through store-bought software. If you do not have a lot of deductions or tax credits, and you are not including a lot of forms and schedules, doing your taxes online or with a computer is a snap—so long as you don't make a mistake and . . . okay, okay, you get the point.

T A X   T I P S

Talk to a Pro

Even if you end up choosing a commercial tax-preparation package, make sure you select one that will make professional tax preparers available to answer your questions. Some tax packages do not have this option—which you may regret at 2 AM on April 15 when you cannot calculate your home office deduction.

What to Look for in Tax-Preparation and Planning Software

Let's begin with a warning.

Using most commercial software tax packages is a great idea—most of the time. However, if you have not done your homework and boned up on tax issues, you may miss deductions online just as easily as you could miss them offline.

Software tax-preparation programs are tools—they will not do your thinking for you. So, the more prepared you are to handle your tax situation, the more benefits and advantages you will derive from a good tax-preparation software package.

As we pointed out above, one idea worth considering is to go ahead and use the software to prepare your taxes, but only use one that offers back-up financial advice and help. Again, not every program offers this.

Once you have decided that online or store-bought tax-preparation software is for you, it's time to pick a package. When you go shopping, do not rely strictly on price (although that is certainly a factor). What you are really looking for are the other two Ps—performance and productivity.

For starters, you want a program that asks simple questions, automatically selects and completes the forms you will need, and double-checks your return. It should also electronically file your return and get your refund faster, or give you the option to print your return and mail it yourself.

Make sure the software is updateable and includes recent tax law changes and updates, helps find missing information and missed deductions, and flags items that might trigger an IRS audit. In addition, the software should provide an up-to-the-minute progress report of your return, refund, or amount due.

With affordability in mind, look for a tax-preparation software program that also offers the following elements:

Tax-Preparation Software Checklist	
☑	**FEATURE**
☐	**Easy-to-read, clean display**
☐	**Easy overall navigation**
☐	**Ability to import data before you get started**
☐	**Uploads your W-2 and 1099 information right into the program**
☐	**Ability to import data from other personal finance software**
☐	**Free telephone support**—even on weekends
☐	**Easy to opt out of tax situations that do not apply**
☐	**Easy to access relevant tax forms**
☐	**Customizable features** (e.g., comparing the benefits of claiming the standard deduction versus itemizing your deductions)
☐	**Schedule C capabilities** (a must for small business owners)

You want a software package that leads you by the hand through whichever tax-preparation process pertains to you. The program should begin by importing your information from last year's return— even if you used a different tax package—along with any relevant information from other financial software packages you own. For example, you will want to import mortgage information from your bank or business expenses from your business accounting software.

The questions should be clearly presented and easy to understand. In addition, they should always steer you toward the tax breaks and deductions you wanted—but were not sure how to get—when you purchased the software in the first place. And most important, if you are stumped, you also want a software program that allows you to stop, pick up the phone or click over to your e-mail, and ask a tax professional for help.

The better tax software packages also have a nice visual look and feel, with plenty of reminders to max out on your IRA when you are working on the investment portion of your tax returns or to remind you to sign your return before you send it off. Hey, it's the little things that add up.

Above all, you should be able to easily install and run the program on your home computer, or it should be accessible on the Internet. You will also want a program that can prepare multiple returns (i.e., five or more), and that can help you complete your state as well as your federal taxes.

Chances are, once you learn how to use tax-preparation software and grow comfortable with the idea of preparing your taxes online, you will wonder why you waited so long to take the plunge.

 TAX TIPS

Deduct Your Tax Assistance— Computerized or Human

Hiring professional tax help? Purchasing tax-preparation software at your local electronic store or online? Write that off as a legitimate deduction.

The Benefits of E-Filing

The government is good at telling people at what to do, and the IRS is no different. That's why soon it may not matter much if you want to file your taxes online or not. This past tax season, Congress asked the IRS to have 80 percent of its returns processed online, and for subsequent tax seasons, the goal may be set even higher.

Why? Because Uncle Sam believes online filing is cheaper, more accurate, and less cumbersome than regular mail, and online filing makes it easier for the IRS to organize and process the approximately 135 million tax forms that pour in each year.

Fortunately, the benefits to you of filing your taxes online are just as important as the perks for Uncle Sam. The IRS claims that millions of Americans already file online, lured by a free, safe, and accurate method of sending returns to the government.

Right up front, taxpayers may be swayed by the fact that, if they have a refund coming, they will get it faster if they file online. According to the IRS, e-filing take two weeks for the agency to process, versus three weeks or longer for snail-mailed tax returns.

E-filing is not only available to professional tax preparers. In fact, there are plenty of commercial software packages—store-bought and online—that enable you to file your taxes electronically with Uncle Sam. The IRS offers free downloads of tax-preparation software packages from participating companies (the IRS calls them partners).

Hiring a Tax Professional to Prepare Your Return

There are instances where the speed, organization, data storage, and quick response time of online or software programs is not enough to justify preparing your own taxes. Trust me. We see it all the time at Roni Deutch Tax Centers.

It could be the newly married couple, Derek and Leslie, finally consolidating their previously separate "universal financial situations." It could be Davis, the former co-worker who earlier in the year burned all his ugly ties, threw a TPS report in his supervisor's face, and started his own business—and now has to pay taxes on said business. In these situations, and many others, you are starting

>>> **FAST FACT**

E-Filing

The IRS is promoting its e-file program as safe and dependable. Here are some areas they are really emphasizing:

Benefit	Explanation
Security	You can select a five-digit personal identification number (PIN) to substitute as an electronic signature before you deliver your taxes online. Or you can sign IRS Form 8453, U.S. Individual Income Tax Declaration for an IRS e-file Return. This ensures that no one else can enter your tax information.
Accuracy	The IRS claims an error rate of under 1 percent with e-file, compared to a long-term average of about 20 percent with regularly mailed returns. That is because authorized software and preparers check for common errors and correct them.
Verification	The IRS will send an electronic verification within two working days to the tax professional that handles your return. For further security, the agency will only work with authorized tax-preparation software or tax preparers.
Speed of Refund	Once the return is processed and the refund amount calculated, the IRS can automatically deposit your refund into your bank account.

Source: Internal Revenue Service ◄

to travel toward the reasons why one should hire a flesh-and-blood professional tax preparer.

Let's start by examining some of the most common reasons why hiring a tax professional might be the best option:

Twenty Reasons You Might Want to Hire a Professional	
1	You work for more than one employer.
2	You are self-employed.
3	You earned more than $1,500 in taxable interest in the current tax year.
4	You have kids or other dependents.
5	You own your home or a vacation home.
6	You will be itemizing your deductions.
7	You will be claiming the Earned Income Tax Credit.
8	You will be completing a Schedule D for capital gains and losses.
9	You will be claiming a home office deduction.
10	You will be completing a Schedule K-1 for your partner's share of income, deductions, credits, etc.
11	You are buying or selling property.
12	You own a business or rental property.
13	You get regular income from a trust or partnership.
14	You trade investments frequently or have a complex portfolio.
15	You have undergone a major financial burden during the previous tax year, such as a divorce, death of a spouse, an inheritance, or a move of more than fifty miles for a new job.
16	You are supporting a child between the ages of nineteen and twenty-four who is a full-time college student.
17	Your income has increased by a considerable amount from the previous year.
18	You are subject to the Alternate Minimum Tax.
19	Your time and effort are better invested elsewhere.
20	You live in California.

The most sophisticated tax-preparation software packages offer a lot of advice and ask you many questions. That's great if you know what to do with the advice and you know how to answer the questions. However, if you don't, it's a problem. Even more so if you are not using sophisticated tax-preparation software. So, if you are leery of spending several hours researching the information you will need to avoid mistakes and/or make a profit, you may be better off spending a half hour with a tax professional.

In addition, if you are a small business owner, at first glance, a tax-preparation software package sounds like a no-brainer. You pop open your laptop, answer a few questions, and send your taxes off. Problem solved, right? But what if you spend so much time on your business (and what business owner doesn't?) that you have neglected to bone up on tax law and your personal tax situation? While there is no shortage of business-oriented online tax options, it may be a bit easier to unload all your tax documents on a tax professional and go back to running your business and making money.

Finally, is it any surprise that the state with the seventh-largest economy in the world would have a complicated tax form? Hardly. California's state taxes are drastically different than the federal forms—which is not the case for most state tax situations. If you do live in California and want to do your taxes online, just make sure you pick a software package that accommodates both state and

 TAX TIPS

Know Your Tax Professional

If you are working with a professional tax advisor or a commercial online tax-preparation program, do not e-mail your return or any important personal financial documents to anyone you don't know. Often, commercial software developers will hire outside advisors to review your taxes and have you e-mail your returns to them, but these e-mails are not always secure or encrypted.

federal tax programs for Californians. Not every software package does.

The Benefits of Hiring a Professional Tax Preparer

You might be the most adamant tooth-brusher in the Western Hemisphere. You've been brushing three times a day for seventeen years straight. However, when it comes time to get your teeth checked and cleaned, you probably go to a dentist, no matter how confident you are in your dental mastery. And while you're there, you also might get some advice about how new tools, like electric toothbrushes or dental tape, compare to conventional brushes and floss.

How about another example? If you own a mutual fund, you just own shares of funds. You will either make money or lose money. That is fine and good, but solely owning mutual funds does not provide an opportunity for you to learn more about them or the market overall. But when you team up and work hand-in-hand with a financial professional, you receive frequent reports that will keep you up-to-speed regarding current market trends and activities. Your financial professional can also educate you on potentially lucrative opportunities you can pursue or better courses of action to take with your current investments.

Similarly, a professional tax preparer can point out things that you miss or update you on the latest news when it comes to the IRS and taxes. He or she can reassure you that your current tax plan is capturing all the tax breaks you are targeting. But be aware that your tax preparer might tell you that it's time to toss your tax plan out the window.

Moreover, just because you're hiring a professional doesn't mean you're taking a back seat. Instead, it demonstrates your commitment to taking an active role in your tax plan by ensuring that you are getting the best advice possible. This not only increases your chances of becoming wealthier, it also makes you a better steward of your personal, financial, and professional life.

Then there's the key issue of timing. If you don't go to the dentist until your teeth are screaming in pain, or if you put off visiting your

TAX TIPS

Getting Beyond Money

Why a professional? Typically, two words—money saved. And if that's not good enough for you, how about these:

	Five More Good Reasons to Hire a Tax Professional
1	You screwed up last year's taxes, and want to avoid doing that again.
2	Tax professionals are up-to-date on the tax laws, know how to act on new ones, and can apply built-in knowledge to your facts and circumstances.
3	You view the tax process as cumbersome, complicated, and time-consuming.
4	You want a competent professional to help you create a tax plan that complements your professional and financial plans.
5	A tax professional can help you if you have to face an IRS tax liability or an IRS audit.

financial advisor until your mutual fund goes belly-up, then you probably waited too long. However, if you plan on regular dental checkups or regular visits to your financial advisor to review your investments, then you are way ahead of the game—good teeth and a fat portfolio. Same with your taxes—an ounce of prevention is worth a pound of IRS collection and audit notices.

Shopping for a Tax Professional

Remember what you're looking for—a tax partner. This partner will not only get you through this tax season, but can also provide

---

>>> **FAST FACT**

Overpaying Is a Big Problem

According to the IRS, out of the approximately 139 million tax returns filed in the 2007 tax year, roughly 115 million Americans overpay their taxes. Tax professionals can help you avoid this problem.

Source: Internal Revenue Service «

---

information about how to better prepare for next season. Thus, you need to investigate the tax professional's performance, organization, level of expertise, motivation, and general availability. Exceeding expectations in those categories is going to translate into exceeding expectations in service.

That is not to say there isn't a benefit to going with a professional tax company over a solo tax professional. It might be cheaper and even more accessible. However, always keep in mind that you are hiring the individual who sits down at that desk with you. You will still need to examine whether that individual scores well in the above traits before you decide to trust him or her with your tax return and tax plan.

Only look to the company for evidence of an efficiently run, profitable organization with low turnover and abundant attention to client service. Find out if the organization provides its professionals with ongoing training and access to tax management research and cutting-edge technology. Again, none of these attributes guarantee a competent professional, but they are good indicators that the organization cares about the service it provides and will not tolerate subpar performance in preparing your tax return.

The Hybrid Approach

Not everything in the tax game is black or white. In other words, there may be some tax solutions that blend both your own efforts and the expertise of a tax professional.

TAX TIPS

Family First

Here are some convenient resources you can tap in to for assistance in finding a tax professional:

- Family
- Friends and coworkers
- Chamber of Commerce
- Employee resource program
- Trade union
- Professional association

For example, you can hire a professional tax preparer to do your taxes this year, and while you work with this person, become a keen student of tax nature. Grill your tax professional about anything you don't understand; ask why that deduction is legit but the other one is not. Ask how he or she arrives at his or her conclusions. And, obviously, reference this book. Once you have gone to school, so to speak, next year you may have the expertise you need to begin handling your own taxes.

Maybe, next year, prepare them yourself. Then bring them into your professional for a thorough quality review. He or she may find that you have hit all the high notes, so to speak. If not, he or she can quickly make changes to the return before you suffer any consequences—like overpaying or getting audited—from mistakes in your return. Learn from the mistakes you made and try again the next year, and so on, until your tax professional gives you a perfect score. And whenever you get in over your head, just call your tax professional and ask for help.

Inside the Ropes: Jackson and Evelyn's Eleventh-Hour Nightmare

It was 9:30 PM on April 14, and Jackson and Evelyn had a problem on their tax return.

"There we were, rushing to complete our return with our tax-preparation software when we hit a snag," explained Jackson. "Evelyn had done some research and knew that we were going to have to account for the AMT (Alternative Minimum Tax) on our return, because we claimed the net operating loss deduction for our side business, among other things. Well, our software didn't account for the AMT. And there was no way I was going to be able to figure it out without some assistance."

At first, Evelyn and Jackson contacted the company that owned the software, but they were no help. "What we needed was in the 'superior' edition," explained Evelyn. "How ridiculous is that?"

So, with nowhere else to turn, they went to the newspaper. There, they happened to find an advertisement for the Roni Deutch Tax Center, which was having a "Forty Hours to Freedom" event: the office was staying open continuously for the last forty hours before the tax filing deadline.

Jackson and Evelyn headed over to the office with a copy of their partially completed return. When they arrived, they met Keith, the manager on duty. Keith was quickly able to complete the IRS Form 6251 worksheet to account for the AMT. In addition, Keith noticed that Jackson had failed to claim an additional first homebuyer's deduction on their return. This brought the couple an additional $7,500 in savings.

"It was a fantastic experience," Evelyn said. "We went there to overcome a minor inconvenience and wound up saving several thousand dollars!"

"Keith was great," said Jackson. "He quickly set aside what he was working on when we got there and dove right into our problem. After solving it, he took the next step and thoroughly reviewed our return for mistakes or tax breaks that we missed. And he found one!"

"I am really looking forward to next month," stated Evelyn. "Keith already set up an appointment to help us plan out our taxes for next year. He wants to make sure that we are aware of and targeting every deduction, exemption, and credit that we can."

➤ ROUND 12

Tax-Cutting Tips You Can Take to the Bank

Anyone may arrange his affairs so that his taxes shall be as low as possible; he is not bound to choose that pattern which best pays the treasury. . . . Everyone does it, rich and poor alike, and all do right, for nobody owes any public duty to pay more than the law demands.

—Judge Learned Hand

Every time someone comes into my office with an IRS problem, the same thing always happens. We research the problem and I make the following comment to my client: "Whoa . . . you are paying *way* too much on your taxes!"

I say that because it is usually true, but I also say that to send a message to my client. Just because the IRS is always dishing it out, that doesn't mean you have to take it.

That's the same message I hope you have gotten from this book. For the past eleven Rounds, I hope I have educated you and taught you the steps you need to take to put your tax life in order. I also hope I have outlined some tax-saving and money-generating tips for you and your family to live by. Ultimately, I hope that you and your family can use this knowledge to understand the IRS, find its weaknesses, and take the Goliath down—all while keeping your hard-earned money in your bank.

To put the icing on the cake, I would like to close the book with a list of handy tips you can use to save on your taxes—year after year after year. I hope you will rip them out of the book, hang them on the fridge, or slide them under your desk calendar and use them to keep more money out of Uncle Sam's pockets and in yours. That's the whole idea, right?

So let's get into some good tips—I can't think of a better way to finish the book!

#1   Take the Long View

I have already told you that tax planning is a year-round sport. So, take a "big picture" approach that allows you to break your tax year down into seasons. In the winter, start preparing your taxes; in the summer, start organizing your records; in the fall, begin calculating your estimated annual income (using November and December to average your estimated income out). Having a year-round plan is perhaps the single biggest factor in saving big bucks on your taxes.

#2   Give Yourself a Nice Present in December

The last month of the year is the best time to figure out how much you can contribute to your 401(k) or IRA. It is also a good time to sell stocks or shares of a mutual fund to lock in capital gains losses for the tax year.

#3   Keep Your Records Clean, Correct, Current, and Complete

I have probably made this utterly clear by this point, but well-organized records make doing your taxes immeasurably easier. And furthermore, I see a frightful amount of money lost each year because people do not have the proper records handy to refute a charge by the IRS. So get a filing cabinet, or even a safe, and back up everything you have online in a safe file on your computer. This way you won't be left holding the bag when the IRS comes calling with their grubby paws out.

#4   Protect Your Most Important Papers

Some financial documents are more important than others. That's why I recommend a safe deposit box for critical documents like your birth certificate, the deed to your home, stock and bond certificates, and your will.

#5   Keep the Necessities

Here is a short list of important tax records to hang on to:

- Paycheck stubs
- W-2 forms/1099 forms
- Receipts for deductible items
- Insurance and medical records
- Charitable records

#6   The Six-Year Rule

The IRS requires you to hang on to your tax records for three years. I say, to be safe, hang on to them for six.

#7 Avoid Under-the-Table Deals

If your employer offers to pay you cash as opposed to a paycheck, just say no. If your employer is paying you cash, he or she is not complying with the tax laws. The employer is not withholding its or your share of your Social Security, federal, and state withholding taxes. This failure to withhold will put you in tax trouble in no time.

#8 Know Your Bracket

The IRS pigeonholes you into a tax bracket, based on the amount of money you earn. The bracket parameters change frequently, so keep up to date on where you fit in.

#9 The IRS Takes Visa

You can pay your tax bill by credit card or debit card. Here's where and how:

Name	Form	Phone #	Website	Fees	Languages
Official Payments Corporation	Debit	1-866-4PAYTAX	www.officialpaymentsdebit.com	$2.95	English Spanish
Official Payments Corporation	Credit	1-866-2PAYTAX	www.officialpayments.com	2.49%	English Spanish
Link2Gov Corp.	Debit	1-866-213-0675	www.incometaxpayment.com	$2.95	English Spanish
Link2Gov Corp.	Credit	1-888-PAY-1040	www.pay1040.com www.pay940.com www.pay941.com	2.49%	English Spanish

#10   Earn it

Do you qualify for the Earned Income Credit? If so, you could save up to $4,700 in taxes (based on 2008 IRS tax figures). You may qualify if . . .

- You earned less than $12,590 ($14,590 if married filing jointly) and did not have an any qualifying children
- You earned less than $33,241 ($35,241 if married filing jointly) and have one qualifying child
- You earned less than $37,783 ($39,783 if married filing jointly) and have more than one qualifying child

#11   Armed and Honored

If you are in the military, you can get help with your taxes from the U.S. Volunteer Income Tax Assistance Program (VITA). Run by the Armed Forces Tax Council (AFTC), VITA gives members of the armed forces (and their families) free tax advice, as well as assistance with tax preparation, return filing, and other tax issues. Call 1-800-829-3676 for more details.

#12   Rules on Alimony

Getting divorced? Among the ten thousand other things on your "to do" list, make sure you know the rules on alimony and child support. In general, alimony payments you get are taxable to you in the year you receive them and deductible in the year you pay them. On the other hand, child support you pay is never deductible, and child support you receive is not taxable.

#13   Double Time

This is the last time I'll say it—*math errors can cost you money*. Make sure to double-check all figures on your tax forms.

#14   Green Machines

If you bought one of those new hybrid cars, make sure you get the full tax credit you have coming. The hybrid vehicle tax credit is worth as much as $3,000 (as of 2008), based on the type of hybrid car you buy.

Make sure to check www.irs.gov often. The IRS adds and deletes vehicles every year.

#15   Home Run

Got a home-based business? If so, you also have a nice little deduction on your taxes. To qualify, you have to use your home office as your principal place of business or as a place to meet or deal with your patients, clients, or customers in the normal course of your trade or business. The amount you can deduct depends on the size of the office or work-related space in your home.

#16   Get Your Transcript

Sometimes the IRS makes adjustments to your tax returns, and you have every reason to see those returns. The IRS charges no fees for transcripts, which are available for the current and three prior calendar years. To get your transcript, either call 800-829-1040, or request IRS Form 4506-T, Request for Transcript of Tax Return, and mail it to the IRS address listed on the form. Allow two weeks for processing. Form 4506-T can be found at www.irs.gov/pub/irs-pdf/f4506t.pdf.

#17　Get Professional Help

Having an experienced tax professional at your side can really help you save money on your taxes. When you start looking, focus on these essential areas:

- **No Fees**
  Stay away from tax preparers who say they can obtain larger refunds than the competition, or those who insist on being paid based upon a percentage of the amount of the refund.

- **In for the Long Haul**
  Work with a tax preparer who is available after your taxes are filed—that is a good sign that your tax pro is on your side.

- **Check Them Out**
  Make sure to poke around and vet any potential tax preparers. Also, get references and follow up on them. Ask the people you call if they are still working with the tax pro—and if not, why not?

#18　Summer Vacation

If you have a child, or know someone who has the summer off, consider hiring him or her to work for your business (if you have one). This can help you lower profits by writing off additional payroll expenses, and can provide a quality working experience to a child or family friend.

#19　Commonly Overlooked Deductions

People are always missing these great deductions. Why be one of them?

- **Medical Expenses**

  If your total medical expenses for a year come to 7.5 percent or more of your Adjusted Gross Income, you can deduct the expenses from your taxable income. Although the total percentage required might seem high, if you carefully plan elective surgeries or other costly medical expenses, you can easily meet the requirement.

- **State Sales Tax**

  The IRS allows you to deduct your total state income taxes paid or your total sales tax paid. If you live in an area without state or local income taxes, deduct your total sales taxes paid.

- **College Tuition**

  The IRS allows you to deduct up to $4,000 in college tuition for yourself, your spouse, or any dependents. This can be especially beneficial to taxpayers whose income is too high to qualify for the Hope or Lifetime Learning credits.

#20   Go Beyond the 1099

Some self-employed taxpayers think that they only need to report income that can be verified by a 1099 form. This is 100 percent incorrect! The IRS requires that taxpayers report *any* income they receive. Don't forget that the IRS has access to bank accounts and other financial data, and they will go after money they are entitled to.

#21   Declare Your Gambling Winnings

You must do this . . . even if you lose. If you won at the poker tables in Vegas, remember to declare your winnings. According to the IRS, taxes must be paid on all gambling income, including but not limited to:

- Lottery winnings
- Raffle prizes
- Horse or dog race winnings
- Any money won at a casino
- Fair market value of non-cash prizes such as cars, trips, etc.

Use line 21 on IRS Form 1040 to list your gambling winnings. And remember, the IRS counts winnings as income the instant you win. So if you follow a $5,000 win with a $10,000 loss, that $5,000 winner is considered income and needs to be included on your return.

#22   Get Foreclosure Relief

Recently, the federal government finally did something to help the thousands of families getting hit with huge tax bills after losing their homes due to foreclosure. According to recent law changes, debt caused by a foreclosure, short sale, or loan restructure will no longer be treated as income. The IRS will now allow for up to $2 million of forgiven debt to be excluded from a person's income (through tax year 2012). However, it is important to note that this only applies to homes used as a principal residence. Vacation homes and property investments are not protected.

For more information, see the Mortgage Forgiveness Debt Relief Act of 2007 or IRS Form 982, available at www.irs.gov.

#23   Make Your January Mortgage Payment Early

Making your January mortgage payment in December will allow you to take a higher interest deduction this year. However, keep in mind that this will result in a lower interest deduction next year.

#24   Collect Your Charity Receipts

If you made any charitable contributions, make sure you have the receipts handy. New IRS restrictions require an acknowledgment (receipt) of your contribution from the qualified organization if the contribution exceeds $250. Gathering the information ahead of time is much easier then frantically searching for receipts before an IRS audit.

To be an acceptable acknowledgement, the receipt must:

- Be in writing (either handwritten or printed from a computer or register)
- Include the amount contributed, whether the organization exchanged any goods or services in exchange for the con-tribution—even if token—and the description and value of those goods and services
- State whether the benefit received was intangible
- Be received on or before either the date you file your return or the due date for filing the return—whichever is earlier

#25   Energy Boost

You can deduct the cost of gas and oil (or the applicable mileage allowance) plus parking and tolls, or bus and taxi fares, used to obtain medical care or perform volunteer work for a charity. With gasoline prices fluctuating hour by hour, this is a nice benefit.

#26   Job-Hunting Expenses

Whether you are working or between jobs, it pays to save your receipts for job-hunting expenses. These expenses are deductible as a miscellaneous itemized expense if they were incurred to locate a new job in the same line of work. For example, telephone bills, résumé advice, and travel expenses may all be deductible.

#27   Investment Portfolio

Build one . . . then take some deductions. Here is a short list of what you can deduct:

- The cost of investment magazines, newsletters, and books
- The cost of trips to your financial advisor or stockbroker's office
- Investment fees, custodial fees, trust administration fees, and other expenses you paid to maintain your taxable investments
- Fees for online trading (restricted to account maintenance–related fees)

#28   The IRS Is Watching

Uncle Sam keeps an eye out for tax fraud, especially for business owners. Watch out for these omissions from your taxes:

- Accounting discrepancies
- Not reporting substantial amounts of income
- Bogus deductions, such as a glaring overstatement of travel expenses or a taxpayer's claim of a large deduction for charitable contributions when no records of the organization exist

#29   Home Office Deduction

These tips can help you earn a home office deduction—and they are almost always overlooked by small business owners.

- Create business cards with your home address
- Have clients who visit your office sign a guest book
- Hang on to office equipment and other business-related receipts

- Keep all your business invoices—with your home address prominently featured
- Keep a time and work log

#30   Go to College

College 529 Plans can be a major tax-saver, but before committing to such a plan, make sure your plan meets the following criteria:

- **A Good Investment Package**
  That means one with plenty of investment, including large- and small-cap stocks and U.S. government bonds.

- **Reasonable Fees**
  If you are paying more in fees for your 529 plan than you are for your mutual funds, look out. Management fees of more than 1.5 percent annually are too high. Most clock in at less than that, with some as low as 0.5 percent. Try to find a plan with expense ratios that are lower than 0.5 percent. Also, keep broker-sponsored 529 plans at arms length. Up-front commissions of up to 5 percent are part of the bargain—and you will be paying higher ongoing expenses.

- **Good Performance**
  Check the plan's historical performance record. A constant track record of underperformance is a big red flag.

#31   Take the Childcare Credit

You might be able to reduce your income tax liability through the Child and Dependent Care Credit if you paid someone to care for a child under the age of thirteen or a qualifying spouse or dependent so that you could work or look for work. With the credit, you can deduct a percentage of the amount of work-related childcare expenses you paid to someone who provided care to your dependent(s). The actual percent you can deduct varies depending on your income, and the maximum is 35 percent. However, you must reduce your qualifying expenses by any benefits provided by your employer for dependent care.

A few restrictions go along with this credit:

- The dependent(s) must be your spouse or your child under the age of thirteen, and must be physically or mentally unable to care for themselves.
- You must have earned income from wages, salaries, tips, self-employment, or any other employee compensation.
- The payments for care cannot be paid to someone you claim as one of your dependents on your income tax returns.
- The payments cannot be made to a child of yours under the age of nineteen, even if he or she is not one of your dependents.
- Your filing status must be single, married filing jointly, head of household, or qualifying widow(er) with a dependent child.
- The care must have been provided for one or more persons qualifying to be claimed as a dependent.
- The qualifying person must have lived with you for more than half the tax year.

For more information on the Child and Dependent Care Credit, check out IRS Publication 503, Child and Dependent Care Expenses.

#32 Get an Extension

If it's tax day and you're not ready, you can file an extension using IRS Form 4868. You can file the form either online through an e-file provider or through standard mail. It must be filed before the tax deadline.

Remember that just because you get an extension to file your return, that doesn't give you an extension to pay the IRS the money you owe. If you are likely to owe money, you should send a payment along with your extension request. To avoid additional fees and penalties, you must pay the IRS at least 90 percent of what you will owe them.

#33 Avoid Direct-Deposit Scams

There are dozens of new scams every day related to the direct deposits of IRS refunds. Many of them use the words *e-file* and *direct deposit* to confuse taxpayers into giving up their financial information. Make sure that you only give your bank account information to the IRS through a secure method. Also, keep in mind that the IRS will *never* e-mail you asking for your financial information. If you receive an e-mail like this, odds are it's a swindle.

#34 Amen to Amended Returns

The IRS corrects simple math errors and will send you a notice when you are missing requested forms or schedules. In these instances, an amended return is not necessary.

However, you should file an amended return if any of the following were reported incorrectly:

- filing status
- dependents
- total income
- deductions or credits

Use IRS Form 1040X, Amended U.S. Individual Income Tax Return, to correct your 1040, 1040A, 1040EZ, or electronically filed return. Be sure to write the year of the return you are amending at the top of IRS Form 1040X.

If you need to amend more than one tax return, prepare a 1040X for each and mail them in separate envelopes to the IRS processing center for the area in which you live. The 1040X instructions list the addresses for the centers.

#35   Substitute a Substitute for Return

If you receive notification from the IRS that they filed a return on your behalf, it should be cause for concern. The IRS typically files single, with one exemption, and claims the standard deduction when filing a substitute for return for a taxpayer. This results in many tax saving exemptions, deductions, and credits falling by the wayside, and often leads to a very large tax bill.

It is in your best interest to immediately prepare and file an original return in such a situation. You may file an original return at any time to correct an IRS-filed substitute for return.

#36   Tax Debts Die

If you have very old tax returns that you never paid, the IRS may not be able to collect on them anymore. That is because the IRS only has ten years from the date the balance due was assessed to collect the underlying debt, interest, and penalties. Called the Collection Statute Expiration Date (CSED)—also known as the Collection Statue of Limitations—it is the date by which the IRS has to collect an outstanding tax liability (debt). Thereafter, the tax debt expires and the IRS can no longer collect the owed taxes or enforce collection efforts against you to collect the debt. If you have multiple years' worth of tax debt, each year will have its own CSED, unless all the tax returns were assessed at the same time.

The CSED is ten years from the date on which the tax debt was assessed. In this case, "assessed" is the date on which the review of your tax return was finalized and an outstanding balance was calculated by the IRS and entered into its system.

Taxpayers with old tax debts are probably curious as to when they will expire. Luckily, you can ask the IRS for the CSED of every tax liability and the IRS has to provide the information. Contact them at 800-829-1040.

However, if you have received a notice or levy from the IRS on your tax liability, the IRS may transfer you to the Automated

Collection Service. If that is the case, it is better to contact your professional tax preparer or a professional tax debt resolution firm to get the CSED for each tax debt.

#37 Owe Taxes? Change Your Withholdings

You should consider changing your tax withholdings for next year if you owe taxes this year. This will assure that the correct amount is withheld. You can even request that extra money be withheld each pay period.

To change your withholdings, complete an IRS Form W-4 with your employer's payroll administrator. The IRS has a useful withholding calculator to determine what you should be claiming. Visit www.irs.gov for more information.

#38 Big Refund? Change Your Withholdings

If you received a large refund this year, you should also adjust your withholdings. Many people mistakenly look at the refund as an easy way to save money, but really you are essentially loaning the government a chunk of change instead of receiving interest on your money. Exercise self-discipline or have the money automatically transferred to a savings account—both options are much better than voluntarily loaning your money to Uncle Sam. Additionally if you qualify for the Earned Income Credit, you can have a portion of that paid to you throughout the year.

#39 Respond to IRS "Proposals"

You may receive a Proposed Tax Change Notice (IRS Notice CP 2000), which shows proposed changes to your income tax return. The proposal is based on a comparison of the income, payments, credits, and deductions reported on your tax return with information on these items reported to the IRS by employers, banks, businesses, and other payers. The Proposed Tax Change Notice also reflects any corrections the IRS made to your original return when it was processed.

This is not a bill. The Proposed Tax Change Notice gives you the opportunity to disagree, partially agree, or completely agree with the proposed changes. The Proposed Tax Change Notice will provide instructions for how to respond. However, if you do not respond by the due date, the changes will automatically go into effect. This could leave you owing the IRS a bit more money or reduce your expected refund.

#40   Reverse Mortgages

A reverse mortgage is a loan against a home in which the homeowner does not have to make a payment on the loan as long as he or she lives in the house. This is very different from a regular mortgage, where you are borrowing to pay for the house, and your monthly payments make your debt go down over time until you have paid off the underlying loan in full. All the while, the equity in your home rises as your property value appreciates.

With a reverse mortgage, the lender sends you money and your debt grows larger and larger as you keep getting cash advances. This will continue to be the case if you make no repayments, and interest is added to the loan balance. Generally, a reverse mortgage does not need to be paid back until the homeowner dies, sells the home, or permanently moves out, as you are in fact borrowing against the built-up equity. There are no monthly payments to be made.

The best part: the money you receive on the reverse mortgage is not considered taxable income.

In order to qualify for a reverse mortgage, a homeowner generally must be at least sixty-two years of age, own his or her home, and the home must have a very low mortgage balance or be owned outright. There is no income requirement to qualify for this type of mortgage.

The homeowner can receive the loan amount in different ways:

- A single lump sum
- A regular monthly payment
- An account that lets the homeowner(s) decide when and how much of the available amount is paid
- A combination of the above methods

#41   Make Your Estimated Tax Payments

All taxpayers are required to pay their taxes throughout the entire year. People with wage-earning jobs have this requirement met for them when their employers withhold taxes from their paychecks. However, this automatic withholding does not happen for self-employed people. If you are self-employed, you are required to make estimated tax payments four times a year.

Many people decide not to make these payments, instead, paying all the taxes when they file their return in April. Unfortunately, for most people, this decision is a mistake. First, the IRS will charge you a penalty for failing to make your estimated payments. Second, many people find they do not have the funds available in April to make a full payment—if you have not saved enough money over the course of three months to make quarterly payments, what makes you think you will save enough money over the course of the year to make a single, lump sum payment?

Consequently, many taxpayers accumulate large liabilities by failing to make estimated payments. But take it from me: *you do not want a tax debt*. It is much easier to learn to budget for four smaller payments then it is to try to scrape together a huge payment once a year or to deal with the collection tactics of the IRS.

#42   Don't Get Injured . . . Tax-Wise

If you're married filing jointly, and your spouse owes back taxes, you can still receive your refund by using the IRS Injured Spouse Relief program. In order to take advantage of it, you must complete and file IRS Form 8379, Injured Spouse Allocation, at the time you file your joint IRS Form 1040 tax return. The IRS will use the Injured Spouse Form to determine the portion of the refund that should be allocated to you. The IRS may then refund the appropriate funds to you and apply the remaining refund to your spouse's back taxes.

To qualify for Injured Spouse Relief, you must meet the following conditions:

- You must not be legally obligated to pay the back taxes
- You must report income such as wages, taxable interest, etc., on the joint return
- You must have made and reported payments—such as federal income tax withheld from your wages or estimated tax payments—or you must have claimed the Earned Income Tax Credit or other refundable credit on the joint return

If you do not complete the Injured Spouse Allocation Form when you file your joint tax return, the IRS will most likely keep the entire refund to pay down your spouse's back taxes. Some people whose spouses owe back taxes solve this problem by filing separately. If you choose to go this route, you will receive your refund, but you may be giving up some important tax advantages. You should probably go back to Round 4 or meet with a qualified tax preparer before making the decision to file separate returns.

#43   Relocated? Reel in the Deduction

If you moved this year, and the distance from your old home to your new job is fifty miles farther than the distance from your old home to your old job, you can deduct moving expenses on IRS Form 3903, Moving Expenses. These expenses include costs associated with:

- Lodging for yourself and members of your household en route from your old to your new location
- Transportation expenses, such as gas and oil, which can be deducted at 27 cents per mile
- Moving your personal effects and household goods (including in-transit storage expenses)

- Storing and insuring household goods and personal effects within any period of thirty consecutive days after the day your things are moved from your former home and before they are delivered to your new home
- Connecting or disconnecting utilities required because you are moving your household goods, appliances, or personal effects
- Shipping your car and pets to your new home

#44   Daycare Deduction

If you pay for daycare, use IRS Form 2441, Child and Dependent Care Expenses, for Form 1040 (or Schedule 2 for IRS Form 1040A) to show the amount paid. You can get a credit of up to $1,050 for one dependent and $2,100 for two or more dependents.

#45   Wait Until Next Year to Buy Your Home

If you plan on buying your first home in the near future and the total of your itemized deductions is smaller than the standard deduction, you will be better off waiting until January of the next year to buy the home. Why? Because any mortgage interest, points, or property taxes you pay when you buy the home will be wasted if the points—when added with other itemized deductions—still do not exceed the standard deduction amount. If you purchase the home in January, you will have the points and one full year of mortgage interest and property taxes to write off as itemized deductions, which is usually more than enough to itemize.

#46   Seek Disaster Relief

If you have been a victim of a natural disaster, the IRS may show some empathy by allowing you to receive an extension on your tax deadlines. Affected taxpayers include those living in disaster areas, those outside the disaster areas whose tax records are located in the areas, businesses located in disaster areas, and relief workers. The IRS will automatically grant disaster tax relief to taxpayers in the covered disaster area. However, if you live or have a business outside the covered disaster area, you will be required to call the IRS disaster hotline (1-866-562-5227) to receive disaster relief.

#47 Avoid "Abusive" Tax Shelter Investments

Tax shelters reduce current taxes by offsetting gains from one source with losses from another. The IRS allows some tax shelters, but will not allow a shelter that it deems "abusive." An abusive tax shelter generally offers inflated tax savings, which are disproportionately greater than your actual investment placed at risk. A legitimate tax shelter typically produces income and involves a risk of loss proportionate to the investment.

Generally, investments are made to make money. However, when an investment generates little to no money while at the same time sheltering other investments that do generate money by offsetting their gains, it probably exists solely to reduce taxes. And if it unreasonably reduces taxes, that could be considered tax evasion. Abusive tax shelters are often marketed in terms of how much you can write off in relation to how much you invest.

#48 Don't Forget to Pay Taxes on Household Employees

According to the IRS, you have a household employee if you hire someone to do household work and that worker is your employee. A worker is considered an employee if you can control not only *what* work is done, but *how* it is done. That's it! It doesn't matter whether the work is full time or part time, or whether you hired the worker through an agency or from a list provided by an agency or association. It also doesn't matter whether you pay the worker on an hourly, daily, or weekly basis, or by the job. Now, if only the worker can control how the work is done, the worker is not your household employee, but is self-employed.

If you have a household employee who you paid $1,600 or more (in 2008), you will need to withhold and pay Social Security and Medicare taxes. You will owe federal unemployment taxes if you pay wages of $1,000 or more in any calendar quarter. You may also owe state employment and disability taxes.

Here are some examples of workers who do household work:

- Babysitters
- Caretakers
- Cleaning people
- Domestic workers
- Drivers
- Health aides
- Housekeepers
- Maids
- Nannies
- Private nurses
- Yard workers

For more information about your responsibilities if you have a household employee, see IRS Publication 926, Household's Employer Guide.

#49 Teachers Deserve It

If you are a teacher, first of all, thank you. You do so much to enlighten the minds and lives of our country's youth. You work a demanding schedule and perform a daunting task. I applaud each of my own teachers and all of you current teachers for all that you do.

The IRS thanks you, too—you can deduct as much as $250 of your classroom expenses per year without having to itemize your taxes. This applies if you are a teacher, instructor, counselor, principal, or aide working in kindergarten through twelfth grade.

Please note that this tax break was supposed to be terminated in 2004 and again in 2006, but Congress recently reinstated the provision to apply through 2009.

#50   Start Your—Or Your Child's—IRA Early

Under our tax system, all that is required to make an IRA contribution is earned income. Age is irrelevant. So if your child earns some dough this summer from, say, cleaning pools, dog sitting, working part-time as a barista, or anything else, he or she is entitled to make an IRA contribution for the tax year.

Specifically, for 2008, a child can contribute the lesser of:

- earned income for the year
- $5,000

Kids can contribute to either a traditional IRA or a tax-free Roth IRA. The contribution limits are the same for both types of accounts. Typically, a Roth IRA is the best alternative because original contributions can be withdrawn at any time for any reason (however, earnings generally cannot be withdrawn before age 59½ without triggering taxes and a penalty).

Now It's Up to You

That's it! For more tax tips and information on improving your personal tax picture, visit my website at www.rdtc.com. In the meantime, I hope you use the information in this book to give you more confidence about your taxes and your personal financial picture—and to stand up and fight back when the IRS comes knocking on your door.

That has been my goal all along, ever since I sat down and started working on this book more than two years ago.

So, stand tall. Get on your toes and get your gloves up. By reading this book and following the instructions it contains, you can confidently enter the ring against the IRS—be it tax day, tax season, or just time to do some tax planning—with the knowledge and skills to float like a butterfly and sting like a bee. Now is the time to fight back. Trust me, the IRS will never know what hit them!

The end . . . of paying way too much money to the IRS!

➤ APPENDIX

Roni's Tax Glossary

*We contend that for a nation to try to tax itself into prosperity is like a
man standing in a bucket and trying to lift himself up by the handle.*
—Winston Churchill

That being said, taxes in America are plentiful and are plenty complicated. To help you navigate, here is a list of terms and definitions that relate to the crazy world of taxes. Knowledge is the key to completing any task, so this list is here to help you out.

Adjusted Gross Income (AGI). Total income reduced by certain deductions, more appropriately known as adjustments, that you claim at the bottom of Form 1040 or 1040A.

Adjustment to Income. A legitimate expense that is deductible even if the taxpayer does not itemize deductions.

Adoption Credit. A nonrefundable credit for qualified adoption expenses.

Advance Earned Income Credit. Prepayments of the Earned Income Credit by an employer to an employee.

Alternative Minimum Tax (AMT). A tax calculation that adds certain normally tax deductible items back into the Adjusted Gross Income. If the AMT is higher than the regular tax liability for the year, the regular tax and the amount by which the AMT exceeds the regular tax are due and payable. Although much maligned, the Alternative Minimum Tax was initially designed to prevent taxpayers from avoiding their fair share of tax liability.

Audit. The process by which the IRS takes a closer look at your taxes, and most taxpayers' worst nightmare. Normally, it is a good idea to have a tax specialist by your side to guide you through the audit process.

Capital Gain. An increase in the value at the time of sale of a capital asset (like a stock or a bond or a home) that gives it a higher worth than the price at which it was purchased. A capital gain may be classified as short-term (one year or less) or long-term (more than one year) and must be claimed on income tax returns.

Casualty Loss. Casualty loss is triggered by the destruction of property from an unexpected event, i.e., a flood, storm, fire, etc.

Charitable Contribution. Money or property donated to a legitimate charity. Charitable deductions are a great way to save money on taxes—and a great way to help society.

Child and Dependent Care Credit. This credit is calculated as a percentage of the money spent on child care.

Child Tax Credit. Also known as the "teenage tax break," this tax credit is available to taxpayers with children under the age of seventeen.

Compensation. Money earned—usually in the form of wages, commissions, tips, fees, or self-employment income—for services rendered.

Credit. A form of tax offset allowed by Uncle Sam for individuals that can cut your tax liability. A tax credit reduces the amount of the tax you owe, dollar for dollar. This is unlike deductions or exemptions, which reduce the amount of the income or Adjusted Gross Income upon which your tax liability is figured.

Deduction. Money or other earnings you can cut, or deduct, from your taxable income.

Dependent. Someone who meets the IRS's criteria for dependency and consequently qualifies as a dependent for tax purposes.

Depreciation. A legitimate deduction for the cost of an item used (usually) for business purposes.

Earned Income. Income that comes from personal services, such as wages, tips, bonuses, and additional compensation.

Earned Income Tax Credit (EITC). A refundable federal tax credit for low-income working individuals and families. Enacted to offset the burden of Social Security taxes and to provide an incentive to work. When the EITC exceeds the amount of taxes owed, it results in a tax refund to those who claim and qualify for the credit.

Employment Expenses. Used mostly by business owners, these are ordinary and necessary expenses required by the employee to do his or her job.

Entertainment Expenses. Sometimes referred to as the "happy-hour deduction," entertainment expenses are job- or business-related expenses necessary to conducting business.

Estimated Tax. What you expect to owe in taxes over the course of the year, generally paid quarterly. Entrepreneurs and other self-employed people usually pay an estimated tax.

Exemption. An elimination or reduction of income that would otherwise be taxed.

Filing Status. The term used for the tax return form that you will use; it is closely tied to marital status. There are five filing statuses: single, married filing jointly or surviving spouse, married filing separately, head of household, and qualifying widow(er) with dependent child.

Head of Household. The filing status used by an unmarried taxpayer who pays more than half the cost of maintaining the home of a qualified individual.

Hobby Loss. A nondeductible loss incurred from a hobby. If you collect baseball cards and they are ruined in a flood, that is a hobby loss. While hobby loss cannot be deducted from other income on your return, it can be deducted against the amount of hobby income on your return.

Home Office Expense. Expenses that stem from operating a business out of your home. Examples include phone charges, office furniture, or meals you eat while on the job.

Internal Revenue Service (IRS). The U.S. government agency directly responsible for collecting taxes.

Itemized Deductions. Expenditures that the IRS deems acceptable for reducing Adjusted Gross Income. The specific deductions that are allowed are outlined by the IRS and include such expenses as mortgage interest, state and local taxes, gifts, and medical expenses.

Married Filing Jointly. The filing status used by a couple who is married at the end of the tax year and uses one tax return between them.

Married Filing Separately. The filing status used by a couple who is married at the end of the year and chooses to file separate tax returns.

Modified Adjusted Gross Income. This is usually the Adjusted Gross Income with various items added back in. It is used for calculations for certain credits and limitations.

Nontaxable Income. Income that is not taxed.

Permanent and Total Disability. A disability that is expected to last at least a year, which keeps a person from working and earning work-related income.

Passive Income. Earnings from a rental property, limited partnership, or other investment enterprise—it usually means the individual is not directly involved with the investment gain, although he or she does benefit from it.

Proprietorship. A business that is owned and controlled by one person.

Qualifying Widow(er). The filing status used by a qualified person for the two years following a spouse's death.

Schedules. IRS forms that are used to report various kinds of income, deductions, and credits.

Self-Employed. A person who individually decides when and where to work and pays his or her own expenses. Self-employed individuals must pay self-employment taxes.

Self-Employment Tax. A tax for the self-employed, who must pay this tax in order to receive Social Security benefits upon retirement. The amount of this tax may be reduced if the individual also pays Social Security and Medicare taxes through another employer.

Standard Deduction. A base amount of income that is not subject to tax. This base amount is used to reduce a taxpayer's Adjusted Gross Income if he or she does not choose the itemized deduction method of calculating taxable income. The amount of the standard deduction is based on the taxpayer's filing status, age, and whether or not he or she is blind or can be claimed as a dependent on someone else's tax return.

Taxable Income. Adjusted Gross Income minus deductions and exemptions.

Unearned Income. Income that is not derived from services performed, such as interest, dividends, and royalties. It is usually taxed at a different rate than earned income.

Worksheet. A document, usually supplied by the IRS, which is used to compile information but is not usually filed with the tax return.

About the Author

Roni Lynn Deutch is the most recognizable tax expert in America known by name to one out of every three over the age of eighteen. The founder of the largest tax-resolution firm in the nation, she is recognized as an experienced tax debt attorney dedicated to resolving IRS back taxes. Her tax law firm, which began as a one-person practice in a small condo, has grown to employ hundreds and has assisted thousands of taxpayers across the country in finding the appropriate relief from the IRS. Today her competitive spirit continues as she reaches out to those in need of help with IRS tax debts.

2Convenient
Tax Preparation Options

Save $50⁰⁰ off Tax Preparation Fees

Select an Option

① At Your Local
Roni Deutch
Tax Center

② Over the Phone

**For more information, visit
rdtc.com/savebigbucks**

© 2009 RDTC, Inc. All rights reserved.

Save Fifty Dollars!

President & Founder
Roni Deutch

This coupon entitles you to:

$50⁰⁰ off tax preparation fees

RD RONI DEUTCH
Tax Center®

rdtc.com/savebigbucks

Here's how to redeem this coupon: Take it to any participating Roni Deutch Tax Center or if calling by phone, mention code: RDBK*

One coupon per customer. Cannot be combined with other offers, discounts, or special programs. Not valid on past services. Must be presented at time of service. No cash redemption value. Photocopy not valid. Redeemable at participating Roni Deutch Tax Center locations. Expires 4/15/2010.
© 2009 RDTC, Inc. All rights reserved.   * Visit rdtc.com/savebigbucks for additional details.   RDBK

Be Your Own Boss!

 RONI DEUTCH
Tax Center®

Listen to what our franchisees are saying about owning a Roni Deutch Tax Center
rdtcfranchise.com

Invest in your financial future, become a Roni Deutch Tax Center Franchisee.

Franchise Opportunities Available
rdtcfranchise.com
866-RDTC-BUY
738-2289

- Prime Territories
- Recession Resistant
- Low Cost Investment
- No Experience Necessary

Seize the Moment.

www.rdtcfranchise.com

© 2009 RDTC, Inc. All rights reserved.